THE
HISTORY OF
CUBA

THE HISTORY OF CUBA

Second Edition

Clifford L. Staten

The Greenwood Histories of the Modern Nations
Frank W. Thackeray and John E. Findling, Series Editors

 GREENWOOD

AN IMPRINT OF ABC-CLIO, LLC
Santa Barbara, California • Denver, Colorado • Oxford, England

Copyright © 2015 by ABC-CLIO, LLC

Library of Congress Cataloging-in-Publication Data

Staten, Clifford L.
The history of Cuba / Clifford L. Staten. — Second edition.
    pages cm. — (The Greenwood histories of the modern nations)
  Includes bibliographical references and index.
  ISBN 978-1-61069-841-2 (hardback : alkaline paper) — ISBN 978-1-61069-842-9
(electronic) 1. Cuba—History—1959–1990. 2. Cuba—History—1990– 3. Cuba—
History. 4. Cuba—Politics and government. I. Title.
  F1788.S695 2015
  972.91—dc23   2014043470

ISBN: 978-1-61069-841-2
EISBN: 978-1-61069-842-9

19 18 17 16 15   1 2 3 4 5

This book is also available on the World Wide Web as an eBook.
Visit www.abc-clio.com for details.

Greenwood
An Imprint of ABC-CLIO, LLC

ABC-CLIO, LLC
130 Cremona Drive, P.O. Box 1911
Santa Barbara, California 93116-1911

This book is printed on acid-free paper ∞

Manufactured in the United States of America

Contents

Series Foreword

The Greenwood Histories of the Modern Nations series is intended to provide students and interested laypeople with up-to-date, concise, and analytical histories of many of the nations of the contemporary world. Not since the 1960s has there been a systematic attempt to publish a series of national histories, and as series editors, we believe that this series will prove to be a valuable contribution to our understanding of other countries in our increasingly interdependent world.

At the end of the 1960s, the Cold War was an accepted reality of global politics. The process of decolonization was still in progress, the idea of a unified Europe with a single currency was unheard of, the United States was mired in a war in Vietnam, and the economic boom in Asia was still years in the future. Richard Nixon was president of the United States, Mao Tse-tung (not yet Mao Zedong) ruled China, Leonid Brezhnev guided the Soviet Union, and Harold Wilson was prime minister of the United Kingdom. Authoritarian dictators still controlled most of Latin America, the Middle East was reeling in the wake of the Six-Day War, and Shah Mohammad Reza Pahlavi was at the height of his power in Iran.

Since then, the Cold War has ended, the Soviet Union has vanished, leaving 15 independent republics in its wake, the advent of the computer age has radically transformed global communications, the rising demand for oil makes the Middle East still a dangerous flash-point, and the rise of new economic powers like the People's Republic of China and India threatens to bring about a new world order. All of these developments have had a dramatic impact on the recent history of every nation of the world.

For this series, which was launched in 1998, we first selected nations whose political, economic, and socio-cultural affairs marked them as among the most important of our time. For each nation, we found an author who was recognized as a specialist in the history of that nation. These authors worked cooperatively with us and with Greenwood Press to produce volumes that reflected current research on their nations and that are interesting and informative to their readers. In the first decade of the series, close to 50 volumes were published, and some have now moved into second editions.

The success of the series has encouraged us to broaden our scope to include additional nations, whose histories have had significant effects on their regions, if not on the entire world. In addition, geopolitical changes have elevated other nations into positions of greater impor-tance in world affairs and, so, we have chosen to include them in this series as well. The importance of a series such as this cannot be under-estimated. As a superpower whose influence is felt all over the world, the United States can claim a "special" relationship with almost every other nation. Yet many Americans know very little about the histories of nations with which the United States relates. How did they get to be the way they are? What kind of political systems have evolved there? What kind of influence do they have on their own regions? What are the dominant political, religious, and cultural forces that move their leaders? These and many other questions are answered in the volumes of this series.

The authors who contribute to this series write comprehensive his-tories of their nations, dating back, in some instances, to prehistoric times. Each of them, however, has devoted a significant portion of their book to events of the past 40 years because the modern era has contributed the most to contemporary issues that have an impact on U.S. policy. Authors make every effort to be as up-to-date as possi-ble so that readers can benefit from discussion and analysis of recent events.

In addition to the historical narrative, each volume contains an introductory chapter giving an overview of that country's geogra-phy, political institutions, economic structure, and cultural attributes. This is meant to give readers a snapshot of the nation as it exists in the contemporary world. Each history also includes supplementary information following the narrative, which may include a timeline that represents a succinct chronology of the nation's historical evolution, biographical sketches of the nation's most important historical figures, and a glossary of important terms or concepts that are usually expressed in a foreign language. Finally, each author prepares a comprehensive bibliography for readers who wish to pursue the subject further.

Readers of these volumes will find them fascinating and well written. More importantly, they will come away with a better understanding of the contemporary world and the nations that comprise it. As series editors, we hope that this series will contribute to a heightened sense of global understanding as we move through the early years of the twenty-first century.

Frank W. Thackeray and John E. Findling
Indiana University Southeast

Acknowledgments

The second edition of this book is partially the result of the substantive questions and comments of the students at Indiana University Southeast who, over the years, have taken either my Latin American Politics class or my special topics class on Cuba. In particular, I want to thank the students who came with me to Cuba in the summer of 2012: Amory Alvey, Katie Ashby, Victoria Bennett, Dale Brown, Cory Cochran, Lorie Gutierrez, John Kummer, Mary Mour, Jenny Reichert, Whitney Reynolds, Adam Sirles, Jerry Stinnett, Dejan Tomanic, Joe Van Horn, Sean Welch, and Ashley Williams. Their eyes and journals helped me see the changes that are taking place in Cuba today through very different perspectives. These students will always be very special to me. I want to thank my friend and colleague, Robert Harding of Spring Hill College, for his very perceptive observations of Cuban society and politics. He and his students also went to Cuba with us and contributed to one of the most wonderful learning experiences in my life. My friend and colleague, Bernie Carducci of Indiana University Southeast, provided invaluable expertise on rum, mojitos, tobacco, food, and the Buena Vista Social Club and kept us all laughing as we traveled across the island that summer.

Over the years other friends and colleagues from Indiana University Southeast have contributed in many different ways. These include the late Tom Kotulak, Stephanie Bower, Tim Ambrose, Linda Gugin, Tom Wolf, and Jim St. Clair. I also mention my mentors from graduate school the late Neal Tate of the University of North Texas and Vanderbilt University and the late Clair Matz of Marshall University. It was Clair who piqued my curiosity concerning Cuba while I was an undergraduate. There are several scholars and authors for whom I owe a major debt in terms of my own knowledge and understanding of Cuba. These include Louis A. Perez, Jr., Julia Sweig, Brian Latell, Hugh Thomas, Jaime Suchlicki, Ada Ferrer, Marifeli Perez-Stable, Susan Eckstein, and Ann Louise Bardach. I am thankful to the Senior Acquisitions Editor, Kaitlin Ciarmiello of ABC-CLIO, who was very patient with me. I want to especially thank the editors of this series, Frank W. Thackeray and John E. Findling, for their continued support of my academic research and writing.

For many years, my children, Joshua, Ryan, Anna, and Glenn, have, without complaining, put up with my stacks of notes, journal articles, and books that are everywhere throughout the house. Joshua, my oldest, who is now in graduate school, has become a keen observer of political processes, and I have come to rely on him in ways that I never anticipated. Ryan, Anna, and Glenn are always there to give me a hug when I most need it. My wife, Shan, is always my biggest fan, and I cannot imagine completing this project without her love and support. Finally, this book is dedicated with love to my mother, Nancy, for her long service to her community through the American Legion and for her love of reading and learning which is so much a part of who I am today.

Timeline of Historical Events

1000 BCE	Ciboney Indians (Guayabo Blanco) migrate to Cuba
1000 CE	Ciboney Indians (Cayo Redondo) migrate to Cuba
1100–1450	Arawak Indians (Sub-Taino and Taino) migrate to Cuba
1492	Christopher Columbus lands in Cuba
1508	Sebastian de Ocampo circumnavigates Cuba
1511–1515	Cuba is settled by the Spanish;
	Several towns are established
1518	Hernan Cortes leaves Cuba for Mexico
1522	First slaves are brought to Cuba
1538	Santiago becomes the first capital of Cuba
1607	Havana is established as the capital of Cuba
1700	Tobacco becomes the primary export
1728	University of Havana is founded
1762–1763	British capture and occupy Havana;

	Liberalized trade, commercial, and maritime laws are established
1763	Spain regains control of Havana
1765	Spain begins to liberalize trade, commercial, and maritime laws
1791	Slave uprising in Haiti eliminates main competitor to Cuban sugar
1800	Sugar becomes the primary export
1818	Royal decree opens Cuban ports to international trade
1837	First railroad in Cuba opens between Havana and Bejucal and Guines
1838–1880	Modernization of the sugar industry begins
1868–1878	First war of independence (Ten Years' War) begins
1880–1886	Spain agrees to gradually end slavery over an eight-year period, but decides in 1886 to end slavery
1890	Cuba becomes even more economically dependent on the United States
1895–1898	Second War of Independence begins; Economic infrastructure is destroyed
1895	Jose Marti is killed in battle and becomes a national hero
1898	Battleship USS *Maine* is blown up in Havana harbor; President William McKinley offers to purchase Cuba from Spain; United States declares war on Spain and intervenes in Cuban war of independence; U.S. armed forces refuse to allow Cubans to take part in Spanish surrender
1898–1902	U.S. military occupation begins
1901	Platt Amendment is imposed on Cuba
1902	Cuban achieves its independence
1902–1906	Tomas Estrada serves as first president of the Republic of Cuba
1903	U.S. naval base at Guantanamo Bay is established

1906–1909	U.S. military occupation begins
1909–1913	Jose Miquel Gomez serves as president
1912	U.S. military intervention begins in Cuba;
	Uprising by the Independent Party of Color is crushed by Cuban and U.S. troops
1913–1921	Mario Garcia Menocal serves as president
1917–1923	U.S. military intervention in Cuba
1921–1925	Alfredo Zayas serves as president
1925–1933	Gerardo Machado serves as president
1933	The Machado dictatorship is overthrown;
	Sergeants' Revolt begins
1933–1934	Ramon Grau serves as president
1933–1959	Cuban politics is dominated by Batista
1934	Platt Amendment is repudiated
1940	Second constitution is proclaimed
1941–1945	Batista serves as president
1945–1949	Ramon Grau serves as president
1949–1952	Carlos Prio serves as president
1952	Fulgencio Batista stages a *golpe*
1953	Fidel Castro and followers attack military barracks at Moncada;
	Castro and followers are sentenced to 15-year prison terms
1954–1958	Batista is elected (no opposition candidate) and serves as president
1955	Batista grants amnesty to all prisoners; Castro and followers are freed;
	The 26th of July Movement is formally created;
	Castro and some followers go to Mexico to prepare for the revolution
1956	Castro and followers land in Oriente Province
1956–1958	Castro wages guerrilla war from Sierra Maestra;

	Underground wages war in the cities
1959	Batista flees;
	Castro arrives in Havana;
	First agrarian reform law is imposed
1959–1961	There is a struggle within the new ruling government over the direction of the revolution
1960	Large foreign and domestic companies are nationalized
1961	Cuban exiles supported by the United States invade Cuba at the Bay of Pigs
1962	U.S. trade embargo is put in place;
	Cuban missile crisis begins
1964–1970	Radical Experiment begins
1965	Popular Socialist Party is reorganized into the Communist Party of Cuba by Castro
1967	Ernesto "Che" Guevara is killed in Bolivia
1968	Small businesses are nationalized;
	The Soviet Union invades Czechoslovakia
1972	Cuba joins the Council for Mutual Economic Assistance trading bloc
1975	First Communist Party Congress is held;
	Cuban troops are sent to Angola
1976	New socialist constitution is enacted
1979	Sixth Non-Aligned Summit meeting is held in Havana
1980	More than 100,000 Cubans leave for the United States from Mariel
1986–1990	Rectification process begins
1989	Communist governments in Eastern Europe collapse
1991–1995	Special period begins
1991	The Soviet Union collapses
1992	Torricelli Act is passed
1993	The dollar is legalized in Cuba;
	Self-employment in various economic sectors begins

1995	Changes in foreign investment law are implemented
1996	Helms-Burton Act is passed
1997	Raul Castro visits China to learn about the Chinese economic model
1998	Pope John Paul II visits Cuba
2000	United States passes the Trade Sanctions Reform and Export Enhancement Act
2002	Former president Jimmy Carter visits the island;
	Cuban government closes 71 of the 156 sugar mills on the island
2003	Cuban government arrests 75 dissidents;
	The Black Spring begins;
	Ladies in White begin their protest;
	Chinese Premier Zhu Rhongji visits Cuba
2004	Chinese President Hu Jintao visits Cuba
2006	Fidel Castro undergoes surgery and gives temporary power to Raul Castro
2007	Raul Castro announces state-run enterprises will operate under market-style management
2008	Fidel Castro officially steps down and Raul Castro becomes president;
	Chinese president Hu Jintao visits Cuba
2011	Raul Castro becomes first secretary of the Communist Party;
	Major economic reforms based upon the Chinese economic model are announced at Communist Party Congress
2014	Chinese president Xi Jinping visits Cuba;
	Yoani Sanchez and Reinaldo Escobar unveil *14ymedio*, the first dissident-run, independent online newspaper that is produced in Cuba;
	President Obama announces that the United States will restore diplomatic relations with Cuba

CUBA

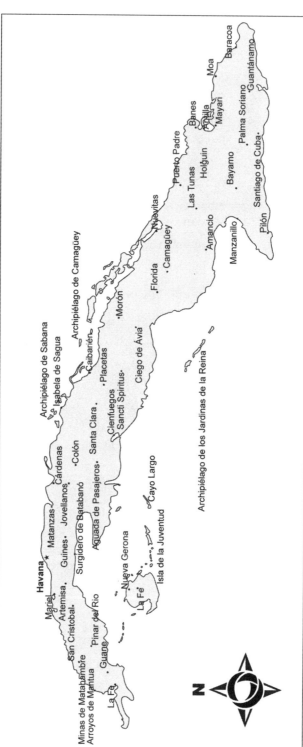

1

Cuba and Its People

It's the Cuban people who make the most profound impression [on visitors to the island]: the Santeria priests and priestesses, the coco taxi drivers, the cabaret dancers, the old women puffing cigars, the mambo drummers, the men and women who have fine-tuned seduction into an art form. A rhythm flows through Cuba, from the tapping of the clave . . . to the drumbeat of the rumba, from vibrant carnivals to political rallies. . . . A tropical undercurrent that pulses through both nightlife and nature [is] central to this country's gregarious people and their unique history. In Cuba, nothing is average; it is either heartbreaking or exhilarating.

                              Maria Finn Dominguez, *Cuba in Mind*[1]

On Monday evening July 31, 2006, the world was stunned when the personal secretary to Fidel Castro, Carlos Valenciaga, announced on Cuban television that Fidel's younger brother, Raul, was now the provisional president of the island nation. Fidel, who had been the face of the Cuban revolution and the country since 1959, was in frail health and had undergone intestinal surgery. Rumors were rampant throughout the anti-Castro community in southern Florida of his impending death. In February 2008, a healthier Castro permanently stepped down and allowed his brother to officially become president. Raul quickly moved to appoint "Raulistas" to leadership positions and by the end of 2010 only three ministers appointed by Fidel remained in office and none held economic posts. When Raul was named as first secretary of the Communist Party on April 19, 2011, the power transition from Fidel to Raul was complete. Yet, this transition predates 2006 and, to some extent, has been taking place since the end of the Cold War. Raul was one of the architects of many of the post–Cold War economic changes that began in the mid-1990s in reaction to the end of the massive subsidies provided to the island by the Soviet Union in 1991. Economic reforms provided incentives for and opened the island to foreign investment as Cuba started a slow, if not haphazard, process toward a mixed economy with China serving as a model. Once Raul came to power the economic reforms became even more dramatic. Some of these include a greater diversity of trading partners, the move to decentralize the economy by providing greater autonomy and responsibility to state-run corporations, the ability of Cuban businesses to enter into joint-ventures with foreign investors, the reduction of government work force, the legalization of an increasing number of private sector businesses and entrepreneurial opportunities, the ability of farmers to rent idle, state-owned land, the ability of Cubans to sell and purchase homes, and the development of the Mariel Special Economic Zone.

Political reforms such as making it easier for Cubans to travel abroad have been implemented. Internationally known Cuban blogger and dissident, Yoani Sanchez, was allowed to travel to the United States and talk openly about the problems faced by the country. Other known dissidents such as Berta Soler and Rosa Maria Paya have traveled abroad. Groups such as the Citizens Committee for Racial Integration are raising awareness of the issue of racial discrimination in Cuba. The Ladies in White movement publicly protests against the continued government policy of detaining political dissidents. Although often intimidated, harassed, beaten, and arrested (in recent years long-term sentences for dissidents are not common), these dissidents operate in a relatively more open Cuban society. Signaling a change in 2012, Raul declared that "the members of the generation who made the revolution have the historic privilege of correcting the errors that they themselves have made." In February 2013 Raul announced that he will step down from the presidency in 2018. He named Miguel Diaz-Canel as his successor. Should Diaz-Canel become president he will be the first leader of revolutionary Cuba from the generation born after the revolution. Communist Cuba is in an economic and political transition and all the world is watching.

CUBAN AND THE UNITED STATES: FAMILY TIES

When Americans hear the word "Cuba," many thoughts, sounds, and images come to mind: the embargo, a bearded Fidel Castro in army fatigues, the song "Guantanamera," Teddy Roosevelt and the Rough Riders, Ernest Hemmingway, mojitos, classic automobiles, the missile crisis, the Bay of Pigs, cigars, rum, sugar cane, the mafia, gambling, *I Love Lucy*, the Malecon, raft people braving the shark-infested waters of the Straits of Florida, Little Havana, and many others. News from Cuba and discussions of the relationship between Cuba and the United States dominate the media in Miami and are never far from the front pages of the major U.S. newspapers on any given day. During presidential elections in the United States, both Democratic and Republican candidates visit the Cuban American community in Florida. They reiterate their support for the U.S. embargo against the island while taking note of Florida's important electoral college votes. Even in the post–Cold War era small or seemingly insignificant events concerning Cuba have a tendency to escalate and directly affect the United States. A case in point was the frenzied media coverage of the struggles of Elian Gonzalez, the small Cuban boy who became the center of an international tug-of-war between Cuba and the Cuban American community in Miami from November 1999 through June 2000. This is a clear illustration of how what should have been a low-profile "nonevent" became a major international story that mobilized Cuban American groups in southern Florida, dominated debate in the U.S. Congress, forced the U.S. attorney general to become involved, and directly affected a presidential campaign.

For better and for worse, Cuba and the United States have developed intimate ties since the middle of the nineteenth century. Within the framework of these intimate ties, the theme of U.S. hegemony (a form of domination) over the island and its people is the primary historical perspective. This hegemony was achieved not only through direct military, political, diplomatic, and economic means but also through cultural and social interactions. It is important to point out that hegemony implies some consent by the Cubans. American values were transmitted via business practices, tourism, movies, radio, newspapers, advertisements, music, consumer goods, education, protestant missionaries, and sports. These values fell upon a receptive people, especially at the time of the Cuban independence movement from

Spain. Spain represented backwardness, and the United States represented progress and civilization. Spanish hegemony was replaced by U.S. hegemony. Even after Fidel Castro's revolution and the rejection of U.S. dominance, it is these values that continue to tie Cuba and the United States together. Cubans are very proud of the major accomplishments of the revolution—cradle-to-grave healthcare, social security, and free education for all—but they still tend to measure their progress or lack thereof by the United States.

Although about one-tenth of the Cuban population has fled to the United States since 1959, emigration has been occurring since the middle of the 1800s. The cigar industry that developed in Key West, Jacksonville, Tampa, and Ocala is a direct result of Cuban immigration in the late 1800s and early 1900s. In addition to sharing a common people, Cubans and Americans share the love of cars, movies, jazz, Coca-Cola, and baseball. The United States brought baseball to Cuba, and it quickly became its national pastime in the early 1900s. Players in the U.S. winter league came to Cuba and played on racially integrated teams prior to their integration in the United States. Noted scholar Louis A. Perez, Jr. points out that integrated baseball in Cuba helped pave the way for the integration of baseball in the United States. Baseball continues to be a source of national pride today with the Cuban national team considered to be one of the best in the world. Cuban ballparks are always full, and watching a baseball game in Cuba is not much different than watching one in the United States. Traveling throughout the island one sees scores of kids playing baseball in fields and alleys and on the side streets—not that different from what one sees every spring and summer in the United States.

THE PEOPLE

Cubans are passionate, gregarious, hard-working, and full of life. They love to tell jokes (*chistes*), especially about themselves. They are extremely resourceful and have a talent for overcoming problems and obstacles. According to scholar Christina Garcia, "Cubans are masters at making the best out of any difficult situation. *Resolver* is probably the most commonly used verb in the language on the island . . .[It] means to survive, to overcome all obstacles with inventiveness, spontaneity, and most important, humor." Perhaps this explains how on a daily basis Cubans have survived the political, economic, and social problems that have characterized much of Cuban history. With three-fourths of its population of 11,167,325 people living in cities, Cuba is primarily an urban society. Life in the larger cities, such as Havana, Santiago, and Camaguey, tends to revolve around the porches, balconies, and verandas of the houses or apartment-style living spaces. Kids, dogs, and cats often play in these areas, while clothes are hanging on the line drying. In the evenings, adults tend to sit on their verandas and balconies and take advantage of the cooler temperatures. Neighbors chat with each other with the noise of the city—cars, trucks, taxis, restaurants, and dance clubs—as a backdrop. Many walk to the local kiosk to purchase the favorite Cuban ice cream, Coppelia. The youth flock to the local dance clubs to hear a wide variety of music, including rap, salsa, jazz, and the more traditional *son*.

The racial and ethnic makeup of the island is listed as 65 percent white or European, 24 percent mulatto or mixed, 10 percent black or Afro-Cuban, and 1 percent Chinese although these numbers are disputed. Most groups on the island argue that at least 50 percent of the population is Afro-Cuban. The vast majority of its people identify as Roman Catholic although it is estimated that only 10 percent attend mass regularly. A large portion of the population practices Afro-Cuban religions. Of these, Santeria, which is a mixture of Catholic and the African Yoruba traditions, is the most common. Over the years the communist government has come to an accommodation with the Catholic Church and religion in general. In 1991 the Communist Party ended its membership prohibition against believers, and a year later Cuba was declared a secular rather than an atheist state. This combined with the historic visits of Pope Paul II in 1998 and Pope Benedict in 2012 has resulted in more visible signs of religion on the island.

Compared to the vast majority of developing countries in the world, Cuba scores extremely well on virtually all indicators of socioeconomic development: life expectancy, access to healthcare and housing, education levels, employment rates, status of women, and infant mortality rates. Its adult literacy rate of 99.8 percent compares very favorably with the wealthiest countries in the world. The security net of free healthcare, education, and social security is rarely found among the developing countries of the world. Cuba has an abundance of doctors—approximately 1 for every 200 people. School attendance is mandatory through the ninth grade. The government invests large sums into day care centers and primary, secondary, and vocational schools. In 1959, there were only three universities. Today, universities, institutes, and vocational schools are scattered across the entire island. The government provides for a wide variety of cultural and literary programs for all citizens.

THE LAND AND THE ECONOMY

Cuba, covering an area of 44,827 square miles, is the largest island in the Caribbean and is about the size of the state of Pennsylvania. It is located south of Florida, north of Jamaica, and to the northwest of Haiti. The island runs approximately 785 miles in an east-west direction and consists mostly of flat to rolling plains with rugged hills and mountains in the southeast. Its temperate, tropical climate and adequate rainfall across the island provide an excellent agricultural base for its economy. The rainy season runs from May to October. The east coast is subject to hurricanes from August to November. The soil is also ideally suited for a variety of crops, including sugar cane, tobacco, citrus fruits, coffee, rice, potatoes, beans, and livestock. Agriculture, which has traditionally been the mainstay of the economy, often suffers from a lack of foreign exchange (internationally accepted currencies) to purchase needed fertilizers, oil, pesticides, and equipment. The island has deposits of cobalt, nickel, iron ore, copper, manganese, silica, oil, and natural gas. It is estimated to have about 10 percent of the world's known nickel reserves with most found in the highlands on the eastern part of the island. Since 1992, the Canadian company Sherritt—which has investments not only in nickel but also in oil, natural gas,

Workers harvest tobacco leaves in the western province of Pinar del Rio. Cuban cigars have historically been considered to be the best in the world and most tobacco, even during the Castro era, is grown on private, family-owned farms although all tobacco must be sold to the government. Tobacco is Cuba's fifth-largest export behind petroleum, nickel, medical products, and sugar. (Corel)

and cobalt—has been one of the largest, single-foreign companies on the island. Cuba's major industries include sugar, oil, food, textiles, tobacco, chemicals, paper and wood products, metals, cement, fertilizers, consumer goods, agricultural machinery, and pharmaceuticals.

Since colonial days, the island has been dependent on trade with the rest of the world. For approximately 150 years, sugar was the dominant industry, but today tourism, services, nickel, pharmaceuticals, cigars, and remittances generate more revenue. Exports include oil, nickel, medical products, sugar, tobacco, fish, citrus, and coffee. Most of its exports go to Canada (17.7 percent), China (16.9 percent), Venezuela (12.5 percent), the Netherlands (5.9 percent), and Spain (5.9 percent). Imports include oil, food, machinery and equipment, and chemicals. Most of its imports come from Venezuela (38.3 percent), China (10.8 percent), Spain (8.9 percent), Brazil (5.2 percent), and, interestingly enough, the United States (4.3 percent). In 2000 the United States passed the Trade Sanctions Reform and Export Enhancement Act, which allows private companies, such as Archer Daniels Midland, to sell food, agricultural products, and medicine to Cuba on a cash-only basis. Today the United States is the largest supplier of food and agricultural products to the island.

When Fidel Castro came to power in 1959, Cuba began to move toward a socialist economic system. By the early 1970s this system, in which the state owns and runs virtually all the major businesses and industries, was fully implemented. The Soviet Union bought Cuban sugar and provided Cuba with needed oil and subsidies. With the collapse of the Soviet Union in 1991, it was evident that the Cuban economy was at a transition point. The island lost about 70 percent of its exports and imports and about $8 billion a year in subsidies and aid. The impact was dramatic. Draconian austerity measures during the so-called special period allowed the island to survive the next few years. Cuba became dependent upon remittances from exiles living abroad in the United States. It needed to find foreign exchange (money accepted on the international market such as U.S. dollars or euros), capital, technology, and markets for its products.

Since the mid-1990s the country has been gradually moving toward a more open, mixed-economy similar to China and Vietnam. Describing these economic changes on the island Raul Castro said, "I'm in no rush. Go slow, but go forward." As head of the Cuban Armed Forces, Raul sent hundreds of military officials abroad to study modern business management in the 1990s. While the majority of the economic enterprises on the island are run by the state, many by the military, all are managed under modern business principles. Cuba began courting foreign investors and trading partners in the mid-1990s and has since then increasingly made it easier for foreign companies to invest on the island. In 2003 Raul invited then Chinese premier Zhu Rongji, who played a primary role in opening up his country to trade and investment, for a series of lectures across the island. Visits by then Chinese president Hu Jintao in 2004 and 2008 and the visit of current president Xi Jinping in July 2014 were symbolic of the deepening economic ties between Cuba and China. Spain, Italy, Germany, Russia, Venezuela, Brazil, the Netherlands, Austria, Jamaica, Mexico, Martinique, Canada, France, and other countries also have investments on the island. Large hotel chains, primarily from Spain, Jamaica, and Canada, have signed joint agreements and are operating in the tourist sector. Two Cuban companies, Cubanacan and Gaviota, were created to manage the foreign investments in tourism. Both companies are funded in part by the Cuban government and in part by foreign investments. Gaviota, run by the Cuban military, is especially known for providing access for foreigners to Cuba's advanced medical technology and eye, open-heart, and plastic surgery capabilities. Billboards and wall murals that used to be covered with revolutionary chants now emphasize hospitality and tourism. Economic reforms have allowed the number of small, private businesses to increase dramatically.

Varadero, just east of Havana, is the tourist capital of the island with its five-star hotels and beachfront properties that attract hundreds of thousands of tourists from Canada and Europe each year. Those Cubans who are fortunate enough to work in the tourist industry earn much more in dollars than they do at other jobs earning Cuban pesos. It is not uncommon for teachers, engineers, and even doctors to moonlight as taxi drivers. It is important to note that tourism is a double-edged sword for Raul Castro. It brings in the dollars that the island needs, yet it contributes to a growing economic gap between those Cubans who have access to dollars and those who do not. The egalitarian nature of the revolution is being threatened, and resentment among those not in the dollar economy is growing. An aging population, with 18.7 percent over the age sixty and the expectation that this will increase to 30 percent in the next two decades, presents major problems such as dramatically increased healthcare expenses and a smaller sized working population with which the country will have to manage.

THE POLITICAL SYSTEM

It is important to note the overlap between the Communist Party and the government to understand the Cuban political system. The Communist Party is the only legal political party. The two most powerful organs in the Communist Party are the Political Bureau or the Politburo and the Secretariat. Almost all of the individuals in these organs have close ties to Raul Castro who is the first secretary of the party. The lowest organ of the Communist Party is the Party Congress, which rarely meets. The Politburo and the first secretary of the Party determine the membership of the Party Central Committee, which is "approved" by the Party Congress. The Party Central Committee meets regularly and serves to approve policies from the Politburo and the first secretary.

Anyone who is "elected" to government or public office is a member of the Communist Party. The lowest legislative body of the national government is the National Assembly of People's Power with 614 members. In the last election in 2013 Cuban voters simply approved a list of 614 nominees who were selected by the Communist Party. The People's Power meets only for a couple of days each year, has little real power, and serves to rubberstamp those selected by the party to serve on the more important governing bodies. The People's Power "elects" twenty-eight of its members to the Council of State. The members who are elected to the Council of State are all part of a single slate put together by the Communist Party, which includes the president and the vice presidents. There are no opposition candidates. The president of the Council of State appoints members to the Council of Ministers, and these appointments are approved by the People's Power. The president and the vice presidents of Cuba are "voted" upon by the People's Power but are all selected by the Communist Party and have no opposition candidates. Raul Castro is the current president of Cuba, and the first vice president is Diaz-Canel. In effect, the Communist Party controls all of the organs of government.

THEMES IN CUBAN HISTORY

There are several interrelated themes that reoccur throughout the history of Cuba. From its colonial era to the post–Cold War era the Cuban economy was primarily based upon the export of agricultural products, especially sugar. The dominance of King Sugar in the Cuban economy played a major role in determining the social class structure, the economy, and the political system. Island infrastructure and the financial system were tied directly into the sugar industry. To be successful, this agro-export model of development requires access to land, labor, and external markets. Historically, the land used for sugar production was controlled by a small group of political and economic elites and foreigners. This also meant that most of the economic wealth was controlled by a small group of local political and economic elites and foreigners, initially from Spain and then from the United States. Since 1959 it has been the Cuban state that has controlled the land and the wealth. The need for labor led to the establishment of slavery shortly after its founding until 1886—longer than any country in the Americas. The post-slavery era meant that control of labor unions that were tied into the sugar industry played a crucial role in the internal politics of the island. Historically, Cuba has depended upon major powers as its primary market—Spain, the United States, and the Soviet Union.

Another related theme that directly affected the politics and economics of Cuba has been the boom-bust cycle of King Sugar. Global demand and supply determines the price of an agricultural commodity like sugar. During the boom part of the cycle, greater demand leads to a higher price which encourages more sugar production and Cuba's economy would then experience growth. Yet, more sugar production eventually brings the price down and leads to the bust cycle in which Cuba would then experience an economic contraction or a recession. The supply of sugar is also affected by the presence of alternatives to cane sugar such as sugar beets and corn sugar. These historic boom-bust cycles often correlated with political instability on the island. Thus, the need to diversify the Cuban economy was crucial so as to avoid the sugar boom-bust cycle and possible political instability. Yet, diversification was contrary to the common interests of the dominant powers and the sugar elites in Cuba.

Dominant powers such as Spain, the United States, and the Soviet Union adopted policies that provided incentives to maintain King Sugar and made it difficult, if not impossible, to develop a thriving and competitive manufacturing sector on the island. For example, the United States managed this through a reciprocal tariff and quota system that gave benefits, such as lower tariffs and a guaranteed quota in the U.S. market, to Cuban sugar producers and, in return, Cuba placed a lower tariff on U.S. manufactured products coming into the country. The United States punished, through higher tariffs and the absence of a quota system, a growing Cuban manufacturing sector based on consumer goods such as food processing, furniture, toiletries, and shoes that began to appear and compete with sugar by the mid-1920s. During this period, the politically dominant sugar elite feared the loss of preferential treatment in the U.S. market and fought politically against local manufacturers who supported an increase in tariffs on U.S. manufactured products coming into the Cuban market. Interestingly enough, the National Association for Cuban Industrialists was able to finally convince the newly elected Gerardo Machado government in 1927 to protect this growing manufacturing sector. Unfortunately, this happened when U.S. government policies and global market forces pushed the entire world economy into the Great Depression. Cuba has always been and will always be economically vulnerable to global forces beyond its control.

Dependence on powerful countries implies a relationship in which Cuba has been vulnerable to actions taken by countries over which it has little control. For almost 400 years Cuba was dependent upon Spain and then from 1898 to 1959 the island was dependent upon the United States. This dependence took the form of a hegemonic relationship. In this relationship Cuba looked to its hegemon, Spain and then the United States, for its identity and its political, economic, social, and cultural values. Cuba's identity was literally tied to Spain and then the United States. To illustrate this fact, under Spain the national pastime of Cuba was bullfighting. Virtually every small town in Cuba had a bullfighting arena of some type. With the defeat of Spain in 1898 and the growth of the relationship with the United States, bullfighting disappeared rather quickly and it was replaced by the new national pastime of baseball. Almost every town in Cuba has at least one baseball field today. Noted scholar Louis A. Perez, Jr. described the relationship between Cuba and the United States in the following manner:

> The two cultures converged on each other, interacting and merging. . . . They intruded on one another as the national character of each was in the process of formation, which is to say they entered each other's national consciousness and henceforth the character of each would retain permanent traces of the encounter. . . . US forms expanded across the island. Important facets of daily life and ordinary social relations with Cuba were influenced by ways and things North American, often with Cuban acknowledgment and acquiescence, for these forms became one of the primary means by which Cubans arrived at self-definition. . . . Many of the values that subsequently gave meaning to Cuban lives, collectively and individually, were of North American origin.[2]

These intimate, pervasive, family-like ties between Cuba and its hegemon were so close that breaking them required a violent process. In the case of Spain it required a thirty-year war of independence and in the case of the United States it required a revolution. Those intimate ties between Cuba and the United States have to some extent even survived the Cuban revolution as President Bill Clinton characterized post-revolution U.S. relations with Cuba as a "terrible family feud."

From 1959 to 1991 Cuba was dependent upon the USSR, but this Cold War dependence took the form of a strategic relationship rather than hegemony. Each received specific benefits from the relationship but neither developed intimate social and cultural ties. Cuba received subsidized oil from the Soviet Union and a market for its sugar. In return, the Soviets gained access to many developing countries in Africa, Asia, and Latin America because of Cuba's leadership role among the non-aligned, developing countries of the world. The Soviets also received the benefit of having a political ally literally ninety miles from the United States. Political scientist Michael Erisman characterized this Soviet and Cuban relationship as one of simply a convergence of interests that came to an end with the end of the Cold War. In the post–Cold War era Cuba is no longer dependent upon a single, major world power such as Spain, the United States, or the Soviet Union. Yet, China is beginning to develop a strong and strategic political and economic relationship with Cuba and in a key sector of its economy—oil and energy—it is still dependent primarily on one country—Venezuela.

A final theme and constant in Cuban history is the search and struggle for a truly Cuban identity or nationalism. As indicated earlier, Cuban identity throughout most of its history was often intertwined with, submerged under, and defined by Spain and then the United States. Yet, Cuban voices often appeared in opposition to Spanish and American hegemony. Creole landowners, those Spaniards from elite families who were born in Cuba and had little to no say in Spanish colonial policy over the island, began to express their identity, separate from Spain, by the end of the 1700s and throughout the 1800s. This Cuban identity was found in organizations such as the Economic Society under the leadership of Francisco de Arango y Parreno and in the first "Cuban" newspaper, which appeared in 1791. Creole intellectuals such as Felix Varela and Jose Antonio Saco expressed a Cuban nationalism and a desire for independence from Spain. During the *Cuba Libre* or independence era of 1868 through 1898, voices such as Carlos Manuel de Cespedes, Antonio Maceo, and the father figure of modern Cuba, Jose Marti, spoke of a Cuban identity. While Marti's nationalism expressed the necessity of independence from Spain and a prophetic fear of U.S. dominance, his nationalism was more inclusive than the previous creole nationalists. He expressed a Cuban identity "that means more than white, more than mulatto, more than Negro."

It is a "revolution [that] will be for the benefit of all who contribute to it" and a vision of a free Cuba "with all and for the well-being of all."[3]

Fidel Castro sought to carve out a Cuban identity separate from the United States. This identity was built upon the three pillars of the revolution—education, healthcare, and social security. It was built upon Castro's ability to stand up to so-called Yankee imperialism and the leadership role that Cuba plays among the developing countries of the world coupled with his ability to take a small island nation and give it influence on the world stage far beyond what anyone could have predicted. Yet, his failure to liberalize the political system, his often brutal suppression of the Cuban voices of dissent, and an economy that is always building for the future have led to other expressions of Cuban identity and nationalism, especially among Cuba's young or the post-revolution generation, such as singer-song writer Carlos Varela and internationally known blogger and dissident Yoani Sanchez. Afro-Cubans, contrary to the rhetoric of the revolution, continue to struggle, just as their ancestors did, to become full and equal partners in the expression of Cuban nationalism. Exiled Cubans living in the United States, who each year at Christmas make the promise of "next year in Cuba," have created an identity counter to that of revolutionary Cuba, while their born-in-America sons and daughters have created yet another Cuban identity. Cubans, divided by geography, generation, and race, continue to search and struggle for that illusive identity that truly reflects all of them.

NOTES

1. Maria Finn Dominguez, *Cuba in Mind* (New York: Vintage Books, 2004), xv.

2. Louis A. Perez, Jr., *On Becoming Cuban* (Chapel Hill: University of North Carolina Press), 7.

3. Louis A. Perez, Jr., *Cuba: Between Reform and Revolution*, 3rd ed. (Oxford: Oxford University Press, 2006), 109, 111.

2

Colonialism, Sugar, and Nationalism: Cuba to 1868

Sugar changes its coloring; it is born brown and whitens itself; at first it is a syrupy mulatto and in this state pleases the common taste; then it is bleached and refined until it can pass for white, travel all over the world, reach all mouths, and bring a better price, climbing to the top of the social ladder.

Fernando Ortiz, *Tobacco and Sugar*[1]

It is quite common today to hear people talk about how events in one part of the world have a direct impact on other parts of the world. People and media commentators often speak of global interdependence as if it were something new. Yet, during the four centuries of Spanish rule over Cuba (1492–1898) one can easily see how events in the Caribbean, Spain, greater Europe, and the United States directly affected the island. One can also see how events in Cuba directly affected the world beyond its borders. It is not insignificant that one of the primary consequences or legacies of Spanish colonialism is that the island became part of an interdependent world never fully in control of its own destiny.

The indigenous peoples of Cuba were either wiped out through disease and Spanish brutality or absorbed through intermarriage in the late 1400s and 1500s. They would not play a significant role in the development of Cuba. The *conquistadores*, after discovering the island did not have significant deposits of gold and silver, quickly moved on to the immense wealth and treasures found in the Aztec and Inca empires in what is today Mexico and Peru. Thus, for nearly 300 years the island of Cuba was relegated to serving merely as a stopping over point between Spain and the riches from its colonies in Spanish America (Mexico and Central and South America). Little change would take place until several events in the 1700s set the stage for the island's transformation. These included an eleven-month occupation of Havana by the English in 1762, the emergence of the United States as a market for Cuba, the Spanish Crown's liberalizing trade reforms of 1778 and 1791, and, perhaps more importantly, a slave rebellion in St. Domingue (Haiti) in 1791 that dramatically affected the world market for sugar. These events set into motion forces that would radically alter the destiny of the island.

With St. Domingue no longer producing sugar, the world market price increased. Increases in sugar production with growing demand in the United States and Europe brought tremendous wealth to the emerging Cuban Creole (Spaniards born in the New World) planter class (large landowners). As the sugar trade expanded dramatically, the United States became the major market for Cuban sugar by the middle of the 1800s. In fact, noted historian Louis A. Perez, Jr. points out that by that time North America had come to replace Spain as a point of reference for most Cubans, the United States had come to represent progress and modernization and Spain, decline and backwardness.[2]

At the same time, there were negative consequences to the sugar boom. It exacerbated the economic inequality on the island. Most did not share in the newfound wealth. Sugar escalated the island's dependence on the slave trade, although ironically this occurred when many countries were banning it and, in fact, Spain agreed to suppress the slave trade in 1817. Of course, it continued and prospered illegally. This also occurred at a time when abolitionist groups were challenging the very institution of slavery. Slave rebellions were common throughout the first six decades of the 1800s. The island's wealthy Creoles came into sharp conflict with the *peninsulares* (Spaniards living in the New World who were born in Spain) over restrictive trade policies and the lack of opportunity to participate in the political decision-making processes. But Cuban nationalism would be hindered by the lack of agreement over the issue of slavery. This divided the nationalist movement and made the struggle for independence (*Cuba Libre*) in the second half of the 1800s most difficult.

PRECOLONIAL AND COLONIAL CUBA

There were three different cultural groups on the island before the arrival of the Spaniards: the Ciboney consisting of the Ciboney-Guayabo Blanco and the Ciboney-Cayo Redondo; the Majari; and the Arawaks consisting of the Sub-Tainos and the Tainos. The earliest cultural group to arrive in Cuba was the Ciboney-Guayabo Blanco who migrated around 1000 BCE and lived primarily along the coasts of western and central Cuba. The Ciboney-Cayo Redondo migrated around 1000 CE. The Ciboney depended primarily on the sea for food. While it is not known how many Ciboney existed at the time of the Spanish conquest, by that time they were largely limited to a few isolated settlements in western Cuba. The Mayari migrated to Cuba sometime between the ninth and eleventh centuries and lived inland along rivers. It was the Arawak Indians from South America who overran and absorbed the Mayari and displaced the Ciboneys from the eastern and central parts of the island. The Sub-Tainos were the first to arrive in the mid-ninth century. While they did depend on the sea and rivers for some of their food, the Sub-Tainos cultivated a variety of crops on plots of land. These crops included maize, sweet potatoes, yucca, tomatoes, pineapples, and berries. They baked cassava, a hearty, unleavened bread that the Spanish called "bread of the earth," used pepper to preserve meat, and cultivated tobacco. Known for their craft skills, the Sub-Tainos carved furniture, weaved cotton, and assembled hammocks, fishing lines, nets, ropes, cord, mats, and mattresses. Tobacco and snuff were used in religious ceremonies, and the Sub-Tainos lived in straw, palm-thatched huts called *bohios*. The Sub-Tainos had three distinct social classes: the chiefs (*caciques*), a small middle class that acted as advisers to the chiefs, and commoners. The second migration of Arawak Indians, the Tainos, began in the fifteenth century but was interrupted by the arrival of the Spaniards. Estimates of the number of indigenous peoples on the island at the time of the Spanish conquest vary from 16,000 to 600,000. The best estimate is about 112,000 with the vast majority being Arawak.[3] Christopher Columbus made landfall in Cuba on the morning of October 29, 1492, somewhere on the north coast between Gibara and Lucrecia Bay. Columbus wrote that he had "never seen anything so beautiful" and later wrote, "It is certain that where there is such marvelous scenery, there must be much from which profit can be made."

Spanish colonialism in the New World was fueled by the missionary zeal to convert non-Christians, the Crown's desire for gold and silver, and the personal motives of the *conquistadores* and settlers. In the late

1400s and early 1500s, Spanish power in the Caribbean was located on the island of Hispaniola (today the island consists of the countries of Haiti and Dominican Republic). The island lacked a reliable labor force and, more importantly, it lacked the gold and silver that Spain wanted. Believing that Cuba had plenty of gold, Sebastian de Ocampo explored and sailed around the island in 1508. In 1511, Diego Velazquez landed near Baracoa and established the first Spanish settlement. He served as the first governor until his death in 1524. The indigenous peoples in the eastern part of the island fought Velazquez but were defeated largely due to the superior weapons of the Spanish. A small amount of gold was found in Cuba, and the indigenous peoples worked the mines at La Mina (close to Havana) and near Bayamo. Others were forced to pan for gold in the Arimao, Escambray, and Holquin Rivers. Velazquez issued *encomiendas* as a method of controlling the Indians. The *encomienda* system legally tied the indigenous peoples to the Spaniards. The indigenous peoples served as laborers, and, in return, were converted to and given instruction in Christianity. Cruelty, physical abuse, and overwork were common practices by the Spanish *encomenderos*. Bartoleme de las Casas, a Dominican Friar and Spanish historian, writing in 1542 stated that the Spaniards are "acting like ravening beasts, killing, terrorizing, afflicting, torturing, and destroying native peoples, doing all this with the strangest and most varied new methods of cruelty, never seen or heard of before."[4] The indigenous population of Cuba was so small by 1513 that the first Africans were imported as slave laborers. It is important to note that although many Indian words made their way into the Spanish language that is used on the island, the indigenous peoples had little impact on Cuban political, economic, and social development. Until the end of the nineteenth century, Cuban cultural identity was shaped primarily by Spanish colonialism, the importation of African slaves, and an economy based upon sugar.

It was from Cuba that Hernan Cortez left for Mexico in 1519. Santiago de Cuba, with its deep water harbor, had been settled four years earlier and was the most important city on the island. By the middle of the century, the focus of Spanish power shifted from the Caribbean to Mexico and South America largely due to the vast amounts of gold and silver found there and the realization that there was little to be found in Cuba. Many on the island left for Mexico and South America with the *conquistadores* in search of fortune and fame. For many years, the population on the island declined. Day-to-day life was extremely difficult and uncertain with the genuine fear of slave uprisings and attack by the English or the French. By 1544, there were no more than

7,000 people on the island and of these 660 were Spanish, 800 were slaves, and the remainder were indigenous peoples.[5] The Catholic Church provided the only education.

It was at this time that Havana with its deep-water harbor became the most important city on the island. It had become the "key to the New World." It served as a transition point for the riches taken from the Americas that were going to Spain because ships could take advantage of the Gulf Stream that helped to carry them eastward and the shifting trade winds between winter and summer. For about a month of each year, the Spanish fleet waited in Havana for the treasure ships coming from Mexico and South America. The fleet then escorted them to Cadiz or Seville. As a result, Havana became a military and shipbuilding center, a provider of supplies (salt beef, leather, vegetables, and fruit) for the fleet's return trip to Spain and a naval seaport. La Fuerza, the first military fortress made of stone in the New World, was built in Havana between 1558 and 1577. Shipbuilding became one of the major industries in the late 1500s. By 1592 the city had constructed a canal that brought fresh water from the Almendares River. According to scholars Roberto Segre, Mario Coyula, and Joseph Scarpaci, this was the first public works program in the New World, and it was funded primarily from taxes on the sale of wine. Two other fortresses, El Morro and La Punta, were completed by 1610.

The vast wealth and riches of Mexico and South America bypassed Cuba, so the island and its inhabitants turned to their primary resource, land. The large forests of mahogany and cedar supported the growing shipbuilding industry in Havana. Mahogany was also exported to Spain to meet the needs of the furniture industry. Spaniards received land grants called *mercedes* from which they were to meet the needs of both the neighboring towns and the Spanish fleet. Sweet potatoes, yams, corn, beans, and yucca were cultivated as well. Sugar cane was introduced as early as the second voyage of Columbus, and there were a few mills (*trapiches*) founded in the 1520s. But sugar would not become important to Cuba for another two centuries largely due to the non-availability of credit, the low demand in Spain, and the expense of providing an adequate labor supply. Large cattle ranches covered much of Cuba, and leather and hides were the largest exports until the early 1700s. Tobacco was initially grown in areas that had easy access to port facilities such as in Havana and Trinidad. Snuff was particularly sought after by the smugglers. It is important to note that under Spanish mercantilism practices, those on the island could legally trade only with Spain. This made it difficult to gain access to European goods at the cheapest prices. Even though the French,

English, and Dutch were maritime and political rivals of Spain and encouraged piracy against the Spanish, merchants of Cuba engaged in some profitable illegal trade with them largely because they offered goods at a lower price than what could be obtained in Seville. It was this desire for access to cheaper goods that began to create a conflict of interest between the Spanish Crown and its settlers in Cuba.

The colonial governing structure in Cuba was headed by a governor who was appointed by the Crown. Initially, the local governing institution of each settlement—the *cabildo*—was given significant autonomy. Members of the local *cabildo* elected a *procurador* who met annually with other *procuradores* in Santiago. These individuals discussed local grievances and issues of importance to their settlement and the island as a whole. This group elected a representative to present these issues and grievances to the governor, the Crown's representative. This practice came to an end in 1532 as the governors sought to centralize the political processes in the Spanish colonies in the New World. The Crown's administrative control over Cuba and the rest of its New World colonies came to reside with the *peninsulares*. Local administrative positions were sold by the Crown at auction. Corruption and patronage became common practice. Creoles rarely achieved political positions of high rank. Over time, this inability of Creoles to participate in the decision-making processes created a growing resentment toward the *peninsulares* that manifested itself in the growth of nationalism and the desire for independence in the second half of the nineteenth century.

From the middle of the 1500s and throughout the 1600s, England, France, and the Netherlands competed with Spain for control of the Caribbean. Spanish cities were under constant threat of attack, and its treasure fleets were prime targets. By the early 1600s, the English, Dutch, and French were also actively seeking new colonies in the region. With the English capture of Jamaica in 1655, the Spaniards in Cuba became quite concerned over the probability of attack. The European countries created their own buccaneers (mercenaries who engaged in piracy during non-war periods) and attacked each other's settlements and colonies. The English buccaneer Henry Morgan attacked the eastern part of Cuba and terrorized it settlers. Spanish buccaneers frequently attacked Jamaica (England) and St. Domingue (France). Recognizing the loss in potential revenues due to these attacks, the English and Spanish sought to end hostilities and trade peacefully. In 1670, Spain recognized England's colonies in the Caribbean, and in 1697 France agreed to end its buccaneer raids in the Caribbean in exchange for recognition of its authority over St. Domingue (Haiti).

By the early 1700s, tobacco had replaced leather and hides as the dominant economic sector of Cuba largely due to growing demand in Europe. Tobacco farms (*vegas*) were located throughout the island but primarily in the western part (Pinar del Rio) along the Cuyaguateje River, where the best tobaccos, such as Vuelta Abajo, are grown. The Spanish created an official monopoly on tobacco in 1717. Local producers had to sell their product to the Crown's purchasing agency (*estanco*) either in Havana or other major cities where it was then sold to Cadiz or Seville. There were protests and even rebellions against these trade restrictions that were met with repression by the Crown. Despite the restrictions, a local cottage industry flourished and much of the tobacco crop and snuff went to smugglers from other countries.

In 1713, the South Sea Company of London was granted both limited trading rights with and an exclusive license (*asiento*) to sell slaves to the Spanish colonies until 1739. A Spanish company was granted a monopoly on the sale of slaves after that, although the company bought the slaves form the South Sea Company. Even with the smuggling of slaves into the island, Creole planters simply could not get enough slaves and this contributed to the limitations on the growth of the sugar industry. They preferred male rather than female slaves to work in the cane fields and believed that regularly replacing slaves through the importation of new ones was cheaper than raising slave children. Females were also seen as less productive and more costly should they become pregnant. This meant that Cuban planters had to depend on a continual replenishment of the supply of slaves. Another problem was that only a few of the wealthy, established Creole families could afford to purchase slaves. Also, much of the land that was converted to the production of sugar in the middle of the 1700s took place on established estates by the wealthiest Creole families. Others converted tobacco lands to sugar when the tobacco state monopoly was created and some converted parts of their cattle ranches. Since there was no banking system in Cuba, the Creole planters often borrowed from local merchants at exorbitant interest rates. In fact, from 1740 to 1760 more than 80 percent of the slaves in Cuba were purchased on credit.[6] Planters were, in more ways than one, dependent upon the merchants not only for loans but also for everything else, from wine and wheat to imported machinery and tools.

The cattle ranchers, the tobacco and sugar planters, and the merchants in the urban areas were at the top of Cuban society during the eighteenth century. Beneath them were small landowners, usually tobacco growers, lawyers, and skilled tradesmen such as carpenters and individuals who managed the large plantations of the Creole planters. Below this group existed a large number of people (Europeans, mulattos, and freed slaves) who worked for wages and lacked the resources to ever own land. Finally, at the bottom of the class structure were the slaves who worked primarily on the sugar plantations. By 1774, the population of Cuba had reached 170,000 of whom about 40 percent were mulatto or African. Havana, a walled and heavily fortified city, had a permanent garrison of Spanish soldiers and a population of about 75,000. It had a large population of free mulattos and Africans estimated to be about 10,000.[7]

SETTING THE STAGE FOR THE RISE OF KING SUGAR

Several events in the late 1700s and the early 1800s set the stage for the growth of the sugar industry on the island. Spain allied with France in its struggle with the English during the Seven Years War (1756–1763). In August 1762, the English under Lord Albemarle attacked and occupied Havana. Juan do Prado, the island's governor and captain-general, the Spanish administrators, and virtually all of the *peninsulares* left the island. The English eliminated the Spanish trade restrictions and more than 700 merchant ships visited Havana during the occupation.[8] This opened Havana to a large number of goods from North America and England. Grain and slave merchants and dealers in sugar equipment such as machetes, cauldrons, and ladles arrived. Items such as hats, stockings, linen, cloth, and wool were available. Eleven months later, the English traded Cuba back to Spain in exchange for Florida in the Treaty of Paris that ended the war. This was largely due to the influence of the English sugar planters in Jamaica who prophetically saw Cuban sugar as a future competitor. But the impact of these eleven months would be felt throughout the island. The Cuban Creoles had received their first taste of free trade and they liked it. They also became aware of the potential of investment from North Americans, the large North American market for their goods, and access to new technology. The Creole sugar planters benefitted immediately from the English occupation largely due to the increased availability of slave labor and equipment. More than 10,000 slaves were brought into Havana, as many that normally would enter in ten years. Sugar exports prior to the English occupation had averaged 300 tons a year and from 1763 through 1769 they averaged 2,000 tons a year.[9]

Conde de Ricla, the new Spanish governor and captain-general, had Havana strengthened by building another fort, La Cabana. This construction required a large increase in the number of slaves and when construction was completed most of them were sold on the market to sugar planters. By 1774, there were more than 44,000 slaves in Cuba.[10] With the Spanish treasure fleets no longer regularly coming to Havana, much of the shipping industry was converted to building cauldrons and ladles for sugar mills. Sugar exports reached 10,000 tons a year during the 1770s.[11] In 1778, the Bourbon monarch Charles III of Spain, in an effort to revive the empire's economic growth, issued his Decree of Free Trade that allowed the twenty-four ports in Spanish America to trade freely among themselves and with any port in Spain. By 1790, sugar production had reached 14,000 tons.[12] In 1791, Charles III agreed to allow the free and unlimited importation of slaves largely due to the lobbying efforts of Cuban Creole planter Francisco de Arrongo. By the next year, the number of slaves on the island reached more than 84,000.[13] When the war between Spain and France started the following year, Arrongo and other Creole planters convinced Captain-General Don Luis de las Casas (who also owned a sugar plantation) that Cuban ports should be open to neutral and allied shipping—in particular, the United States and England.

In 1791, a slave rebellion started in the French colony of St. Domingue (Haiti). St. Domingue was the largest producer of sugar in the world at that time. By the time the slaves, who were led by Toussaint-Louverture and Jean-Jacques Dessalines, had won their independence in 1804, more than 180 sugar and 900 coffee plantations had been destroyed. More than 2,000 Europeans and 10,000 African slaves had lost their lives. Sugar exports declined from 70,000 tons in 1791 to 2,020 tons in 1825.[14] This situation created a tremendous opportunity for the expansion of the Cuban sugar industry. Many of the French planters fled to Cuba and brought with them their sugar expertise to areas around Cienfuegos, Nipe, Banes, and Nuevitas. By 1796, the price of sugar had more than doubled, and England provided one-third of the island's imports and purchased one-half of its exports. At the same time, Cuba began turning more and more to the United States for its exports and imports. In the same year, only 100 U.S. ships arrived in Cuba, yet by 1800 that had increased to 606 ships. By 1805, there were twice as many sugar mills in Cuba as there were before the English occupation of Havana and sugar production reached 34,000 tons.[15]

Arrongo, who had traveled secretly to Liverpool in 1788 to spy on England's technology improvements such as the steam engine, Conde de Casa Montalvo, Jose Ricardo O'Farrill, and other modernizing Creoles were intent on creating a rich, sugar-based economy in Cuba. It was to be based on the expansion of slavery, better infrastructure, modern sugar mills (*ingenios*), and greater access to capital or finances and the world market. They helped create Cuba's first newspaper and came to represent a Cuban nationalist rather than a Spanish point of view. This reform-minded and nationalist viewpoint manifested itself in the creation of the Economy Society (*Sociedad Economia de Amigos del Pais*). The members of the society were well educated, urban, and internationalist in their orientation. They played the primary role in developing an intellectual climate with the support of Creole planters that resulted in dramatic changes to Cuban economic policies of the early 1800s. In particular, the Economic Society was responsible for the land reform that set the stage for the growth of the sugar industry. Land that was previously held in usufruct (a condition in which a person did not own the land but could profit from the crops grown on the land) became private property as long as the person could show he had been in possession of the land for ninety years and had been cultivating it for forty years. Cattle ranchers holding *mercedes* were no longer required to provide beef for the neighboring cities and could manage their lands as they saw fit. Fighting a war against France and needing to replenish its treasury, the Crown agreed to begin to sell its land to Cuban Creoles. Trees, especially hardwood forests of mahogany, could now be cleared for agricultural production. These reforms increased the number of land owners and allowed property owners greater freedom in the use of the land.

The sugar boom in the aftermath of the slave rebellion in St. Domingue came to an end just after the turn of the century. With high prices during the 1790s, sugar production increased throughout the Caribbean and in Europe where the sugar beet had been introduced. This created a sugar surplus on the world market and drove the price down. Other factors also made it difficult for the growth of the sugar industry during the first two decades of the century. These included the wars of independence in Spanish America, the campaign to end the slave trade, and the growth of the coffee industry. By 1808, Napoleon Bonaparte occupied the Iberian Peninsula and placed his brother Joseph on the Spanish Crown. This event was the catalyst for the wars of independence in the Spanish colonies in the Americas that lasted through the mid-1820s. But, the Creole planter class in Cuba remained "ever faithful" to the Crown and did not join this struggle for several reasons. Large numbers of Spanish troops who were involved in the fight against the revolutionaries were stationed in Cuba. It would have been difficult to defeat these troops. The growing wealth from tobacco, coffee, and sugar and greater control over the use of their own land led the Creole planters to believe that the risk and cost of failure was too great. Finally, the memory of the tremendous destruction during the slave rebellion in St. Domingue also weighed on their decision because by this time there were more Africans (slaves and free) than Europeans on the island.

In 1808, Denmark, England, and the United States banned the slave trade. Sweden, France, and Holland quickly followed. This abolitionist movement was clearly a threat to the future of the island in the eyes of the Creole planters. Arrongo and the other Cuban Creoles extensively lobbied the Spanish government not to abolish the slave trade. Nonetheless, Spain, under tremendous pressure from powerful England, who played the dominant role in the coalition that defeated Napoleon, agreed to end the slave trade by 1820. In reaction to this, Cuba imported more than 100,000 slaves from 1816 to 1820—as many or more than those who were imported in the previous 300 years.[16] Creole planters encouraged the governor to "turn a blind eye" to the ban and it was common practice for illegal slave traders regularly to pay tribute or bribes to the governors and captain-generals in Cuba after 1820.

During the first two decades of the century, the price of coffee remained high and many coffee planters saw no reason to plant sugar cane. Coffee plantations (*cafetales*) were largely the result of the French exodus from St. Domingue. The best coffee growing regions were in Pinar del Rio, the area southwest of Havana, and the region around Santiago. By 1827, Cuba was exporting 20,000 tons of coffee, and there was more land devoted to the production of coffee than sugar.[17] Yet, many of these planters also owned sugar estates and, according to historian Hugh Thomas, by 1829 they realized that the return on their investment in coffee was less than the return on their investment in sugar. Coffee production in Cuba declined until 1834 and then remained constant until the mid-1840s. Production then declined precipitously largely due to growing competition from Brazil. More and more *cafetales* were converted to the production of sugar cane. Coffee would continue to be grown on the island but the stage was set for the dominance of sugar. It is important to note that coffee producers on the eastern part of the island came to blame sugar for the decline of their fortunes. They came to see the sugar industry, sugar planters, slavery, and the Spanish Crown in the same negative light. Some of them would initiate the independence movement in the 1860s.

With the Crown's monopoly on tobacco ending in 1817, it also continued to be a major product of Cuba. By the middle of the century, Cuban cigars were in great demand in Europe and the United States. By this time, as they are now, they were considered to be the best in the world. In 1860, there were 11,500 *vegas* on the island with 130 cigar factories in Havana.[18] But tobacco was never a large user of slave labor and typically the work on the *vegas* was done either by free men or the family of the owner. According to Thomas, *vegas* were usually no more than thirty three acres in size with plantains and vegetables being grown on half the land. Thus, tobacco never competed with the growth of sugar on the island.

THE RISE OF KING SUGAR

By 1818, Cuban ports were opened to all nations of the world, and a small number of sugar planters installed steam engines at their mills. Increasingly, the planters turned to North America for their necessary technology and capital and for a market for their sugar. Modernization was necessary in order for Cuban cane sugar to compete with European beet sugar. Steam engines arrived from Merrick and Sons of Philadelphia, Novelty Iron Works in New York, and Isaac and Seth Porter of Boston. American engineers and technicians arrived regularly to operate and maintain them during the harvest season. New technology and investment funds from the United States began to transform the sugar industry and Cuba's trade relationships. Cuba became more and more oriented toward the United States.

During the first part of the century, the increase in sugar production was achieved largely through the growth in the number of mills rather than an increase in the size of the mills and plantations. Sugar plantations remained small, largely due to the lack of roads and railroads to get the cane from the fields to the mills. It should be noted that after the cane is cut, it must reach the mill within two days or the fermentation process begins. The trees around the mills were used as fuel and it was difficult to transport wood over long distances. Thus, the lack of adequate infrastructure led to an increase in the number of mills and plantations rather than an increase in their size in the early 1800s. By 1827 there were about 1,000 mills across the island.

The sugar wealth exploded after 1830 with the growth of the railroads (imported from the United States) through the important sugar growing areas of Matanzas to Union de Reyes, Puerto-Principe to Nuevitas, Cienfuegos to Santa Clara, Cardenas to Colon, Remedios to Caibarien, Matanzas to Jovellanos, Casilda to Trinidad, and Havana to Matanzas. Havana was linked to New York, Philadelphia, Baltimore, Mobile, New Orleans, and Key West via regular steamship service by 1836 and by 1850 there were more than 600 miles of railroad linking the sugar growing areas to Havana and the major port cities.[19] Planters typically built feeder lines directly from their plantations into these major railways. Transportation costs were reduced dramatically. The wealth derived from the tax revenues from sugar was easily visible in Havana. In the 1830s, Governor Miguel Tacon engaged in public works programs that paved many of the roads, installed public lighting, built a theater house, created wide boulevards with trees on each side, installed sewer lines, repaired port facilities, dredged the harbor, and constructed a train station. The captain-general's palace in the Plaza de Armas was remodeled. In 1837, a passenger service railroad line was established between Havana and Bejucal.

In addition to the engineers and machine operators, U.S. retailers, shipping agents, and freight handlers began to appear in Cuba, primarily in Havana and the other port cities. They provided manufactured goods, foodstuffs, and insurance. Merchants extended credit to sugar planters. This was often done in exchange for sugar and molasses that were then exported to the United States. Some Americans owned and operated sugar estates. Others were responsible for developing the telegraph service both within Cuba and between Havana and Key West.

Due to the growth of technology in sugar production, the arrival of railroads and other infrastructure improvements, and competition from the rest of the Caribbean and sugar beet producers in Europe, Cuban planters began building larger sugar mills (*centrales*). Modern, large mills could process more sugar but they required more fuel and employees. The need for more cane for their mills led the *centrales* either to acquire their own cane fields or to assume greater control over the tenants (*colonos*). Some of the owners of the *centrales* were owners of large sugar plantations; others were not. Typically, the land on these plantations was cultivated either by resident laborers (slaves) or by *colonos* who worked the land for a salary or for a share of the crop. By 1860, there were 1,365 sugar mills on the island, and Cuba was producing almost one-third of the world's sugar.

One could identify three different groups of sugar planters by the middle of the century. The first were the old oligarchs such as the Cardenas, Alfonsos, Betancourt, O'Farrill, Iznagas, Arrongos, Calvos, and Herreras families, whose ancestors had bought their land prior to the nineteenth century. The second group included self-made immigrants, mostly from Spain. They typically were merchants before becoming planters and usually had more technologically advanced mills than the oligarchs. Tomas Terry who came from Venezuela and settled in Cienfuegos was the first planter in Cuba to use electricity at his mill Caracas. A third group of sugar planters consisted of estates that were owned by companies such as the Noreiga Olmo and Company of

Havana and Barcelona. The sugar planters often built opulent mansions, although many actually lived in their homes in Havana, Santiago, or Matanzas and visited the plantations only during the sugar harvest. The plantations were typically run by an administrator who may or may not have been a member of the planter family. The homes frequently had marble fountains, baths, and large staircases. Planters often bought titles of rank such as count, marques, or gentleman from the Crown, which accorded them a certain social status and rights such as the protection from arrest for debt. It was almost a competition among the planters as to who could adorn their carriages with the most jewelry, silver, and gold. They spent much money on entertainment, especially masked or costume balls and dances. Cockfighting and bullfighting were other favorite pastimes of the planters. Many invested their wealth in the United States and Europe and continued to engage in the illegal slave trade.

The growth of the sugar economy in Cuba created an ever-increasing tension among elite groups that were dependent upon one another. In addition to the Creole planters, the other elites in Cuba consisted of the *peninsulares* merchants and government administrators. Creole planters depended upon the government administrators for political and social order and needed Spanish support for the continuation of the illegal slave trade and slavery. They depended upon merchants to market and sell their products abroad, provide them with necessary imports, and service their loans. The merchants needed the products of the Creole planters to make a living in the business of international commerce. The colonial administration (and the Spanish Crown) needed the revenue generated by taxing both the merchants and the Creole planters. All three groups were dependent upon the perpetuation of sugar and slavery. But, there was a growing divide among the groups. Creoles represented a growing "Cuban" nationalism or identity that was separate from Spain. Merchants and government administrators represented Spain and supported a continuation of its dominance. Creoles were excluded from the colonial administration and *peninsulares* merchants dominated all foreign trade transactions. *Peninsulares* merchants typically overcharged for imports and underpayed for exports.[20] The merchants and the government administrators reinforced each other. While the three groups had a common goal of perpetuating sugar and slavery in Cuba, the tension between Creoles and the *peninsulares* administrators and merchants would eventually lead to conflict. Of course, this immense sugar wealth that supported the Creole planters, the government administrators, and the merchants was built on the institution of slavery.

THE ISSUE OF SLAVERY

It is estimated that most of the approximate 400,000 slaves imported illegally into Cuba after 1820 worked on plantations producing sugar, molasses, and rum. The remainder worked on coffee plantations, cattle ranches, and in the cities. Many in the cities were able to earn enough money to purchase their freedom, and the large non-slave African population was involved in trades such as driving the carriages (*volantes*) of the wealthy planters, carpentering, tailoring, laundering, shoe making, and cigar making.

For the sugar planters, slaves represented the largest single investment. The high price of the slaves even offset the money-saving technological advances, such as steam engines and vacuum boilers, which came to be seen on the larger plantations by the mid-1850s. Plantation slaves worked under desperate conditions especially during the five to six months of the sugar harvest (*zafra*). Twenty-hour workdays were the norm. Many died from overwork, accidents, or sickness. On the large plantations, most slaves were typically housed in large barracks. The only form of entertainment was dancing. Drum dances held on Sundays or during fiestas were frequently attended by the planters and the plantation overseers. African religions mixed with the official religion of Catholicism. Slaves developed their own folklore that reflected their lives in Africa and Cuba.

There was a constant fear among the sugar planters that either Great Britain or a weak Spanish government being pressured by Great Britain would force them to live up to the treaty obligation of 1820 and free all the slaves imported illegally. They also lived in constant fear of slave uprisings and most had long memories of the slave revolution in St. Domingue (Haiti). Major slave rebellions had occurred as early as 1727 but accelerated in the 1800s with rebellions occurring in 1826, 1837, 1843, and 1844. The uprising in Matanzas in 1844 resulted in 4,000 arrests, including freed slaves and mulattoes and at least seventy Creoles. Seventy-eight conspirators were shot and more than 100 were whipped to death by local authorities.[21] It came to be known as the "Year of the Lash." Cuban planters, mostly those of the so-called Club de la Havana, turned to the United States, especially the southern slave states. Some were hopeful of a permanent relationship that would protect the institution of slavery on the island. They were convinced that the Spanish government was going to give in to English pressure to free all the slaves imported illegally into Cuba. Proslavery groups in the southern United States saw the annexation of Cuba as a way of increasing their power within the Congress. Others in the United States supported annexation based on claims of manifest destiny. President James Polk tried to purchase the island in 1848, as did President Franklin Pierce in 1854. Some of these groups, both within the United States and Cuba, encouraged armed expeditions (called filibusters) with the hope of overthrowing Spanish control of the island. All of these filibusters, the most famous led by Narciso Lopez in 1850 and 1851, ended in failure. The U.S. Civil War ended the talk of annexation as Cuban planters were forced to depend solely on the Spanish Crown to continue to protect the institution of slavery and to overlook the illegal slave trade. Many came to see that the illegal slave trade was coming to an end and that Cuba would not be able to replenish its slave labor. Without the ability to replenish its slave labor, they believed that the institution of slavery would eventually die out for economic reasons.

The U.S. Civil War also destroyed the sugar plantations in Louisiana and paved the way for an expansion of Cuban sugar production in the 1860s. By this time, advances in technology were making the larger plantations more efficient in the refining of sugar and creating an economic disincentive in the use of costly slave labor. Only the largest plantations could afford slaves and new technologies. Small sugar plantations could afford neither the technology nor the necessary number of slaves to produce sugar at a competitive price. By 1865, the first actual slave strike occurred. Slaves demanded payment for their work and peacefully asserted their right to freedom because they had arrived in Cuba after 1820. Troops ended the strike but this was a clear indication of the growing difficulty of using slave labor for Cuba's main export. Finally, an increase in Asian immigrants increased the pool of wage laborers available to plantation owners who were willing to experiment in non-slave labor. This was especially true in eastern Cuba (Oriente Province) where the smaller, poorer, and less modern sugar planters had experimented with wage laborers. Some had already freed their slaves and then hired them as wage laborers. Some, seeing their economic fortunes decline compared to the modern plantations of central and western Cuba, saw rebellion as an option.

THE GROWTH OF NATIONALISM

Cuban Creoles remained loyal to the Crown during the wars of independence and the growth of sugar wealth early in the century retarded the growth of nationalism among the sugar planters. Yet, Creole elites were becoming increasingly dissatisfied with the trade limitations and restrictions associated with its colonial status, the lack of a real voice in the political processes on the island, and the corruption of the local government officials. As discussed earlier, the Economic Society was the first institution to become a voice of Cuban nationalism and its members successfully pressured the Spanish government for several economic reforms. Bishop Diaz de Espada, one of the founders of the society, liberalized the curriculum at the Real Colegio Seminario de San Carlos in Havana, which served as a breeding ground for soon-to-be prominent Cuban Creole intellectuals such as Felix Varela and Jose Antonio Saco. By the 1830s Cuban poets such as Jose Maria Herdia, Juan Clemente Zenea, Hernandez Echerri, and Miguel Teurbe Tolon became the voices of those desiring independence from Spain. Some Cuban planters, as discussed earlier, promoted annexation to the United States as an alternative to Spanish colonialism. Others, such as Saco, questioned the development of a closer relationship with the United States. They came to fear U.S. dominance as much as Spanish dominance. Other groups came to support reform within the existing colonial relationship. Reform rather than rebellion was preferred by many planters because the Crown was still the best protection for the institution of slavery on the island.

In an effort to sway a growing nationalist movement, the administrations of Captain-General Francisco Serrano (1859–1962) and Domingo Dulce (1862–1865) were more tolerant of Cuban Creole demands. Proposed political reforms were published in *El Siglo*, and Serrano even proposed that Cuban Creoles be given the right to participate in the Spanish Cortes. The reform movement in Cuba reached a peak in 1865 with the creation of the Reform Party, which wanted Cuban Creoles to have the same political rights as the *peninsulares*, greater economic freedom and limits on the power of the captain-general. *Peninsulares* formed their own party, the Unconditional Spanish Party, to counter the demands of the reformists. Spain, in an attempt to moderate some of the demands, then called for the election of a reform commission that was charged with the task of discussing the political and economic needs and reforms on the island within the colonial framework. The reform commission, which consisted of no fewer than twelve Creole reformers, adopted several reforms in late 1866 and early 1867, including representation in the Spanish Cortez, freedom from arbitrary arrests, and the requirement that Creoles be given equal access to government positions.[22]

The commission also called for the gradual end to slavery which represented a change in planter thinking on the subject. Planters recognized that the rising costs of slave labor coupled with the diminishing returns of slave maintenance made the slave labor system not viable in the long run. The increasing uncertainty of the slave trade made it impossible to replace slave laborers on a consistent schedule. They also came to see that on this issue Spain held the upper hand. A planter rebellion could be met with an immediate decision by Spain to emancipate the slaves. In this case much of the wealth of the planters would disappear unless they were compensated for their emancipated "property." Also, there was no alternative to slave labor that could be instituted in the short run. The decline in coffee production in the 1850s meant there were fewer planters defending the continuation of slavery. The economic panic of 1857 left many planters unable to service their loans, and many lost their land to the *peninsulares* merchants. Thus, the planters believed that a gradual end to slavery with reimbursement from Spain was the preferred solution. This would allow them to overcome their loss of property (slaves), pay off their debts, and purchase new equipment and machinery that would enable them to survive without a slave-based labor system.[23]

Hope for reform was quickly ended as a new, reactionary government in Spain disbanded the commission and refused to implement the proposed reforms. It also appointed Francisco Lersundi as the new captain-general of Cuba. Lersundi asserted an iron-fist rule by censoring the local press and clamping down on all forms of political activity. It was clear to many that reform was not possible and the stage was set for a violent struggle for independence. It would begin in the east near Bayamo and be led by Carlos Manuel de Cespedes, the patriarch of a sugar planter family that traced its roots in Cuba to 1517.

CUBA AT THE BRINK OF THE WARS FOR INDEPENDENCE

By 1861, the population of Cuba had reached 1.4 million people of whom 30 percent were African or of African descent. There were ten cities that had a population in excess of 10,000, including the large port cities of Havana and Santiago. With the original city walls coming down in the early1860s, the growth of elite neighborhoods, and a thriving commercial and port center, Havana was a metropolis of more than 390,000 people. Tourism in Havana was a growing industry with an estimated 5,000 U.S. vacationers arriving annually by 1860.[24] The number of North American ships arriving in Cuban ports increased annually from 529 in 1792 to more than 2,088 between 1851 and 1856. By 1850, more than one-half of Cuba's sugar was exported to the United States. Foreign trade, most of it passing through Havana, amounted to more than $92 million by 1862.[25] Sugar production reached more than 500,000 tons between 1862 and 1864 and more than 600,000 tons by 1867. It was the largest producer of sugar in the world. Cuba's wealthy planter class stood in dramatic contrast with the majority of Cubans who benefitted little from sugar wealth. This was easily seen in Havana with its new elite neighborhoods and large numbers of poor immigrants, Creoles, mulattos, and freed slaves who survived on diets of plantains, jerked beef, fish, tobacco, cheap Spanish wine, and *guarapo* (cane juice). Begging and prostitution were common. Shanty-towns on the outskirts of the city continued to expand. In sum, Cuba's economic growth during the first half of the century was impressive by any measure. The increase in sugar production, the greater use of technology, the development of the infrastructure on the island, the growth of tourism, the rise of Havana as a major world trading center, and the growth in trade with other countries clearly indicated tremendous progress. Yet, at the same time it is also important to point out that the benefits of that growth and progress were clearly not shared very evenly among its population. In particular, the slave population of Cuba continued to suffer.

By 1868, many Cuban elites had come to the conclusion that only a break with Spain would give them the political and economic freedoms they so desperately sought. In the countryside, a restless and more assertive slave population could form the basis of an army that could be mobilized against its Spanish colonial masters. At the same time, it served as a threat to the economic well-being of wealthy planters who continued to defend the use of slaves in the production of sugar. This double-edged sword would play a major role in Cuba's first attempt to win its independence from Spain from 1868 to 1878.

NOTES

1. Fernando Ortiz, "Tobacco and Sugar," in *Cubanisimo*, edited by Christiina Garcia (New York: Vantage Books, 2002), 11.

2. Perez, Jr., *On Becoming Cuban*, 6–15.

3. Perez, Jr., *Cuba*, 13–14.

4. Bartoleme de las Casas, *A Brief Account of the Devastation of the Indies* (1542). Quote taken from <http://www.swarthmore.edu/SocSci/bdorsey1/41docs/02-las.html>.

5. Jaime Suchlicki, *Cuba: From Columbus to Castro*, 2nd ed. (Washington, DC: Pergamon-Brassey's, 1986), 28.

6. Hugh Thomas, *Cuba: The Pursuit of Freedom* (New York: Harper and Row, 1971), 33.

7. Ibid., 65.

8. Ibid., 51.

9. Ibid., 61.

10. Ibid., 65.

11. Ibid., 61.

12. Suchlicki, *Cuba: From Columbus to Castro*, 45.

13. Thomas, *Cuba: The Pursuit of Freedom*, 92.

14. Ibid., 76, 77.

15. Suchlicki, *Cuba: From Columbus to Castro*, 45.

16. Thomas, *Cuba: The Pursuit of Freedom*, 95.

17. Ibid., 129.

18. Ibid., 134.

19. Perez, Jr., *On Becoming Cuban*, 18.

20. Perez, Jr., *Cuba: Between Reform and Revolution*, 48.

21. Thomas, *Cuba: The Pursuit of Freedom*, 205

22. Suchlicki, *Cuba: From Columbus to Castro*, 63.

23. Perez, Jr., *Cuba: Between Reform and Revolution*, 84–85.

24. Perez, Jr., *On Becoming Cuban*, 23.

25. Louis A. Perez, Jr., *Slaves, Sugar, and Colonial Society* (Wilmington, DE: Scholarly Resources, 1992), xvii.

3

The Wars of Independence and U.S. Occupation: 1868 to 1902

> The truth about the United States must be made known to our America . . . the crude, unequal, and decadent character of the United States, and the continual existence within it of all the violences, discords, immoralities, and disorders of which the Hispanoamerican peoples are accused.
>
> Jose Marti, *The Truth about the United States*[1]

Wars for independence are often precipitated by the desire of economic and political elites to have greater control over their own destinies. These wars are typically associated with the growth of nationalism, and they tend to create heroes who are venerated by subsequent generations. Wars for independence also often come with unanticipated consequences. All of these characteristics fit *Cuba Libre*, the Cuban struggle for independence from Spain. The growth of a Cuban identity and nationalism was tied to the desire of the island's economic elites to have more control over their own political and economic futures. The struggle created national heroes such as Carlos Manuel de Cespedes, Antonio Maceo, and the father figure of modern Cuba, Jose Marti. The tremendous damage done to the economic infrastructure and the elimination of many of the island's primary economic elites—the Creole sugar planters—had the unanticipated outcome of making it possible for a more than willing and opportunistic United States to expand its economic presence and, ultimately, its political and cultural dominance over the island. Cuba freed itself from Spain but not the United States.

THE BEGINNING OF THE TEN YEARS' WAR

Cuban discontent increased dramatically with the rapid decline in the price of sugar in 1866, the failure of the reform movement to achieve Creole political demands from Spain in 1867, an increase in Spanish taxes, and an increase in taxes by the United States on Cuban sugar. All of this occurred during the oppressive rule of Captain-General Francisco Lersundi and a period of political instability in Spain beginning with the deposal of Queen Isabella II in 1868. It was no accident that the rebellion began in the eastern part of the island as the plantations there were smaller and less modern than those of central Cuba. New taxes were unacceptable as land owners were generally poorer and lacked both modern machinery and the funds to purchase a large number of slaves. In fact, slaves accounted for no more than 8.5 percent of the population and a majority of the population was white in the eastern provinces. According to scholar Ada Ferrer "Slavery had ceased to be a pivotal social or economic institution" in the eastern regions that sustained the initial uprising.[2] Many land owners had already experimented with freeing their slaves and paying them as contract labor during the sugar harvest (*zafra*). Eastern sugar planters had not benefitted near as much as the planters in central Cuba from the wealth generated by the growth of the sugar industry. Rebellion and independence was seen as a way to increase their wealth.

The rebellion was started by Creole landowners in Oriente Province under the leadership of Carlos Manuel de Cespedes. Cespedes was from a prominent plantation family near Bayamo and had studied law in Spain. While in Spain, he became involved in the political turmoil by joining the conspiratorial forces of army general D. Juan Prim. After the failure of the 1843 uprising, he returned to Cuba and opened a successful law office in Bayamo. He was arrested because of his anti-Spanish statements and forced to leave Bayamo. He began to organize for a war of independence in Oriente. After learning that his conspiratorial activities had been discovered by the Spanish, Cespedes decided that it was time to act.

From his plantation, *La Demajagua*, on October 10, 1868, Cespedes issued his famous *Grito de Yara* proclaiming Cuban independence and freeing his slaves in his rebel army. Cespedes cited several reasons for the rebellion against Spain. They included the inability of Cuban Creoles to serve in their own government, excessive taxation, corruption, the lack of religious liberties, suppression of the press, and the denial of the rights of petition and assembly. Leaders in the eastern provinces in 1869 formed a provisional government with Cespedes as the president. Rebel leaders, such as Agnacio Agramonte from Camaguey in the central region, insisted on a legislative assembly with the ability to check the power of the president and to decide the future of slavery. Maximo Gomez, a Dominican, was selected as the leader of the rebel army forces because of his expertise in military strategy, in particular, guerrilla warfare. Gomez trained the mulatto leader Maceo, who became the most important rebel commander in the field.

Although many factors worked against the success of the Cuban rebels, the lack of unity and dissension between the eastern and central planters within the rebel leadership was probably the most crucial. Leaders were divided over the issue of slavery. Wealthier sugar planters from central Cuba relied more upon slaves on their plantations. They were less likely to join a rebellion that would immediately free their slaves or encourage the emancipation of their slaves. Cespedes, who had promised freedom to all slaves who took up arms in rebellion, recognized the necessity for the central landowners to become a part of the rebellion. In the written manifesto of the rebellion, Cespedes only promised a "gradual and indemnified emancipation." This was done to encourage central planters to take up arms against the Spanish and join the revolt in the east.[3]

Yet, Cespedes continued to urge slaves to revolt and join the rebels (*mambises*) in Oriente. Thousands of slaves joined the rebellion in the east. Local rebel leaders were often men of humble and nonwhite backgrounds such as Policarpo Pineda, a fugitive from the law and better known as Rustan or the Indian; Quinton Bandera, a laborer and the son of free black parents; Guillermo Moncada, a black carpenter; and Maceo, a former mule driver. This created a backlash by some wealthy, conservative, and central region Creole planters. Cespedes was later removed from office by the revolutionary legislative assembly and was killed by the Spanish in Oriente Province in 1874. The new rebel president, Salvador Cisneros Betancourt, a cattle rancher from Camaguey, and the next president, Tomas Estrada Palma, led rebel governments largely made up of conservative landowners. It was during the early 1870s that Maceo was identified as a threat not only to the Spanish but also to the central region sugar planters who were now largely in the political leadership positions of the rebellion.

Today, Maceo, the Bronze Titan, is one of the most beloved and revered men in Cuban history. Born in 1845, he was the son of a Venezuelan, mulatto-immigrant farmer, Marcos Maceo and a free Cuban black woman, Mariana Grajales y Coello. Maceo had three younger brothers and a sister. He grew up on his father's small but prosperous farm, known as Jocabo, outside of Santiago and worked as a mule driver taking products back and forth between the farm and Santiago. Maceo was educated at home by private tutors. He was well read largely due to family readings during dinner. He was fascinated with the French revolution and read the novels of Alexander Dumas and biographies of Simon Bolivar and Toussaint Louverture, who led the 1791 slave revolution in St. Domingue (Haiti). Maceo became a Freemason in 1864. When the Ten Years' War broke out, he joined the rebel army immediately. He so impressed his superiors that he was shortly promoted to sergeant. Fighting under Gomez, Maceo became an expert in guerrilla warfare tactics and by 1872 he had become a general in the rebel army.

THE END OF THE TEN YEARS' WAR
AND ITS AFTERMATH

Many western landowners, especially sugar planters in Las Villas Province, remembering what had happened in Haiti, feared that Maceo would create a black republic after independence was won. They also feared that the scorched earth policies of Gomez and Maceo toward the sugar plantations in Oriente, if carried out in the central and western parts of the island, would destroy their wealth. This fear was heightened in early 1875 when Gomez burned eighty-three plantations around Sancti Spiritus and freed the slaves. In reaction to this, the rebel legislative assembly, now dominated by the more conservative Creole elites, was able to strip Gomez of many of his troops and prevent him from burning plantations in the prime sugar growing area of central Cuba between Matanzas, Cardenas, and Colon. Some rebel leaders were jealous of Gomez's success and others resented the fact that a Dominican was in command of rebel armies. Gomez was forced to resign his military post in 1876. He wrote in his diary, "I retired that same day with my heart broken by so many deceptions."[4] Other factors also worked against the rebels. Weapons, supplies, and money from exile groups in the United States arrived sporadically due to the fact that the U.S. government refused to recognize the movement for independence. It was difficult for the United States, which had just fought a civil war over the issue of slavery, to support a rebel movement in Cuba whose leadership was at best ambiguous and at worst divided on the issue of slavery. Finally, Spain controlled the sea lanes and had a large number of troops in Cuba, thereby making it difficult for the rebels to win a major victory in the field. The rebels were largely limited to fighting a protracted, guerrilla war.

The bulk of the war was fought in the eastern part of the island. Maceo fought a successful guerrilla war against the larger Spanish forces. He gained the admiration of his own troops, fear from the Spanish troops and, at the same time, he became a threat to the more conservative rebel leadership who opposed him on the slavery issue. Maceo freed many slaves who rallied behind the rebel cause in the east. The rebels controlled much of the eastern countryside, while the Spanish controlled the cities. Neither side could win a decisive victory. Brutality and arbitrary executions were common. The symbol of the war or *Cuba Libre* became the machete. With the political instability behind Spain in 1876, a new offensive led by General Arsenio Martinez Campos was launched against the rebels. This offensive with more than 70,000 troops was coupled with a diplomatic effort aimed at the more conservative elements of the rebel leadership. Amnesty was guaranteed to all rebel troops who surrendered before an end to the conflict. Rebel morale was very low by this time. An armistice, the Peace of Zanjon, was finally agreed to in February 1878 by the rebel political leaders who represented the interests of the large landowners. Maceo referred to the peace as "shameful," the conditions as "dishonorable," and the pact as "humiliating."[5] He refused to surrender. He wanted nothing less than Cuban independence and an end to slavery. Facing the brunt of the Spanish forces alone with his small army, Maceo realized he could not prevail. He traveled to New York and worked with Calixto Garcia in organizing a new rebellion. The so-called *Guerra Chiiquita* in 1879–1880 ended in disaster. The Spanish were very successful in labeling it a race war, which caused many former and important white landowning rebels to oppose it. After ten long years of war, the Cuban people were not prepared to fight anymore.

The war and the subsequent collapse in the world price of sugar in the 1880s dramatically changed the political, economic, and social systems of Cuba. Spain was afraid that if it returned all the "freed" slaves in the rebel army to a status of servitude this would cause nothing but problems for their new owners. Spain freed the approximately 16,000 slaves who had fought in the rebel army. After this, large numbers of slaves throughout Cuba simply fled their plantations. Slavery was gradually phased out between 1879 and 1886. With slavery gone, the Creole planters no longer had a reason to be loyal to Spain. Although voting was limited due to property qualifications, Cubans were elected to the Spanish Cortes and local councils. There was enormous property damage to both the Creole loyalists and separatists. Very prominent, separatist Creole elite families had all their property seized by the Spanish government. This included savings accounts, stocks, bonds, and personal property, as well as the cattle ranches, tobacco farms, coffee estates, and sugar plantations. The Spanish government parceled out some of these seized plantations to pardoned revolutionaries, soldiers who had served in the Spanish army, and Spanish immigrants.

The large sugar plantations that remained faced an uncertain future. Almost all were severely in debt to bankers, merchants, and shippers. Interest rates skyrocketed. An 1880 law allowed creditors for the first time to seize the land of those planters who were in default. According to Hugh Thomas, the U.S. consul in Havana reported in 1884 that "out of the twelve or thirteen hundred planters on the island, not a dozen are said to be solvent." In that same year, sugar production had increased worldwide due to the development of the sugar beet industry in Europe. The price of sugar dropped dramatically. Many Cuban sugar plantations slipped into bankruptcy. It was clear that the smaller plantations with the outdated sugar mills could no longer compete on the world market. It was also clear that significant changes were going to take place on the large sugar plantations. Cuba had no alternative but to turn to a more than willing United States for a market for its sugar and for capital (investment funds). Capital was needed to modernize both the sugar industry and the economic infrastructure that supported it.

U.S. investors quickly took advantage of the situation in Cuba. U.S. companies acquired many Cuban and Spanish businesses, as well as many of the bankrupt tobacco and sugar plantations at rock-bottom prices. With this, the Creole sugar planters for the most part disappeared in the 1880s. U.S. capital and technology was used to modernize the sugar mills and make them more efficient. For example, Atkins and Company of Boston became the proprietors of the Soledad Plantation near Cienfuegos and several other surrounding plantations. By 1894, Adkins Soledad was one of the largest sugar plantations in the world with 12,000 total acres, 23 miles of private railroads, 5,000 acres of cane, and 1,200 men employed at harvest time.[6] This *centrale* represented a combination of foreign capital, technology, and efficiency that changed the social organization of sugar production in Cuba.

Most small sugar plantations could not afford to modernize their mills, so many simply began supplying cane to the *centrales*. Many of the large plantations with modern sugar mills leased their land to the tenants (*colonos*) who took care of growing the cane. In effect, there was a clear division of labor between the cane growers (typically small farms and *colonos*) and the cane processors (*centrales*). Cheap U.S. steel allowed the *centrales* and the larger plantations to build private railways to get the cane to the mills more efficiently and to carry the processed sugar from the mills to the sea to private port facilities for export. By 1895, there were more than 350 miles of private railroads built in Cuba.[7] The *centrales* had access to capital and often made loans to the *colonos*. *Colonos* needed capital to pay wages, food, and lodging for their workers and other costs. Small sugar planters and *colonos* were almost always in debt to the *centrale*. This created a patron-client relationship between the *centrales* and the *colonos*. *Centrales* began competing with each other for access to sugar cane for the first time in Cuban history.

A growing sense of Cuban identity and nationalism was heightened by both the Ten Years' War and the realization by the Cubans after the war that Spain had no intention of allowing them to have any substantive say in its political and economic decision making. The rebel armies had been a mixture of rich and poor, black and white, peasant and workers, and Chinese and mulatto. During the war the words that would eventually become the Cuban national anthem were written and the Cuban flag first appeared. The machete became one of the nation's symbols. Although the bulk of the fighting was on the eastern part of the island, the fact that Creole leaders fought on parts of the island they had never seen before helped to overcome regional loyalties and develop a stronger sense of nationhood. By the early 1890s, the Autonomous Liberal Party (*Autonomistas*) of Cuba had become frustrated with Spain's lack of response to its demands for greater local control. Some Cuban nationalists, such as Marti, Gomez, and Maceo, fled in exile to begin plotting their return and a new rebellion against Spain.

The McKinley Act of 1890 ended U.S. import duties on raw sugar and molasses. This greatly facilitated the growing trade between the United States and Cuba. By 1894, the United States had invested more than $50 million in Cuba, purchased 87 percent of Cuba's exports, and accounted for almost 40 percent of the island's imports.[8] A downturn in the world's economy in the early 1890s reduced the demand for

Cuban sugar. Many Cubans and American investors in Cuba came to blame Spanish imperial authority for their problems. The stage was set for another rebellion.

THE SECOND WAR OF INDEPENDENCE AND THE UNITED STATES

Marti, Gomez, and Maceo arrived in Cuba in April 1895 to continue the rebellion against Spain. Estrada organized the exile community in the United States and began a public relations campaign to gain the support of the U.S. government. Although a revolutionary government was created, most decisions were made by the generals in the field. Marti was killed in a skirmish with Spanish forces near Bayamo in May. Making use of the expert horsemanship of their soldiers, living off the land, and using guerrilla tactics they had developed during the Ten Years' War, Gomez and Maceo took the offensive. In September, Gomez and Maceo, leading rebel armies made up primarily of Africans and mulattos, expanded the war into the west. They reached Las Villas by November and were near Matanzas by Christmas. By January, Gomez was nearing Havana and Maceo was moving into the west into Pinar del Rio Province. Gomez and Maceo once again employed scorched earth policies against the large plantations and *centrales*. When U.S. holdings were burned, many Americans complained to Estrada in the United States. He indicated that when the United States formally recognized the rebels, U.S. property would be protected. Recognizing the difficult situation, Spain sent General Valeriano Weyler to Havana to take control of its forces.

Estrada very effectively used the media to gain the support of the United States. With increasing competition for readership by the major newspapers (such as William Randolph Hearst's *New York Journal*) and the rise of yellow journalism in the United States, reports of Spanish cruelty and atrocities became commonplace as the American public began to demand that President Grover Cleveland do something about Cuba. General Fitzhugh Lee, the U.S. consul general in Havana and a nephew of Robert E. Lee, sympathized with the rebels and actively pushed the U.S. intervention into the war. By June, U.S. naval intelligence had prepared a war plan against Spain.

General Weyler concentrated on trying to isolate Maceo in the west. He hired Cuban counter-guerrillas to fight against the rebels. He devised a plan in which people were forced into internment centers (concentration camps) in urban areas throughout the island and anyone outside these centers was considered to be a rebel. Local

Spanish commanders were given the power to execute rebels and anyone who refused to relocate to these centers. Rural villages and homes were destroyed by the Spanish. Planted fields were burned and livestock that could not be taken back to the internment centers was slaughtered. Anything that could possibly support the rebels was destroyed. Maceo and Gomez also waged a brutal war against the economic infrastructure and the large plantations that refused to contribute to their rebel forces. Maceo used his speed and maneuverability to avoid major battles with Weyler's larger forces. In April, Gomez ordered that all mill owners who continued to grind sugar cane should be hung. Some mill owners, including many U.S. owners, hired Spanish forces to protect them from the rebels.

By the middle of 1896, the Cuban economy had come to a standstill with sugar production coming to a halt. Smallpox and yellow fever had reached epidemic proportions in areas where populations were interned, such as in Cienfuegos. Typhus, dysentery, cholera, and measles raged through the 100,000 people who were interned in the shantytowns of Havana. Tens of thousands died in these internment centers. This policy backfired as peasants who at one time were not part of the rebellion now joined the rebel armies. By the end of 1896 rebel forces numbered 50,000.[9] While Maceo was killed trying to break out into the central provinces as were several other rebel leaders throughout the island, the war came to a stalemate as the Spanish occupied the large, fortified urban areas largely in the west. The urban areas were under complete Spanish martial law with urban families forced to house the Spanish soldiers. Rebels controlled the countryside and all of the eastern provinces. Weyler began arresting not only those associated with the rebel cause but even those Creoles who supported autonomy under the Spanish Empire. These political arrests turned the "moderate" Creole *autonomistas* against the Spanish. Hundreds of political prisoners were deported to Spain. By the middle of 1897, most believed that the Spanish could not win the war and the rebels had put into motion plans for attacks on the urban areas. Garcia successfully defeated the Spanish in the eastern cities of Bayamo, Las Tunas, Guisa, Guimaro, Jiguani, and Loma de Hierro in the last six months of 1897. In early January 1898, Assistant Secretary of State William Day concluded that Spain's struggle in Cuba had become hopeless.[10]

By this time, General Weyler's reputation in the United States as a butcher appeared to make intervention likely. Recognizing the tremendous cost of trying to continue the war (Spain was also fighting a rebellion in the Philippines) and fearing a U.S. intervention, the Spanish government changed its policy toward Cuba favoring limited autonomy within the Spanish Empire, self-government, and universal suffrage. General Weyler resigned and was replaced by Ramon Blanco. President William McKinley was open to the change in Spanish policy and a political settlement in Cuba. In fact, most U.S. businessmen who had investments in Cuba preferred a political settlement. Yet, the rebel leadership and most in Cuba could not accept a political settlement without complete independence—something that the Spanish government could not grant. Rioting broke out in Havana by rebel supporters who were opposed to a limited political autonomy settlement. President McKinley believed that U.S. citizens and property were in danger. In January 1898, he sent the battleship USS *Maine* to Havana and fate intervened.

On February 15, 1898, the *Maine* blew up in Havana harbor. Two hundred sixty men out of 355 died. Although the cause of the explosion was never satisfactorily explained, the sensationalist U.S. press with its yellow journalism blamed Spain and created a near anti-Spanish hysteria within an American public that already disliked the Spanish. "Remember the *Maine* and to Hell with Spain" became the mantra of an American public which increasingly supported a U.S. intervention. This hysteria played into the growing imperialistic desires of many leaders in the United States such as Theodore Roosevelt, the deputy secretary of the navy. President McKinley, desperately trying to avoid war, offered to buy Cuba from Spain for $300 million. Spain refused and McKinley capitulated to those who supported U.S. intervention. On April 19, the U.S. Congress demanded Spain give up its authority over Cuba. A U.S. blockade went into effect on April 21. Spain made overtures to the rebel commanders, but neither Gomez nor Garcia was willing to accept. Gomez rejected an offer to join with Spain to "repel the North American invaders." He and Garcia welcomed U.S. support, something Marti and Maceo probably would never have done if they had lived. The U.S. Congress declared war on Spain on April 25. According to Louis Perez, "This changed everything . . . a Cuban war of independence was transformed into a U.S. war of conquest."

The fighting was over rather quickly. The U.S. Navy blockaded the outnumbered Spanish fleet in the harbor at Santiago. The demoralized Spanish troops fought bravely but were overwhelmed. In the most famous battle of the war at San Juan Hill in Santiago, the Spanish lost 102 men with 552 casualties. The United States lost almost 10 percent of its total forces—223 dead, 1,243 wounded, and 79 missing—while Roosevelt and his Rough Riders became famous.[11] The Spanish fleet was sunk trying to run the blockade. Malaria, yellow fever, and dysentery wreaked havoc with the U.S. troops. The Cuban forces under Garcia were almost entirely African and mulatto, while the American troops were almost all white. The American journalist, H. Irving Hancock, made the observation at the landing of U.S. troops at Daiquiri that the Cubans had "the raggedest uniforms conceivable" and "none of them had the strong, sturdy look of our own people." The Americans treated the Cubans with paternalistic contempt and, according to Hugh Thomas, in many ways preferred the company of the defeated Spanish to the black "inferior and uncivilized" Cubans. U.S. general Rufus Shafter even suggested that they should serve as laborers rather than as soldiers in battle. Spanish general Juan Jose Toral surrendered in Santiago on July 17 to the U.S. forces. The United States did not allow the black Cuban troops, who fought the Spanish for three years, near the city to participate in the surrender ceremony. Garcia himself refused an invitation to participate because the United States did not remove Spanish municipal authorities from power. The war ended officially on December 10 with the signing of the Treaty of Paris. Cuban officials were not asked to participate. The exclusion of Cubans from the decision-making process at the end of the war foreshadowed future Cuban relations with the United States.

Cuba had won its long struggle against Spain, but the cost was enormous. Almost two generations of Cuban families suffered directly from the thirty-year struggle. In the aftermath of the most recent struggle, thousands were left homeless and destitute. Those whose homes or farms had escaped the destruction of the war fell victim to tax collectors and creditors. Pawnshops proliferated. Entire families became beggars. The economy had come to a virtual halt. The economic infrastructure of the island had either been destroyed or was in disrepair. Almost one-third of the sugar plantations had been burned through the scorched earth policies of the armies. Matanzas Province, the center of sugar production, had virtually collapsed with the number of operating mills falling from 400 in 1894 to 62 in 1898. Only 207 sugar mills on the entire island were operating at the end of the war. This was down from 1,100 working mills in 1894.[12] The few remaining sugar elites were heavily in debt and could not make their mortgage payments. Literally thousands of small farms, cattle ranches, tobacco farms, and coffee farms disappeared. General Lee said, "The great fertile island of Cuba in some places resembled an ash pile, in other the dreary desert."[13] It was estimated that more than two-thirds of Cuban wealth had been consumed during the war. Given its vulnerable situation and desperate needs, Cuba was unable to counter the growing power and manifest destiny of the United States.

OCCUPATION AND CONDITIONAL INDEPENDENCE

On January 1, 1899, the Spanish flag was lowered and the U.S. flag was raised over El Morro, the fortress that had protected Havana's harbor since 1610. It was a humiliation and an insult to the many Cubans who had fought the Spanish for their independence. The newspaper, *El Nuevo Pais*, described the state of the country as "neither a colony nor a free state, Cuba suffers all the disadvantages of the former and none of the advantages of the latter."[14] Cuba was placed under U.S. military occupation led by General John Brooke from January until December 1899 and then under General Leonard Wood until May 1902. The United States did not allow the Cuban rebel army to participate in the final Spanish exit from the island in ceremonies held in Havana and Santiago. The stated reason for this insult was the possible threat to life and property should the victory celebrations become excessive and end up as riots, although it was clear that the U.S. belief in its mission of bringing civilization to the "inferior" people of Latin America played a role in the nature of its policies toward the Cuban people. The policies often reflected arrogance, paternalism, and racism that upset many Cuban nationalists. U.S. general Shafter commented, "Those people are no more fit for self-government than gunpowder is for hell." General Samuel Young stated that the "insurgents are a lot of degenerates, absolutely devoid of honor or gratitude."[15] This upset almost all Cuban nationalists, but given the harsh economic and political realities of 1899, there was little they could do.

The U.S. occupation had three interrelated goals: to maintain political stability, to rebuild the primary economic infrastructure of the island to attract U.S. investments, and to keep Cuba within the sphere of influence of the growing political and economic power of the United States. The U.S. military appropriated the Cuban treasury and its public revenues. The exhausted rebel army, which had not been paid, disbanded when the United States offered to purchase its equipment and weapons. It also helped that certain rebel leaders were offered well-paid positions within the new administrative structure. The United States created a Rural Guard, the majority of which were non-Africans who had served in rebel armies. It is very telling to note that the purpose of the Rural Guard was to protect U.S. property in rural areas. The judicial branch of the Cuban government was reorganized and an electoral system was established that gave the vote to male property owners who were over the age of twenty, able to read and write, and had personal property worth at least $250. The reason for these stipulations on voting was, according to U.S. secretary of war Elihu Root, to exclude the "mass of ignorant and incompetent" Cubans. As a result only 5 percent of the Cuban population could vote.[16]

Three parties, the Republicans, the Nationalists, and the Democratic Union competed for municipal elections in June 1900. The Republicans, led by former rebel commander Jose Gomez and based in Santa Clara, favored immediate independence. The Nationalists, led by former rebel General Maximo Gomez and based in Havana, favored immediate independence and a strong central government. The Democratic Union supported annexation to the United States. The Republicans and Nationalists were the overwhelming winners. The outcome of the elections upset U.S. general Wood who stated, "The men whom I had hoped to see take leadership have been forced into the background by the absolutely irresponsible and unreliable element."[17]

Roads, bridges, and railways were rebuilt. Port facilities were improved. Food distribution was an immediate priority and the United States focused on improving the health and education sectors of Cuba. Hospitals were built and the sanitary and health conditions improved in many areas on the island. The American Sanitary Commission eradicated yellow fever, although its success was based largely on the research of Cuban scientist Carlos Finlay, who correctly linked the disease to mosquitoes. General Wood, who believed the Cubans would ask to be annexed to the United States, began to reorganize the education system based on the U.S. public school model. Cuban teachers adopted U.S. teaching methods, and U.S. textbooks were translated into Spanish and adopted by the schools, although no attempt was made to make them understandable within the Cuban culture and context.

Cuban business owners, farmers, and planters appealed to the U.S. military for assistance such as low-interest loans or subsidies to make it through the difficult economic times. All were rejected by General Brook, who argued that these types of public subsidies and charities would do nothing but encourage dependence, increase pauperism, and destroy an individual's self-respect. Cuban property owners were forced into bankruptcy. Between 1898 and 1900, farms changed owners at a rate of almost 4,000 a year.[18] Estates were abandoned, and property values fell dramatically. Land could be purchased at one-tenth to one-twentieth of its value prior to the rebellion. Thousands of Americans came to Cuba looking to purchase land cheaply and make their fortunes.

In September 1900, thirty-one delegates were elected to participate in a constitutional convention for Cuba. The Cuban Constitution that was

A Cuban sugar train takes cane to the Victoria Sugar Mill near Yagauajay to be processed during the U.S. occupation in 1901. U.S. investors came to dominate the Cuban sugar industry after the Spanish-American War and benefited from U.S. tariff reductions and a growing demand for sugar by the American public. (Library of Congress)

developed called for universal suffrage for all males, a complete separation of church and state, a powerful presidency, and a weak legislature. General Wood, who doubted the ability of Cubans to govern themselves and had already antagonized former rebel leaders, wanted a provision in the new constitution or a treaty that would spell out the future relationship between the United States and Cuba. General Wood made this recommendation to Secretary of War Root. Root wanted to secure U.S. rights of intervention to maintain an "adequate government" in Cuba. An adequate government meant one that was stable and fiscally responsible; one that would not enter into agreements with European powers that might "interfere with the independence of Cuba"; one that would allow the United States the right to intervene to protect the independence of Cuba; and one that would allow the United States to maintain a naval presence on the island. He then recommended to Secretary of State John Hay that the new Cuban Constitution should spell out this relationship between Cuba and the United States. This came to be known as the Platt Amendment to the Cuban Constitution. It allowed the United States to intervene into the domestic politics of Cuba whenever it believed the government lacked the ability to govern or should its independence ever be threatened. In 1901, the Cuban constitutional convention voted 16–11 with four abstentions to accept the Platt Amendment without any modifications, largely due to President McKinley's threat of not withdrawing the U.S. Army from Cuba and Root's effective diplomacy and characterization of the amendment as simply a restatement of the Monroe Doctrine.

General Wood used money from the Cuban treasury to mount a public relations campaign in the United States to encourage investment in both the sugar and tobacco industries and to lower U.S. tariffs on these products. Before 1899, almost all tobacco companies were either Cuban or Spanish owned. By May 1902, North American companies controlled more than 90 percent of the export trade in Cuban cigars and more than 50 percent of the manufacture of Cuban cigars and cigarettes. The United Fruit Company of Boston created the first great sugar *centrale* (called Boston) in Cuba on the edge of the Bay of Banes. In 1900, it invested more than $20 million in Cuba. Texas investor R. B. Hawley and former Cuban general Mario Garcia Menocal created the Cuban American Company and built the *centrale* Chaparra on the north coast of Oriente. It became the largest sugar estate in the world.[19] General Wood then maneuvered to gain the support of the U.S. Congress to lower the tariff on Cuban sugar. Wood also granted more than 218 mining concessions to U.S. companies, who were exempted from property taxes. By 1902, U.S. investment capital in Cuba totaled more than $100 million and by 1905 nearly 13,000 Americans had bought land in Cuba.[20]

In December 1901, Estrada was elected the first president of the Republic of Cuba and on May 20, 1902, the Cuban flag was raised for the first time over Cuba. By this time, the United States had already replaced Spain as a point of reference for most Cubans. Cuba was now independent, but the stage was set for the United States to dominate the political and economic processes of the island and to reshape its politics, economics, society, culture, and identity. Spanish hegemony had been replaced with U.S. hegemony. Marti's dream of a truly independent Cuba remained just that—a dream.

JOSE MARTI

Jose Marti, a literary figure, poet, revolutionary, and freedom fighter, is considered by most to be the father-figure of modern Cuba. Marti was born in 1853. His father, Mariano Marti Navarro from Valencia, Spain, was a city official and a policeman in Havana and his mother was Leonor Perez Cabrera from the Canary Islands. He was influenced throughout school by Rafael Maria Mendive, an educator, poet, and prominent supporter of Cuban independence. Marti founded his first newspaper, *La Patria Libre*, in 1869. Due to his passionate, pro-independence articles, editorials, and poems, Spain found Marti guilty of treason and sedition and sentenced him to six years hard labor. After one year in labor, his parents intervened and he was exiled to Spain. While in Spain, he studied law and wrote articles and poems about national independence. He traveled to France with his longtime friend and fellow revolutionary

Jose Marti was the public voice of Cuban independence and father-figure of modern Cuba. He spent much of his adult life in the United States where he became suspicious of its imperialistic designs toward Cuba. He prophetically warned Cubans of the possibility of winning the war against Spain only to fall under the dominance of the United States. (Hulton Archive/Getty Images)

Fermin Valdes Dominguez. He traveled to Mexico in 1875 where he established himself as a literary figure and a vocal supporter of an independent Cuba. He briefly returned to Cuba in 1877 but then went to Guatemala where he married Carmen Zayas Bazan. He returned to Cuba in 1878–1879 and was exiled once again for his pro-independence activities. He ended up in New York with the exiled Cuban community. There he served as a consul for Uruguay, Paraguay, and Argentina and wrote for several newspapers published in the United States and Latin America. He also wrote several volumes of poetry while raising awareness and support for the Cuban independence movement.

Marti was a supporter of a free, universal, secular, and public education system in Cuba. He believed it was necessary for the establishment of democracy and he saw it as a counter to the Catholic education which he believed promoted loyalty to Spain and the Church. It was Marti who laid the groundwork for Cuban independence through his intense opposition to the idea of the U.S. annexation of Cuba and his distrust of the *autonomistas* (Creole planters who desired either an accommodation with Spain or an annexation of the island by the United States). He became well known throughout Latin America. He organized Cuban American tobacco workers in Florida to contribute monetarily to the cause of *Cuba Libre*.

By this time, it was clear that Marti was concerned about independence not only from Spain but also from the United States. He was witness to the growing economic and military power of the United States, coupled with an imperialistic and missionary belief system that found an outlet in the newspaper industry led by William Randolph Hearst. Marti then worked with Gomez and Maceo and returned to Cuba in 1895 to renew the Cuban struggle for independence. Marti died in a small battle near Bayamo in May and became a martyr to *Cuba Libre*. He was the foremost spokesperson for Cuban independence. Marti feared that Cuba would win its independence from Spain only to lose it to the United States. He wrote, "It is my duty to prevent through the independence of Cuba, the U.S.A. from spreading over the West Indies and falling with added weight upon other lands in Our America." The Platt Amendment was a confirmation of Marti's worst fear. The Cuban wars of independence were lost to the United States.

NOTES

1. Esther Allen, ed. *Jose Marti: Selected Writings* (New York: Penguin Books), 331.
2. Ada Ferrer, *Insurgent Cuba: Race, Nation, and Revolution 1868–1898* (Chapel Hill: University of North Carolina Press, 1999), 18, 21.

3. Ibid., 23.

4. Suchlicki, *Cuba: From Columbus to Castro*, 63.

5. Ferrer, *Insurgent Cuba*, 64.

6. Thomas, *Cuba: The Pursuit of Freedom*, 274.

7. Ibid.

8. Ibid., 289.

9. Perez, Jr., *Cuba: Between Reform and Revolution*, 128.

10. Ibid., 136.

11. Thomas, *Cuba: The Pursuit of Freedom*, 393.

12. Ibid., 425.

13. Perez, Jr., *On Becoming Cuban*, 101.

14. John Paul Rathbone, *The Sugar King of Havana* (New York: Penguin Press, 2010), 52.

15. Ferrer, *Insurgent Cuba*, 189.

16. Perez, Jr., *Cuba: Between Reform and Revolution*, 140.

17. Ibid.

18. Perez, Jr., *On Becoming Cuban*, 106.

19. Thomas, *Cuba: The Pursuit of Freedom*, 466–468.

20. Ibid., 466, 600.

4

U.S. Dominance, the Failure of Reform, and the Rise of Batista: 1902 to 1952

The destiny of Cuba cannot be to sell sugar in order to buy automobiles.

Hilda Perera, *Manana es 26*[1]

Politics and economics are so intertwined that it is impossible to understand one without the other. Nowhere is this more evident than in the history of Cuba during the first half of the twentieth century. The Platt Amendment and the growing political and economic power of the United States made a mockery of Cuban independence. Cuba was strategically important because it allowed the United States to control access to the Panama Canal. The United States also believed that the maintenance of political stability, although not necessarily democracy, was the best way to protect its growing economic investments and its dominance of the Cuban sugar industry. U.S. trade agreements with Cuba encouraged the export of sugar and, in effect, limited the diversification of the Cuban economy because other products faced a high tariff.

Given its increasing dependence on the export of sugar, the Cuban economy was acutely vulnerable to changes in the world market price and the boom-bust cycle of an island agriculture-based export economy. Economic hard times were often associated with political instability on the island. Labor unrest was common. Political instability was viewed as a direct threat to the Cuban political and economic elites and, perhaps more importantly, to U.S. investments on the island. Cuban elites came to rely on a politicized army and a more than willing United States to maintain political stability. Corruption became pervasive and the standard way of doing business in Cuba. Politics became a way of accumulating wealth and, thus, elections often turned into political crises that invited U.S. intervention.

When the corrupt and repressive Gerardo Machado became a second-term president through fraudulent elections in 1928, students entered the Cuban political scene as the heirs to Jose Marti's dream of a truly independent Cuba. Student-led reform peaked with university professor Ramon Grau San Martin becoming president in 1933. Grau's nationalistic reforms, pro-labor policies, and proposals for agrarian reform were opposed by groups on the Right such as the United States, the Cuban military, and economic elites and those on the Left including radical students who claimed his reforms were too moderate. Political instability at this time marked the entry of the military as the decisive actor in the political decision making processes of Cuba. By 1934, the United States came to see Fulgencio Batista and the military as the only guarantee for the necessary political stability and the protection of the vast U.S. interests on the island.

Growing wealth during World War II created a surplus of government revenue that allowed political elites to pay for modern social reforms while elite patronage, corruption, and graft worsened. Economic growth created a growing middle class that adopted an American consumer culture with rising economic expectations and the hope of political reform. Batista would end the hope of meaningful political reform with the *golpe* (illegal takeover of the government either by the military or with the support of the military—a coup d'etat) of 1952 and the rising economic expectations that would never be fulfilled due to the inability of the sugar industry to provide the necessary economic growth and development on the island by the mid-1950s.

CUBA DURING THE PLATT AMENDMENT YEARS

Tomas Estrada Palma, a former teacher, rebel president, and leader of the Cuban exiles in the United States, was elected without opposition as the first president of the newly independent Cuba in 1902. He sought favor with the United States and used patronage to maintain the support of various elite groups. Corruption, intimidation, fraud, embezzlement, and graft became a staple of his administration. More importantly, the origins of a new Cuban elite class—a largely political class—began to take shape. It was organized around the control of the state and dependent upon the control of public administration as the major source of wealth and means to property ownership. Politics became the means to economic wealth for the Cuban political class.[2] Two political parties—the Liberals and the Conservatives—stepped into this competition to control the government to gain access to economic wealth. Liberals were typically of modest economic means and largely made up of officers and enlisted men from the army of *Cuba Libre*. Conservatives, mostly European or white and with greater economic means, were often former government administrators within the provisional government.

In 1903, the Commercial Treaty of Reciprocity gave Cuban sugar and other agricultural products exported to the United States a 20 percent tariff preference and gave American manufactured products preferential treatment when exported to Cuba. This agreement worked against the development of a Cuban manufacturing sector and discouraged the diversification of its economy. It consolidated an agro-export model of production that continued the monoculture of King Sugar based upon large landholdings. It also facilitated a growing and pervasive American presence on the island that could be seen in clothing fashions, education, architecture, business practices, sport and leisure, and the growth of language schools specializing in English. In the same year, Cuba agreed to lease Bahia Honda and Guantanamo Bay to the United States. Guantanamo Bay would serve as a coaling station and naval base for the United States.

The 1904 elections for the Cuban national legislature were marred by fraud and in 1905 Estrada intimidated his opponent into withdrawing from the election and he was reelected president. The Liberal Party led by Jose Miguel Gomez and veterans of *Cuba Libre* cried foul and organized a rebellion. The rebels had 15,000 troops in the field against Havana by the end of August and destroyed the communications network of the island so as to isolate the small Rural Guard units. The Rural Guard, created by the United States during its occupation of the island, amounted to nothing more than police units designed to protect the property of wealthy landowners and was not capable of fighting the rebels. Not having a standing army to counter the rebels, Estrada asked President Theodore Roosevelt for support. Roosevelt dispatched Secretary of War William Taft to Havana to negotiate a settlement between the two parties. Taft was unimpressed with Estrada

A sentry stands guard on the grounds of the U.S. naval base at Guantanamo, Cuba, around 1919. Leased from Cuba in 1903, Fulgencio Batista affirmed in 1934 that the leasing agreement not be terminated without mutual consent. The Castro brothers have refused to cash the approximately $4,000 monthly rental check from the United States. Fidel referred to it as "a knife stuck in the heart of Cuba's dignity and sovereignty." (National Archives)

and believed that he should resign. He also came to the conclusion that none of the Liberals were capable of governing the country. Estrada and his supporters in the Cuban legislature resigned on September 28, 1906, and effectively left Cuba without a government. Two thousand U.S. Marines landed in Havana the next day. Taft commented that the Cuban government had "proven to be nothing but a house of cards." Cuba was once again occupied by the United States.

Roosevelt placed Charles Magoon, the former governor of the Panama Canal Zone, in charge of the American occupation. Magoon, with support from the Liberals, created a permanent standing army while preserving the function of the Rural Guard. Magoon believed that a large standing army would serve to deter any internal rebellion and provide the necessary political stability for U.S. strategic and economic interests while the Rural Guard would continue to function as a police force to protect private property. It was believed that this standing army would eliminate the need for the use of U.S. troops in Cuba. Note that standing armies are primarily created to deter an external threat to the country. Cuba's army was specifically created to deter internal opposition to the government. The United States provided supplies, weapons, training, and advisers to the Cuban military. Cuban military officers began attending service academies in the United States. Magoon also reformed the electoral system by developing qualifications for voters and candidates for public office. Election boards were created to maintain the lists of eligible voters. A racist immigration policy was adopted by favoring "whites," in particular Spaniards, and restricting "races of color" into Cuba. The sinecure system (a system of providing people jobs with minimal or no duties, yet with substantial financial reward) was expanded to pacify elite groups and by the time the Americans left in 1909, elite opposition to U.S. dominance had, for the most part, come to an end. Magoon granted several major public works contracts to major American firms and continued to work on improvements to the economic infrastructure such as roads to the tobacco-growing region of Pinar del Rio. Local elections were held in August 1908 and national elections in November. Not surprisingly, Gomez, leader of the Liberal Party, was elected president and the U.S. occupation ended with Magoon leaving on the newly rebuilt battleship the USS *Maine*.

With a cock on a plough as a symbol of the Liberal Party, Gomez, in one of his first acts, reinstated the traditional past time of cockfighting. Public corruption and graft increased, especially in the awarding of government contracts for infrastructure improvements such as sewage and waste systems, railroads, roads, telephone lines, bridges, port facilities, and military barracks. Underpaid public officials viewed graft (*chivo*) as a way of supplementing their incomes. Cuban newspapers received government subsidies or grants and could not be relied on for objective and accurate reporting. The national lottery was reinstated and provided the government with money for patronage purposes. Officers in the military who were loyal to Estrada were dismissed. Officer appointments and commissions were based on loyalty to the ruling Liberal Party, although factions appeared between the supporters of Gomez (*Miguelistas*) and the supporters of Vice President Alfredo Zayas (*Zayistas*). This practice of politicizing the military came to be a permanent feature in Cuban politics and over time served to undermine its professionalism, discipline, and morale.

The U.S. government periodically reminded Gomez that failure to protect life and property of U.S. investors could lead to an intervention. The army was used to meet the needs of the rural landowners. Calvary units patrolled the sugar districts during the harvest season. The United States continued to influence and, in some cases, to interfere in the decision-making processes on the island. For example,

President Taft prevented an attempt by Great Britain to gain a contract to build a railroad between Nuevitas and Caibarien. He offered new loans to the Cuban government with conditions that increased U.S. control over the Cuban treasury and he finalized the Guantanamo Treaty in December 2012, which gave the United States a naval base on the island for a total rent of $2,000 a year in perpetuity.

This Independent Party of Color (PIC) had been organized in 1908 in response to growing complaints against the dominance of the economy by foreigners (not only Spaniards who were favored in the immigration policies but also Americans who dominated the sugar industry) and white Cuba elites. The primary purpose of the party was to defend interests of Afro-Cubans. Black or mulatto Cubans made up about 30 percent of the population in 1907 and were the majority in the relatively large cities of Santiago, Jovellanos, and Guantanamo. Blacks and mulattos had twice the illiteracy rate as whites, were underrepresented in the professions, and most practiced either African religions or religions that represented a syncretism between Catholicism and the African religions.[3] The PIC was led by Evaristo Estenoz, a former slave and veteran of *Cuba Libre* and the Liberal Party uprising of 1906. With the passage of the Morua Law in 1911, which banned all political parties based on race, the PIC led an uprising consisting largely of labor strikes and demonstrations throughout the island on May 20, 1912. Panic spread, especially in Havana, where the fear of the "Negro uprising" was greatest. The army was able to put down the uprising rather quickly, except in Oriente Province where the largest number of blacks and mulattos lived. The United States, fearing the destruction of American property, sent the battleship USS *Nebraska* to Havana and landed U.S. Marines in Daiquiri (Oriente Province) on May 31. Four thousand blacks under the command of Estenoz were defeated in a battle in June, and the uprising quickly disintegrated. This was the last race-based uprising in Cuba. After this defeat, Afro-Cuban elites and politicians tended to associate with the existing political structure. The vast majority of Afro-Cubans were never integrated into the general political development of the island.

The Liberal Party, split between supporters of Gomez and Zayas, led to the election of Cornell University–educated General Mario Garcia Menocal as president in 1913. He was the manager of the Chaparra sugar mill and plantation and leader of the Conservative Party. Menocal, who had strong support by the United States, was even more corrupt than Gomez. He pursued several loans from the United States and began to purge the military of its Liberal Party supporters. With the beginning of world war in 1914, European beat sugar came to a standstill and the world market price of sugar almost doubled during the months of July and August. That year, three *centrales* were founded and the next year twelve new mills were built with U.S. owning eight of them. A total of twenty-one new mills were built between 1907 and 1919, most taking advantage of U.S. technology using multiple rollers and electricity. This allowed Cuba to become the largest exporter of sugar in the world.

More lands came under sugar production, including some of the virgin forests of cedar, mahogany, and mastic in Pinar del Rio. This led to a labor shortage and the need to import laborers from Haiti, Jamaica, and China. Another outcome of the Cuban sugar boom was the merger of sugar mills and plantations with companies that were large users of sugar such as Coca-Cola, Hershey, and Hires (root beer).[4] Hershey even purchased the Havana-Matanzas electric railway. American ownership of sugar mills increased to an estimated 35 to 50 percent of all the sugar mills in Cuba. The Cuban Cane Sugar Corporation founded in New York purchased fourteen mills in 1916 that included the following *centrales*: Conchita, Asuncion, Mercedes, San Ignacio, Agramonte, Jaguayal, and Lugareno. By 1918, it was the largest sugar enterprise in the world.[5] The sugar boom brought prosperity to the island. Conspicuous consumption could be seen in the wealthy Havana districts of Vedado and Miramar. Cars could be seen regularly on the streets of Havana and the tourist industry developed around gambling.

Continued divisions within the Liberal Party coupled with a fraudulent election count allowed Menocal, the U.S. favorite, to win reelection in 1916. Violence marked the election. Candidates and election board officials were shot. As many as fifty people died in preelection violence. In the end, Menocal won an election in which more votes were cast than the number of people who were eligible to vote. *Miguelista* and *Zayista* military officers with Liberal Party politicians plotted a *golpe* against Menocal and the Conservatives in 1917. Even though they were able to seize control of Camaguey and Santiago for a short period, the *golpe* failed largely due to their inability to seize the main military camps (Camp Columbia and La Cabana) in Havana. Five hundred U.S. Marines landed in Santiago and occupied Guantanamo, El Cobre, Manzanillo, and Nuevitas. This failed *golpe* allowed Menocal to continue to fill the military with his loyalists. With U.S. encouragement, Menocal declared that Cuba would no longer be neutral in World War I. He used the excuse of world war as a reason to continue to exercise the near dictatorial powers he had adopted during the *golpe* attempt. Menocal's corruption knew no boundaries and imaginary roads and bridges were built over rivers that did not exist. Government officials ran their own businesses with money from the treasury. U.S. Marines remained in the country until 1923.

In the 1920 election, Zayas, who had been expelled from the Liberal Party by Gomez, was elected by joining forces with the Conservative Party under Menocal. Menocal's support was won with the promise that Zayas would support him in the 1924 election. Menocal was able to buy off Gervasio Sierra, the leader of the growing trade unionists. The threat of officer purges should the Liberals win the election was used to gain military support for Zayas. The military harassed and intimidated Liberal Party leaders and voters. In some areas, the military was used to supervise and rig the election outcome. This effectively eliminated the power of the Liberal governors in these areas. In some areas, more votes were cast than there were voters. By this time, it was clear to all that the Cuban military could determine the outcome of an election.

During World War I, an international committee made up of representatives from the United States and Great Britain supervised the sugar supply to the allies. By 1918, it had basically set the world market price of sugar at 4.6 cents a pound and purchased the entire Cuban crop.[6] This was much higher than the prewar price but lower than what could have been obtained in a free market situation. Price controls ended in 1920 and the "Dance of the Millions" began. The price of sugar increased from 9 cents a pound in February to 22 cents a pound in May. The value of the sugar crop in mid-1920 was $1 billion, more than twice what it was the previous year. The price of sugar then collapsed as quickly as it had risen. By December, it had fallen to less than 4 cents a pound. This devastated most of the sugar mills that had contracted to purchase large quantities of sugar at high prices and borrowed money to expand operations based on the promise of higher prices. Then, when the price of sugar dramatically fell, they were faced with having to sell their processed sugar at a much lower price. Many went bankrupt and could not pay off their loans. By the end of 1921, the First National City Bank of New York had foreclosed more than sixty sugar mills in Cuba.

The economic crisis caused many big investors to withdraw their accounts from Cuban banks who were already overextended in loans. The entire banking system was near collapse when the U.S. government sent Albert Rathbone, a financial adviser, to Cuba in December 1920. Rathbone stayed two weeks, recommend a U.S. loan to the Cuban banking system, and billed the Cuban government $50,000 for his services. The United States sent Special Ambassador Enoch

Crowder to Havana in January on the battleship USS *Minnesota*. The National Bank of Cuba closed its doors in April 1921 with its debts exceeding its ability to pay by more than $65 million. One month after the inauguration of Zayas in May, eighteen Cuban banks had collapsed with a combined debt of $130 million. Government workers and teachers went unpaid.[7]

The United States made a difficult situation worse when it raised the tariff on Cuban sugar by a little more than 1 cent a pound. This was largely due to the growing influence of the American sugar beet industry. By September, tons of unsold sugar remained in Cuba. The situation was critical. Zayas agreed to cut the Cuban budget and a group of U.S. banks under the direction of J.P. Morgan provided a short-term emergency loan of $5 million until a long-term financial package could be worked out. Cuba's sugar crop of 1921 sold for less than it had generated in 1915 even though it was the second-largest crop in the history of the country. A financial package from the United States was contingent on Zayas meeting some of the reforms demanded by Crowder. Crowder insisted on reform of the lottery, the firing of the "corrupt" members of Zayas's cabinet and further budget cuts. New York bankers under Morgan also insisted that Crowder must stay on in Cuba for another two years as ambassador. Zayas agreed and was awarded a major financial aid package consisting of $50 million loan to keep the government running and pay its employees, a $7 million loan to pay Cuba's war debts, and $6 million for public works debts. With this financial package, the corrupt Zayas enriched himself, his family, and supporters and maneuvered to put his own people back in his cabinet.

The economic problems of Cuba resulted in a growing nationalism that expressed itself in resentment toward U.S. interference in Cuban affairs, demands to repeal the Platt Amendment, opposition to the growing U.S. economic presence, and support for tariffs to protect and promote Cuban businesses. Newspaper articles and cartoons depicted Zayas as a puppet of the United States. This nationalism would eventually spill over into demands for an end to the massive political corruption and a call for greater social justice on the island. Zayas was able to take advantage of this nationalism and negotiate the return of the Isle of Pines to Cuban control. U.S.-controlled sugar companies in Cuba urged the United States to stop an attempt by the Cuban senate to close all private railways and ports. A compromise brought an end to the construction of all private railroads and ports after 1923.

Various groups began calling for more progressive policies, such as increased taxation on the wealthy, a national healthcare system, government control of the sugar industry, a new trade treaty with the United States, and an end to the massive political corruption. In particular, these groups rallied around the call to repeal the Platt Amendment. The crisis of 1920 and 1921 spurred a growing Cuban manufacturing sector that began to demand state support of Cuban-owned businesses. Groups such as the Commercial Association of Havana, the Committee of One Hundred, the National Association of Cuban Industries, and others began lobbying the political elite class to adopt protectionist policies (import substitution policies) and negotiate a more favorable trade agreement with the United States. Crafts and trade workers, including cigar-workers, typesetters, construction workers, bakers, port-workers, and railroad employees, organized into local unions. By the early 1920s unions had created national organizations. The Havana Federation of Workers organized strikes in favor of better wages and working conditions. Veterans groups, organized initially due to the threat of cuts to their pensions, became advocates of political and economic reforms. Faculty at the University of Havana complained of Cuba's educational backwardness and began demanding greater support for university programs that would be more attuned to the development needs of the island. University students were influenced not only by their faculty but also by the Mexican and Russian revolutions and the success of the students in Argentina during the Cordoba reform movement. They began to speak out for the less privileged sectors of Cuban society. A University Student Federation (FEU) was organized in 1923 and student leader Julio Antonio Mella became a national figure. A nationalistic literature, journalism, and music scene developed that was led by scholars and writers such as Fernando Ortiz, Carlos Trelles, Ruben Martinez Villena, and Jorge Manach and composers such as Amado Roldan.

The corrupt Zayas benefitted from a 4-million-ton sugar harvest in 1922 and an increase in the world market price of sugar in 1923 to 5 cents a pound. Sugar would not command this price again until 1956. Cuban sugar production topped 4 million tons in 1924 at a price of 3.82 cents a pound and 5 million tons in 1925 at a price less than 3 cents a pound. In the 1924 election, the Conservatives nominated Menocal again while Zayas threw his support to the Liberal Party candidate Gerardo Machado. Machado, a former cattle thief, member of Gomez's cabinet, vice president of the American-owned Cuban Electric Company, and owner of the Moulin Rouge Theatre, won the fraudulent election by promising "roads, water, and schools" for Cuba. In response to demand for reform from the business class, labor, veterans, and students, the Liberal Party called for the abrogation of the Platt Amendment.[8]

By this time, American influences in Cuba were readily visible and pervasive. U.S. racist policies that were put in place during the first occupation (1898–1902) continued to have an impact on the social norms of the island. Resident Americans and businesses openly practiced discrimination against mulattos and Afro-Cubans. This practice was increasingly found among Cuban businesses as well. The Cuban government openly discriminated against Cubans of color in its hiring practices. American tourism increased dramatically from 33,000 in 1914 to 56,000 in 1920 to 90,000 in 1928.[9] New U.S.-owned hotels and restaurants catered to American tourist interests. Cuban-owned hotels were often managed by Americans. During the American prohibition era, large numbers of bartenders and bar owners moved to Havana. U.S. tourist agencies advertised Cuba as a tropical paradise where Americans could indulge themselves in actions that were forbidden at home—gambling, playing the lottery, drinking, or romancing with an exotic lover. Horse racing, boxing, prostitution, and baseball became prominent features of the Cuban landscape. American films were well known and became very popular throughout Cuba. A U.S. company created the first theatre chain on the island and by 1920 Havana had more than forty movie theaters. Movie advertisements helped sell American beauty products, clothes, cigarettes, breakfast foods, beverages, and detergents. U.S. department store chains, such as Woolworth's, appeared in major Cuban cities. The rapid expansion of electrical power during the 1920s fed the growing demand for American appliances such as toasters, electric clocks, mixers, and fans. Radios became a highly sought-after item for almost all Cubans. In a case study of the General Electric in Cuba, historian Thomas O'Brien traces the transfer of American corporate culture and values in Cuba such as modern management and production techniques. At the same time, he provides evidence of the standard American racist view of the natural inferiority of Cuban workers.[10]

U.S. companies outside Havana made their presence felt as well. They came to own vast tracts of land. Comfortable, modern, and well-kept American communities sprang up near the U.S. companies across the island. These communities isolated themselves from Cuban life, preferring to maintain the American way of life rather than becoming part of Cuba. Cuban employees sometimes lived in company towns in which the company owned and provided virtually everything including housing, retail and food stores, and loan facilities. The best (or worst) examples of this existed at the large, American sugar mills with their segregated American and Cuban zones. The sugar mill was the dominant force in these areas providing virtually all the local employment and becoming a transmitter of American values. In addition to working as laborers and as low- to mid-level administrators, Cubans were hired as surveyors, accountants, clerks, teachers, engineers, technicians, and physicians for the mill. The local holidays and social calendar set by the sugar mill typically reflected American products. Cubans came to adopt the American consumer culture. The sugar mill and its surrounding was a self-contained region capable of providing its own law enforcement. The mill provided grants and contributions to local towns to build schools, libraries, and roads. It provided scholarships to send the children of its employees to universities. Yet, this came at a price. Local Cubans became totally dependent on the sugar mill. With dependency also came a sense of powerlessness. Workers had no recourse to arbitrary dismissals. Mill owners fought labor organizers. Locals working in the mill adminis-tration rarely moved beyond mid-level positions that were reserved for Americans. They endured the humiliation of racist remarks by the American employees. Finally, the mill was in a position to make deals with corrupt, local political elites. The mill could do as it pleased in Cuba. As historian Louis Perez points out, "The sugar company was emblematic of almost everything that was wrong in Cuba's relation-ship with the United States: the powerlessness, the degree to which the mill constituted a world into itself in which Cubans had no rights except those conceded by the company and to which existed neither remedy nor redress."[11]

MACHADO AND THE GENERATION OF 1930

President Machado quickly moved to gain both the control and support of the military and opposition politicians. Military officers supportive of Menocal were quickly retired and replaced with *Machad-istas*. Promotions and appointments were contingent on loyalty to the governing party. Other officers were bribed with extra pay and bene-fits. The few professional Cuban officers educated at the U.S. military academies found their authority undermined by Machado, who fre-quently turned to the "interests" of the noncommissioned officers—the sergeants—for his support. Machado increased the military budget and the number of soldiers, built new training facilities, created an air corps, and improved housing conditions on military bases. The mili-tary began supervising physical education and marching classes in the secondary schools. Graft within the military increased as it controlled the production, distribution, and sale of meat and milk throughout Cuba. Kickbacks from private companies who supplied the military became common. With the promise of an arrangement for sharing the graft and control of the lottery (*cooperativismo*), most of the old politicians from the "independence generation" in the legislature, including many Conservatives, were bought off by Machado. In this way he came to control the competition among Cuban political elites. Those who did not support this arrangement were sent into exile. Machado banned opposition parties. He began an extensive public works program with work on the Central Highway in 1927 while a private building boom in Havana had also started.

It is important to note that Machado came into office a wealthy man and did not need to use political office to gain wealth. He owned the Santa Marta sugar mill, a construction company, a paint factory, newspapers, a bank, a shoe company, a contracting business, a market, a soap factory, a beer brewery, and other local enterprises. He supported the diversification of the economy and the growth of local industry.[12] In 1927, the Customs-Tariff Law was enacted, which provided state support and subsidies to Cuban industries while a tariff was placed on imported goods that may compete with local industries. It was perhaps the first time that the sugar elites, who opposed the tariff on imported goods from the United States, had lost a public policy struggle in Cuba. These reforms, unfortunately, were negated by his immense corruption and the Great Depression, which came early to Cuba. Machado's decision to seek an extra term was met with student demonstrations and riots and labor unrest across the island. Machado quickly closed the university and exiled the Spanish labor leaders as undesirable aliens. Endorsed by President Calvin Coolidge, Machado won an uncontested, fraudulent election in 1928.

The Great Depression devastated the export-oriented, sugar-dominated Cuban economy. It began with a drop in the price of sugar by almost 60 percent between 1924 and 1928 to about 2.5 cents a pound. By 1929, the price of sugar was down to one and eight-tenths cents per pound. The Smoot Hawley Tariff, which added 2 cents per pound on sugar exported to the United States in 1930, effectively cut Cuba's share of the U.S. sugar market in half by 1933.[13] Economic hard times set the environment for the growing opposition to the increasingly repressive Machado government and his secret police, the *porra* (translated literally as the bludgeon). This also alarmed the United States. The opposition to Machado centered along two major groups that were outside his governing arrangement of *cooperativismo*—labor and students. Labor and student opposition took the form of an urban underground that waged a war consisting of strikes, work stoppages, demonstrations, assassinations, gun battles, bombings, riots, and propaganda.

Students, many of whom were the sons, grandsons, daughters, and granddaughters of those who fought in *Cuba Libre*, had entered the political arena during the Zayas administration with the formation of the University Student Federation. In 1927, the University Student Directorate was formed in reaction to Machado's decision to seek another term. It organized a large demonstration in September 1930 that ended in a riot and the death of its leader Rafael Trejo. Machado closed the university and all high schools across the island. According to historian Jaime Suchlicki, it was the martyrdom of Trejo that led most Cubans to come to support the student opposition to Machado. This student opposition movement came to be known as the Generation of 1930. A more radical and secretive group led by middle-class professionals called the ABC Revolutionary Society (the letters A, B, and C refer to its cell-based organizational structure) was founded in 1931 with the goal of killing Machado. This group, led by Harvard-educated Cuban intellectuals, adopted the terrorist technique of assassination through bombings and published a manifesto demanding limits on U.S. control of Cuban land, nationalization of public services, and an end to large landholdings on the island.

Labor or working-class groups in Cuba were located primarily in the export-oriented, foreign-owned industries, so that labor unrest was not simply a domestic issue. Labor unrest among the tobacco, sugar, construction, railroad, and dock workers brought the possibility of U.S. intervention and had historically been repressed by various Cuban governments after independence. Prior to 1925, Cuban labor was typically tied to or led by veterans of the Spanish anarcho-syndicalist labor movement. It is also important to note that rural (primarily workers on the sugar plantations) and urban workers often maintained contact with each other. This made it possible for a unified labor movement that could be mobilized for political purposes if a Cuban leader could somehow capture control of it. The National Confederation of Cuban Workers, the first national organization of trade unions, was created in 1925 and represented 128 trade unions and more than 200,000 workers. In 1925, several local communist groups united to create the Communist Party of Cuba. By 1929 it had expanded its influence into constituent unions and the National Confederation of Cuban Workers. Machado responded with violence to strikes by the textile and railway workers in 1925. The secretary general of the National Confederation of Cuban Workers was literally thrown to the sharks by the *porra* in 1926. Machado continued to assassinate militant labor leaders while trying, unsuccessfully, to capture control of the labor organizations. As the depression deepened, labor became more militant and 200,000 workers went on strike in March 1930. By 1931 the Communist Party of Cuba had gained control of the majority of leadership positions within the National Confederation of Cuban Workers.

The Cuban military was called on by Machado to carry out more and more of the repression against the opposition. Those charged with activities against the government were often tried in military courts. Students and faculty members of the University of Havana were arrested on charges of conspiracy to overthrow the government in early 1931. Among them was Ramon Grau San Martin, a popular physiology professor. The ABC Revolutionary Society, the University Student Directorate, the Communist Party, and the National Confederation of Cuban Workers responded to Machado's violence with more violence of their own. Daily political murders and increasing urban violence coupled with a disastrous sugar harvest characterized Cuba of 1932. Unemployment was at an all-time high. The United States gave Machado emergency loans to pay Cuba's debts. In September, the ABC Revolutionary Society assassinated the president of the Cuban Senate. This was followed by an unprecedented campaign of terror against students and other opposition groups.

In January 1933, more than 20,000 sugar workers went on strike and it was evident that by that time the army was the only institution that kept Machado in power. It was against this backdrop that the United States and newly elected President Franklin Roosevelt decided to act. Fearing a threat to American investments and being lobbied by exiled Cuban elites, Roosevelt sent Sumner Welles to mediate between Machado and the opposition in May. Welles's decision to talk to the opposition legitimized these groups and empowered them to play a major role in the post-Machado government. When Machado rejected the mediation efforts, Welles threatened to withdraw U.S. support for the government and hinted at the possibility of an armed U.S. intervention.

A bus driver's strike in Havana during the summer culminated in a general strike across the island in early August. According to Suchlicki, the Communist Party lost all credibility, especially with students, during the general strike because it made a last-minute deal with Machado promising to call off the strike. The Communist Party believed it could head off an immediate U.S. intervention on the island that would result in a pro-U.S. government. In the passion of the moment, the workers ignored the return-to-work order. For the next twenty-five years, the discredited communists worked primarily with the more conservative forces and the military in Cuba.

By the end of the first week in August, Cuba was ready to collapse into anarchy. Welles suggested a plan in which Machado and all his cabinet would resign except General Alberto Herrera, the secretary of war, who would become the interim president until a civilian could be selected. Realizing that the United States no longer backed Machado, the Cuban military became concerned about its repressive activities in support of Machado and there was a growing fear of an antimilitary backlash in a newly constituted government. After receiving a promise from Welles and the other opposition leaders that any future government would not engage in retribution against the military, the local commanders at military installations in Havana told Machado they could no longer support him. On that same day, August 12, Machado and his cabinet resigned. Machado left for Nassau with seven bags of gold, his family, and five revolvers.[14] General Herrera became the interim president who quickly turned the presidency over to Carlos Manuel de Cespedes, the son of the hero of *Cuba Libre* and the favorite of Welles and the U.S. government. Vengeance against the supporters of the Machado government, the *porristas*, and the police was carried out with impunity in the streets of Havana and across the island. It is estimated that 1,000 people were killed and 300 houses were looted on April 12 and 13 in Havana. The ABC hunted down and murdered as many *porristas* as possible by staging neighborhood executions complete with witnesses and drum rolls. In rural areas, wealthy landowners were threatened by workers. Cespedes faced an almost impossible task of trying to restore political order in the midst of the depression. In fact, Welles reported that as late as August 24 the country was still in chaos.

This American-backed deal was not received well by some of the opposition. Cespedes and his cabinet were viewed as nonreformist, made up of individuals perceived to be extremely pro-American and did not have representatives from some of the major groups that fought against Machado—the ABC Revolutionary Society, the University Student Directorate, the National Confederation of Cuban Workers, university professors, and former president Menocal and his supporters. Cespedes refusal to do away with the 1901 constitution, which included the Platt Amendment, provided enough evidence to the opposition groups that he was standing in the way of the more progressive and nationalistic reforms for which they had fought. A devastating hurricane hit the island in early September and foreshadowed the events of the next few days. It was at this point that the "sergeants" revolt occurred.

The Cuban military was in a difficult situation. It was reluctant to enforce law and order, fearing that the anti-Machado groups would use this as an excuse to restructure and reduce the size of the military. There were increasing demands to purge the military officer corps of its *machidistas*. When upper-level officer vacancies did occur, Cespedes filled them with supporters of former president Menocal rather than current junior officers. This upset many junior officers who were seeking promotions. They began protecting themselves by demanding that vacancies in the junior officer corps be filled only with graduates of the military academy and the army agreed to their demands in late August. Sergeants would no longer be allowed to fill vacancies in the junior officer level. At Camp Columbia in Havana, the mulatto Sergeant Fulgencio Batista, upset with the order that would restrict the promotions of enlisted men to junior officer positions and a proposed reduction in pay, led a mutiny against the officers and seized control of the camp. Enlisted men at La Cabana joined the mutiny. The sergeant's revolt clearly had racial overtones as a white officer corps tied to a corrupt government was replaced with predominantly nonwhite noncommissioned officers and enlisted personnel.

With the cabinet fearing an attack on Cespedes in Oriente observing the hurricane, the opposition student groups met with Batista and signed the "Proclamation of the Revolutionaries," which called for a restructuring of the political and economic systems of Cuba based upon justice and democracy. The students and the military had united in an uneasy alliance to seize control of the destiny of Cuba. Batista and his sergeants were largely from lower-class backgrounds with little education, whereas the student and labor leaders were largely middle-class professionals. On the night of September 4, Cespedes turned over the government to a five-man group that included Professor Grau, who had the support of the students. Ambassador Welles, viewing the ruling group as "frankly communistic," began organizing the opposition groups, including the deposed officer corps. He asked Roosevelt to send naval ships to Cuba. The five-man ruling group dissolved when one of the members of the group promoted Batista to colonel and commander of the army. Batista then met with the students from the University Student Directorate and created a new government. On September 10, Grau became the president of Cuba.

The new president represented the hopes of the nationalistic students, the Generation of 1930, who saw themselves as finally realizing the dreams of Jose Marti. Grau immediately abrogated the 1901 constitution, demanded that the United States abrogate the Platt Amendment, and called for a constitutional convention for April of the next year. He began purging the government of the followers of Machado and met student demands for greater autonomy at the

University of Havana. He instituted a 40 percent cut in utility prices and pro-labor policies consisting of the creation of a department of labor, an eight-hour workday, a minimum wage, and restrictions on the importation of cheap laborers from the Caribbean. Cuban citizenship became a requirement for all union leadership positions and half of the workforce industries and commercial enterprises had to be made up of native Cubans. This directly affected Americans, Spaniards, Jamaicans, Haitians, and others from the Caribbean who made up some 21 percent of the population of Cuba. Workers marched on and seized sugar plantations, especially those owned by foreigners. By the end of September more than one-third of the plantations were occupied. Due to labor problems, Grau seized two American-owned sugar mills (*Chaparra* and *Delicias*) in December and temporarily took over the American-owned Cuba Electric Company in January 1934.

These "leftist" actions were not supported by the United States or American businesses in Cuba. Welles recommended that the United States not recognize the new government and continued to encourage opposition groups consisting of the ABC, the deposed officer corps, the old-line Liberal and Conservative political parties, prominent politicians Menocal and Carlos Mendieta and the Communist Party. The officer corps, which had taken up residence in the magnificent National Hotel, continued to refuse to negotiate with Batista, whom they derogatorily referred to as *guajiro* or country boy. Batista declared the officers to be deserters and brief hostilities broke out on October 2. The officers surrendered although several were massacred during the panic. With this victory and the subsequent victory over an ABC Revolutionary Society-led revolt on November 8, Batista had strengthened his position as commander and was now able to reshape the officer corps of the Cuban military. By this time Welles had already come to the conclusion that Batista represented the only authority in Cuba capable of preserving stability and protecting U.S. economic interests. In November, Welles was replaced with Jefferson Caffery who began working with Batista to get a government in Cuba with which the United States could work. Student leader Antonio Guiteras demanded even more social reforms. Grau, the reformer, was caught between the demands of both the Right and the Left and had no prospect of gaining U.S. support.

By 1933, the standard of living in Cuba was one-fifth what had been in 1925. Sugar mills were not producing, and bandits in the countryside were common. With the sugar harvest beginning in December, Batista realized that the United States would never recognize the Grau government. In the middle of the depression, he knew that sugar exports to the United States were essential. In January 1934, Batista informed Grau that he and the army were no longer able to support him. A general strike on January 17 led Batista to install Mendietta, the U.S. favorite, as president of Cuba. Five days later, the U.S. government recognized the new Cuban government, although most realized that the real power in Cuba was Batista and the army. To the Generation of 1930, it became quite clear that for a revolution to succeed in Cuba, it would have to take on the United States.

BATISTA AND THE FAILURE OF REFORM

With the belief that the crisis in Cuba was over and that Batista and the military were more than capable of protecting its interests, the United States abrogated the Platt Amendment in May 1934. This was consistent with Roosevelt's Good Neighbor Policy toward Latin America. He declared the United States would no longer intervene into the internal affairs of the countries of the region. Of course, this only referred to outright military intervention. This policy reflected the growing reality that the United States could exercise as much, if not more, influence by manipulating the growing economic dependence of the region as it could through outright military intervention. The United States then guaranteed a market for its agricultural products via a quota and lowered the protectionist tariff on Cuban sugar, but the growing manufacturing and light industry sector of Cuba did not receive the same trade benefits. In effect, U.S. policy helped to maintain the dominance of sugar and agriculture in the Cuban economy and worked against the economic diversification of the island.

With the old political institutions largely discredited, the new civilian government of Cuba became more and more militarized over the next few years. The military was used to suppress labor strikes with the support of the United States and the economic elites of the island. As strikes hit the transportation and utility industries, military personnel stepped in to replace the striking workers. In order to prevent the possibility of strikes by government workers, the government made them all military reservists who were under military supervision during any type of political unrest. Utility companies would often only hire people who were military reservists. In the provinces outside Havana, the military commanders controlled virtually all government functions. The military continued to provide protection for the sugar plantation owners during the sugar harvest. These landowners often provided lists of labor leaders and suspected troublemakers to regional military commanders who would arrest them. Provincial and rural civilian authorities were often replaced by members of the military. Mill owners and businesses clearly recognized the military as the real power in Cuba. According to historian Louis A. Perez an American consul in Santiago commented that the reach of the Cuban army was so great that it could even control insignificant city jobs, such as street sweepers. With its dominance of the political system, corruption within the military increased dramatically. The family members of military personnel received jobs through a massive patronage system. The former sergeants who were now the military elites of Cuba became the primary beneficiaries of this corrupt system.

Opposition to the militarization of the government appeared with students from the Generation of 1930 and national labor organizations. Some students created the Cuban Revolutionary Party, also known as the *Autentico* Party. The *Autenticos* were led by Grau, who was living in exile in Mexico. Other students believing that only violent methods would lead to success joined the *Joven Cuba* led by Guiteras. *Joven Cuba* led an urban underground against Batista similar to the one waged against Machado. Violence reappeared in the streets. In March 1935, a teacher-led movement objecting to poor educational conditions at elementary schools was joined by the *Autenticos* and national labor organizations. The outcome was a nationwide strike against the corrupt and pervasive military dominance in Cuba. With transportation, utility, and hospital workers on strike in Havana and work stoppages at the sugar mills in the countryside, President Mendietta was unable to control the situation. Martial law was declared and the strike was crushed by the military. The suppression continued with military firing squads appearing for the first time in Cuban history. Guiteras of the *Joven Cuba* was killed by the military in May. Many student and labor leaders were exiled. This successful repression further entrenched the military into virtually every part of the Cuban government. Mendietta's government collapsed in late 1935, and Jose Barnet was appointed president to oversee new elections in 1936.

Miguel Mariano Gomez, son of the former president, was elected president in 1936. He assumed that he had full authority and immediately began appointing his loyal supporters to military and government positions and dismissing individuals who gained their jobs largely due to the influence of the army and Batista. These actions clashed with Batista, who pressured the Congress to impeach Gomez. He was successfully impeached in December and Federico Laredo Bru, the vice president, assumed the presidency. He, just as Mendietta, was a figurehead as Batista and the army continued to function as a shadow government. Batista began catering to labor by providing pensions, insurance, and a minimum wage. By this time, the new national labor organization, the Cuban Confederation of Labor, was effectively controlled by the Communist Party, now referred to as the Communist Revolutionary Union, and its leader Blas Roca. Batista, who had made overtures to the Communist Revolutionary Union and gained its support in 1938, effectively brought the Cuban Confederation of Labor under the control of the minister of labor. Public works programs were developed in Havana. The government approved a sugar tax that provided funds for a civic-minded school system in rural areas with military personnel serving as teachers and schoolmasters. The military directed rural programs that provided healthcare, housing assistance to orphans, and support for the elderly. These activities improved life in rural Cuba. They also served to improve the image of the military in these areas as well as increase the popularity of Batista, who had his eyes on the presidency. With the firm entrenchment of the military in the political system, exiled politicians were allowed to return to Cuba and Laredo Bru called for the drafting of a new constitution.

The constitution of 1940 was written by an elected assembly led by the *Autenticos*. Student representatives of the Generation of 1930, such as Eduardo Chibas and Carlos Prio Socarras, were rewarded with a very progressive document that guaranteed the protection of civil liberties and women's equal rights. It provided for extensive social welfare provisions, paid vacations for workers, and minimum-wage guarantees. It also guaranteed the autonomy of the University of Havana. The new constitution represented a New Deal for Cubans. Perez notes that the constitution of 1940 was, in reality, a "statement of goals." It lacked enforcement provisions and became a "dormant document." Yet, its significance is that it would serve as an ideal with which to mobilize future political support and the standard by which to measure future political performance. That same year, Batista, with the support of the economic elites of the island and a coalition of parties including the communists, was elected the first president under the new constitution.

The Batista government of 1940–1944 collaborated with the United States during World War II and received increased economic aid for agricultural and public works programs and loans to increase its sugar crop. The United States bought the entire sugar crops of 1941, 1942, and 1943. Cuba and the United States signed at least nine military agreements during the war. Most of these allowed the United States to use Cuban military bases. German submarine activity in the Caribbean actually sank several sugar tankers. World sugar shortages worked to Cuba's favor. Increased U.S. demand for manganese from the Bethlehem Steel Mines in Oriente also proved to be a windfall for the Cuba economy. Batista moved to gain the support of the nonmilitary sectors of Cuba. Administrative posts that were under military control such as customs houses, lighthouses, and the civic-military rural educations projects were returned to civilian authorities. These moves upset many in the military who were benefitting from the military dominance that Batista had orchestrated in the 1930s. With Batista's dismissal of the police chief of Havana, military officers became anxious. Fearing a military intervention led by army chief Jose Pedraza, the United States intervened by insisting that political stability and the support of Batista were of utmost importance to it. This demonstration of American support cut short the plot to overthrow Batista. Remarkably, by 1944 Batista had restored civilian control over the government of Cuba. He had won the confidence of the wealthy elite, labor, and many other groups. The political process was relatively open, and Batista appointed communist leader and member of the Popular Socialist Party (note that this was the newly adopted name of the Communist Revolutionary Union/Communist Party), Carlos Rafael Rodriquez, to his cabinet. Corruption and graft were still common throughout the government, as Batista left office in 1944 and moved to Florida. He lived near the headquarters of mafia leader, Meyer Lansky, whom he had met and befriended in the 1930s. Batista was now an extremely wealthy man.

Grau, back from exile, representing the *Autentico* Party, and promising everyone "a pot of gold and an easy chair," was elected president in 1944. It was made very clear to him by Batista that he should not do anything to threaten the Cuban military and, in fact, Grau won the trust of the military with the support of the United States. He expanded professional development programs, raised the pay of the enlisted men, and arranged for more Cuban officers to attend U.S. military academies. By the end of 1944, Grau was able to retire more than 200 officers who were associated with the September Sergeant's Revolt of 1933. Key positions in the military came to be occupied by those loyal to the *Autenticos*.

Grau benefitted from high sugar prices, and production in 1946 reached its highest level since the depression. He placed a small tax on sugar that financed public works programs, especially roads. Havana's population expanded dramatically in the 1940s, while U.S. investments in light industry in the city also expanded. J. M. Bens Arrarte, a specialist on Cuban agriculture, estimated that Grau spent almost $80 million annually on public works projects that built parks, roads, houses, schools and hospitals, roads in Havana's suburbs, and upgraded water and sewage systems. These programs provided jobs for the sugar workers in the off season. Grau encouraged the formation of unions and by the end of his term 30 to 50 percent of the workforce was organized and most of these were in key industries such as sugar, tobacco, textiles, transportation, and light manufacturing. *Autenticos* in the Cuban Confederation of Labor came to collaborate with the communist leadership.

Grau betrayed the revolutionary and nationalistic ideals that he had exhibited in 1933 by presiding over one of the most corrupt governments in the history of Cuba. The lottery, the sinecure system, kickbacks from public works contracts, gambling, and outright thefts or misappropriations of public funds were used to enrich *Autentico* supporters. Because of the low salaries paid to the majority of government employees, corruption permeated every level of government. It became the way of doing business in Cuba. In addition to corruption, violence reappeared in the form of *gangsterismo*. Gun battles in the streets of Havana, assassinations, kidnappings, and violence on the University of Havana campus became common as the remnants of the more violent anti-Machado groups and the *Joven Cuba* maneuvered to take advantage of the widespread corruption. These pistol-bearing action groups were used by various parties and government officials to intimidate and gain support for their corrupt activities. One of the most feared of these groups, the Guiteras Revolutionary Action, controlled the bus-driver's union and one of its leaders, Fabio Ruiz, was appointed chief of police of Havana by Grau in return for election support. Another group, the Revolutionary Insurrection Union, also had ties to the Grau administration as its members sometimes served as body guards for the president. Its leader, Emilio Tro, was appointed the chief of police of Marianao. All of these groups had ties to students at the university. Campus politics came to be characterized by competition among these gun-toting action groups for the presidency of the University Student Federation and the control of the sale of textbooks and exam papers.

With the Cold War becoming the dominant force in world politics in 1947, the cooperative relationship between the *Autenticos* and the Popular Socialist Party became strained. Grua and Prio, the minister of labor, moved to eliminate the Socialist Party's control of the Cuban Confederation of Labor. Two competing leaderships were selected—one communist and the other *Autentico*. The majority of labor groups on the island were undecided as to which to follow. In July, Prio used force to take the Cuban Confederation of Labor headquarters from Lazaro Pena and the communists. Prio turned it over to the *Autentico* unionists and by the fall almost all trade unionists had recognized the noncommunist leadership.

The *Autentico* corruption under Grau was so great that the charismatic Eduardo Chibas, the son of a wealthy family from Guantanamo, former leader of the University Student Directorate and *Autentico* leader, created his own *Ortodoxo* Party. Making "honor against money" as his slogan and demanding Cuba "free from economic imperialism of Wall Street and from the political imperialism of Rome, Berlin, or Moscow," he challenged Prio, the Autentico candidate for the presidency in 1948. Ricardo Nunez Portuondo was the candidate representing the interests of Batista who had returned from Florida. *Gangsterismo* characterized the campaign as Prio openly used the gunmen of the Guiteras Revolutionary Action. Prio won the election with Nunez coming in second. Batista was elected to the senate.

Prio benefitted from continued high prices of sugar through 1949 and he represented a continuation of the Grau administration with massive corruption and *gangsterismo*. Trying to divert the public's growing dissatisfaction and disillusionment with what was happening, Prio began trying to place the blame on Grau, his predecessor. He also resorted to the time-honored Cuban tradition of massive public works programs with the promise of jobs. In September 1949, he began negotiating a $200 million loan to finance a new aqueduct in Havana and the dredging of the harbor. In a vain attempt to end the violence, Prio exchanged "government jobs" for an end to the violence by placing more than 2,000 members of the action groups under the massive sinecure system within the Ministries of Health, Labor, Interior, and Public Works. With the outbreak of the Korean War, the price of sugar remained high in 1950. Evidence of new wealth could be seen in the growing number of new cars and television sets in Havana.

Chibas effectively exposed the massive corruption of the *Autenticos* and played a major role in undermining their legitimacy. On August 5 during his very popular weekly Sunday night radio broadcast at 8:00 P.M. on the CMQ station, Chibas, who was a gifted orator, ended his show shouting, "People of Cuba, awake! This is my last call!" He then shot himself. The event, which has never been fully explained but was probably an accident, left the *Ortodoxo* Party without leadership. This effect was to further erode the legitimacy of the Cuban political system. The *Autentico* candidate for president was the respectable Carlos Hevia, an engineer who was closely connected to the Bacardi Rum Company. *Autentico* hopes increased when it was reported that the 1952 sugar production would hit 5.9 million tons with the United States willing to buy more than the normal Cuban quota due to the inability of the Philippines to fill its quota. The *Ortodoxos*, stunned by the death of Chibas, selected Roberto Agramonte as their candidate, although most believed that he could not win. Rumors were rampant of an *Autentico*-sponsored *golpe*. The third candidate was Batista, who had been using all of his abilities to gain the support of his old followers, especially the military and those living in rural areas. It was clear to many that he could not win the election. In December 1951, a group of junior officers gained the support of Batista to plan the overthrow of the discredited *Autentico* government. There was fear among the remaining Batista loyalists in the army that if the *Autenticos* should win the election they would be purged and would no longer have access to the benefits of military graft and corruption. Batista and his supporters went into action on March 9 and in the early morning hours of March 10, 1952, Batista and his supporters staged a perfectly coordinated and bloodless *golpe*. Prio escaped Cuba by driving his Buick to the Mexican embassy. Batista declared, "The people and I are dictators." The *golpe* marked the end of all hope for democracy in Cuba and ushered in a new era that would have unforeseen consequences for Cuba, the United States, and the world.

FULGENCIO BATISTA

Fulgencio Batista, known as *el mulato lindo* (the pretty mulatto), was born in 1901 in the Veguitas section of Banes, the major port serving the United Fruit Company in northeastern Cuba. He was the son of a sugar worker, Belisario Batista, who had fought with Jose Maceo (Antonio Maceo's brother) during the Ten Years' War. Of very humble origins, the family lived in a two-room *bohio* (a small hut) with dirt floors and neither running water nor a toilet. Batista attended both public and private schools at night while cutting cane during the day. With the death of his mother, Carmela Zaldivar Gonzalez, he left home at the age of fourteen. He worked at many odd jobs (water boy at a plantation, timekeeper of a work gang, charcoal vendor, fruit peddler, dockworker, carpenter and tailor's apprentice, hand boy at a barber shop, and brakeman on the railroad) but primarily as a sugar cane cutter until he joined the army in 1921, where he studied law. This background and knowledge of virtually all parts of Cuban society served him well in his ability to manipulate and dominate Cuban politics for almost thirty years. He was clever, fast-thinking, personable, and charming when he wanted to be. He left the army briefly in 1923 to work as a teacher but reenlisted shortly thereafter. While working as a sergeant stenographer, Batista came to lead the Sergeant's Revolt, which propelled him into the labyrinth of Cuban politics in the 1930s from which he emerged as the greatest political broker on the island. After he came to power through a *golpe* on March 10, 1952, he appeared on the cover of *Time* magazine in April with the caption: "Cuba's Batista: He Got Past Democracy's Sentries."

NOTES

1. Perez, Jr., *On Becoming Cuban*, 445.
2. Perez, Jr., *Cuba: Between Reform and Revolution*, 162–163.
3. Thomas, *Cuba: The Pursuit of Freedom*, 515.
4. Benjamin Keen and Keith Haynes, *A History of Latin America*, 6th ed. (Boston: Houghton Mifflin, 2000), 434; Thomas, *Cuba: The Pursuit of Freedom*, 541.
5. Thomas, *Cuba: The Pursuit of Freedom*, 538.
6. Ibid., 539.
7. Ibid., 549–550.
8. Perez, Jr., *Cuba: Between Reform and Revolution*, 184.
9. Perez, Jr., *On Becoming Cuban*, 167.
10. Thomas F. O'Brien, "The Revolutionary Mission: American Enterprise in Cuba," *American Historical Review* (June 1993): 765–785.
11. Perez, Jr. *On Becoming Cuban*, 237.
12. Perez, Jr., *Cuba: Between Reform and Revolution*, 188–189.
13. Keen and Haynes, *The History of Latin America*, 436.
14. Rathbone, *The Sugar King of Havana*, 87.

5

The Fall of Batista: 1952 to 1959

What is measured at the hour of the battle for freedom is not the number of the enemy's weapons but the number of virtues in the people. . . . Search for them and you will find them; guide them, and they will march ahead, no matter how hard the road. The masses are ready; all they need is to be shown the true path.

Fidel Castro, letter to Luis Conte from Isle of Pines Prison[1]

Revolutionary struggles are rare throughout history. Successful revolutionary struggles are even more rare, and they are the result of many factors the come together in a given place at a given time. Cuba was no different. The stage for the violent upheaval was set by the existence of striking political, economic, and social inequalities with more than one-third of the population considered to be poor and lacking social mobility, coupled with the growth of a frustrated middle class whose rising expectations could no longer be met by a stagnant, sugar-based economy. A corrupt and repressive government supported by the United States had alienated its own people and spurred the growth of a Cuban identity and nationalism divorced from the United States.

Yet, with all of this it still took the appearance of a charismatic leader in the right place at the right time to light the fuse and bring all these ingredients together to make a revolution in Cuba. That leader was Fidel Castro.

BATISTA SEIZES POWER

On March 10, 1952, Fulgencio Batista with the support of the army seized power from President Carlos Prio in a swift, bloodless, and masterful *golpe*. Batista had been encouraged in late 1951 by loyal officers in the military who were not satisfied with the state of affairs in Cuba. In fact, there was little opposition to Batista's seizure of power. Prio and his *Autentico* Party had lost much of their credibility due to widespread violence, *gansterismo*, and corruption. The *Ortodoxo* Party was very effective in rallying public opinion against the *Autenticos* by exposing its corruption, but lacked strong leadership after the death of Eduardo Chibas. Many Cubans were ambivalent about Batista's seizure of power. They wanted an end to gang violence and believed his promise of holding election in 1953.

Batista filled the military ranks with loyalists. He gave military personnel a pay increase, increased the military pensions of senior officers, and purchased modern jet fighters from the United States. Navy officials regained control of the customs houses and regional army commanders replaced governors and mayors. He hired 2,000 new national policemen. Batista declared himself loyal to the 1940 constitution but then suspended all constitutional guarantees and the right to strike. He put forward a new constitution in April that enabled him to deny freedom of speech, press, and assembly at any time for a forty-five-day period. Political parties were no longer recognized and an eighty-member consultative council with Batista supporters replaced the Cuban Congress. Batista began censoring the newspapers and jailing or exiling those who came to oppose him.

The end of gang violence and the promise of political stability brought Batista support from economic elites such as the Banker's Association, the Association of Land Owners, the Association of Industries, the Association of Sugar Mill Owners and Planters, the cattle industry, and local and foreign business owners. The U.S. government recognized the new Cuban government on March 27. A visit by officials of U.S. Steel Company with the promise of investment in the mining sector signaled strong and continued U.S. economic support. U.S. investment in the mining sector increased. Batista started a new public works program that upgraded roads and built a sorely needed water system for Havana. He used bribery, flattery, and intimidation to win the support of some labor leaders while continuing the pro-labor policies of the Prio government. The Cuban Confederation of Labor led by Eusebio Muhal supported the administration. The Popular Socialist Party (communists) initially denounced the *golpe*, but many continued to work in the Ministry of Labor. The Catholic Church hierarchy tolerated the new government.

With the celebration of the fiftieth anniversary of the Cuban Republic, much of the literature and print media lamented the inability of Cuba to live up to the promise of independence and the ideals of Jose Marti and the other founding fathers. Guilt and pessimism permeated the Cuban people as Batista tightened his control. Several small plots to topple Batista within the military were discovered in late 1952 and early 1953. Opposition to Batista also appeared among the students at the University of Havana and took the form of demonstrations and riots, although they were sporadic and uncoordinated at this time. With increasing repression and censorship of the media, many students came to the conclusion that violence was the only viable means of removing Batista from power. They also realized that the overthrow of Batista would lead to a confrontation with the United States.

Fidel Castro had run for the Cuban House of Representatives in 1952 as a member of the *Ortodoxo* Party. He had been a supporter of Chibas, the *Ortodoxo* leader who was killed during a radio broadcast. When Batista seized power, Castro began organizing a group in Artemisa with the purpose of toppling Batista. Many in the group had been active in the *Ortodoxo* Youth Movement. The group included Abel Santamaria, an employee of an American sugar refinery, his sister Haydee Santamaria, Jesus Montane, an accountant for a Cuban branch of General Motors, and Melba Hernandez, a lawyer who would later marry Montane. Santamaria and Montane had published a secret political newsletter entitled *Son Los Mismos* (They Are the Same). Most of Castro's followers in 1953 were not university educated, as they were primarily workers and farmers. Only one person in Castro's group was an official member of the Popular Socialist Party.[2]

The plan, which was worked out in Abel Santamaria's office in Havana, was to attack the Moncada Barracks at Santiago in the early morning of July 26. It took place during the month-long and very popular carnival in Santiago that had become closely associated with the Santiago-based Bacardi Rum Company. It was hoped that the dancing, partying, and drinking during the carnival on Saturday night would make it difficult for the soldiers to respond effectively to an attack early Sunday morning. The purpose of the attack was to capture weapons that would enable Castro to arm his movement in the future and spark a popular uprising in Oriente Province that had a long tradition of revolutionary activities. Castro invoked Marti's ideals and Chibas's policies of promising land reform, sugar reform (such as workers having shares in the company profits and strict Cuban ownership of the sugar industry), the nationalization of the utility companies, a pay increase for teachers in rural areas, and rent reductions.

The attack at Moncada was doomed from the very beginning given that Castro's group was vastly outnumbered and poorly armed and had little military training. Only a few men were killed in the actual attack, but sixty-eight were captured, brutally tortured, and executed. Thirty-two ended up in prison and another fifty escaped. It should be noted that the much smaller barracks at Bayamo was attacked at the same time. This attack failed just as it did at Moncada. Castro's brother, Raul, was captured trying to escape to his family's farm. Castro initially escaped but was later captured by Lieutenant Pedro Sarria, who did not approve of the torture that was taking place at Moncada Barracks. He took Castro to the civil prison in Santiago under the spotlight of the local media. This probably saved Castro from torture and death. Castro was tried in October and acted in his own defense. He gave an impassioned plea ending with the statement, "Sentence me, I don't mind. History will absolve me." The speech would later be smuggled out of his jail cell one sentence at a time on matchbox covers. Later, it would be rewritten and his "History Will Absolve Me" speech was put into a pamphlet and used as an effective propaganda tool. Castro, his brother Raul, and the other conspirators who were not executed were sentenced to prison on the Isle of Pines. While the attack at Moncada failed, it placed Castro as a contender for the anti-Batista forces on the island and, according to scholar Louis Perez, "reaffirmed armed struggle as the principal means of opposition."[3]

During his prison stay, Castro wrote many letters that gave clues as to the future of the revolution that he would lead. In these letters he focused on the themes of Marti and Chibas. He emphasized the corruption, greed and repression of the Batista government; the need for land reform given the terribly unequal distribution of land; the problems with an economy based primarily on sugar; and the dependence of Cuba on the United States. Other letters focused on the use of propaganda and the media as tools of a revolutionary. Finally, reflecting one of Marti's themes, Castro emphasized the need for Cuban unity. He spoke of "the gigantic, heroic enterprise of uniting the Cubans" and the necessity of "uniting in an unbreakable bundle."

In Castro's absence, women assumed much of the leadership of the 26th of July Movement. They included Haydee Santamaria, who was with Castro at Moncada, and Hernandez, who had helped to defend Castro during his trial. They formed contacts with other women's groups opposed to Batista, such as the Association of the United Cuban Women and the Women's Marti Civic Front. They also distributed Castro's "History Will Absolve Me" speech in a pamphlet form.

Batista finally agreed to hold elections and stepped down from the presidency on August 14, 1954, so he could campaign to be officially elected as president. He started his campaign by announcing that $350 million in newly issued government bonds would be used for public works projects. He received large sums of money from companies and wealthy Cubans for his campaign. The *Autentico* candidate, Grau, withdrew from the election that was a sham from the very beginning. Batista was elected without any opposition on November 1 and assumed office in February. He claimed that a constitutional government had been restored. Vice President Richard Nixon visited the island and gave the government U.S. support. Believing he was in control and feeling invulnerable, Batista made a fateful decision. He granted general amnesty to all prisoners. Castro and his comrades walked out of the prison on the Isle of Pines on May 15, 1955.

That same year the moderate opposition parties in Cuba attempted to negotiate with Batista to secure the promise of new elections and the guarantee of participation by all Cubans. This so-called civic dialogue failed when Batista simply refused. Moderates were now pushed to support an armed confrontation. Castro, now free, immediately began attacking Batista in speeches at public meetings and on the radio. He wrote articles for various newspapers, the journal *La Calle*, and the magazine *Bohemia*. These came to be censored by Batista. Castro decided, once again, that the use of violence was the only way to topple Batista. Raul Castro and others left from Mexico to begin preparations for an armed invasion of Cuba. Castro met with those supporters who were to remain on the island. They included not only those from the ill-fated attack at Moncada, such as Haydee Santamaria and Pedro Miret, but also Frank Pais, Celia Sanchez, Faustino Perez, Armando Hart, and Carlos Franqui. These supporters formed the basis for the 26th of July Movement on the island. Castro left for Mexico on July 7, 1955. Enough money was raised to purchase some arms and a farm outside of Mexico City to begin the military training of Castro's group of revolutionaries. Among these revolutionaries was Ernesto "Che" Guevara, a young Argentine doctor who would become second in command and play a major role in Castro's revolution. The Mexican government frequently harassed Castro and his group by seizing their arms and arresting some of them.

Meanwhile, the students at the University of Havana, led by Jose Echeverria, began a more violent campaign against Batista after the failure of the "civic dialogue." Police arrested and brutalized many students at anti-Batista rallies in Havana and Santiago in November. Echeverria organized a nationwide student strike. By the end of 1955, Echeverria organized the Revolutionary Directorate, a clandestine student organization whose goal was to topple Batista. Student rioting continued through the early months of 1956 across the island. Batista retaliated with increasing violence. Many students were killed and became instant martyrs.

Dissident officers in the army led by the nationally known and decorated Colonel Ramon Barquin conspired against Batista in April 1956. Barquin's supporters represented the best of the Cuban military. Two hundred twenty officers were implicated in the conspiracy, and most were tried and thrown in jail. This conspiracy surprised Batista and publicly exposed the open dissension within the Cuban military. Batista became obsessed with loyalty to him as the major requirement of his officers. This increasingly led to the Cuban military coming under the control of political appointees—officers who lacked the professional qualifications that were needed to gain the confidence of the men serving under them.

Echeverria then traveled to Mexico and met with Castro. He agreed to support Castro's invasion with diversionary riots and student demonstrations in Havana. Frank Pais, the leader of the 26th of July Movement's national urban underground also traveled to Mexico to work out the details of the invasion. Pais was to organize a general strike and plan for a general uprising that would coincide with Castro's landing in Cuba. Castro and eighty-two companions crowded onto a small yacht, the *Granma*, and left Mexico on November 25. The faculty and administrators cancelled classes at the University of Havana while Pais and the 26th of July Movement staged an uprising on November 30 in Oriente Province by attacking several military installations and engaging in several acts of sabotage, such as derailing trains and cutting down power lines. By the time Castro and his followers landed near Niquero on December 2, the uprising in Oriente had been crushed by Batista's forces. Castro's men made it to a sugar cane field in Alegria de Pio on December 5 where Batista's troops surprised them. Castro, his brother Raul, and ten others (Che Guevara, Camilo Cienfuegos, Juan Almeida, Efigenio Amejeiras, Ciro Redondo, Julio Diaz, Calixto Garcia, Luis Crespo, Jose Ponce, and Universo Sanchez) were the only ones to escape the ambush. With the assistance of some local peasants, the revolutionaries avoided capture for the next several days and made their way up into the mountains of the Sierra Maestra. A few days before Christmas, the group cooked two pigs and celebrated the "commencement of the victory of the revolution."

THE STRUGGLE AGAINST BATISTA

On Christmas Eve, the 26th of July Movement encouraged strikes and bombed several facilities in Oriente, causing a blackout in several cities. On New Year's Eve, bombs were exploded in several hotels in Havana and in the city of Santiago. Batista responded with torture and brutality toward anyone associated with the opposition, but the bombings continued. Still, the rebellion was not considered to be a major problem by either Batista or the United States, which continued to support him politically and economically. In fact, it was widely reported that Castro was dead and that his small group of supporters would be captured very shortly.

It was in the Sierra Maestra, the rugged, jungle-covered mountains of southeastern Cuba, that Castro waged a guerrilla war against Batista. It was here that *Radio Rebelde* began broadcasting the revolutionary propaganda that he would use so successfully. It was here that the legend of Castro started. The hardships suffered by the bearded guerrillas (*los barbudos*), the constant moving from one place to the next to avoid a major confrontation with the Cuban army, the harassment and hit-and-run tactics used by the guerrillas against the army, the support given to Castro by the local peasants and the ability to attract new recruits to the revolutionary group added to the growing heroic image of Castro over the next two years.

With about twenty men, the *Fidelistas* successfully attacked a small military outpost on January 17 at La Plata and obtained some needed supplies. Even with this, the morale among Castro's small force was low due to the hardships of the mountains, the presence of planes above them, and the necessity of dealing with traitors in the group. Castro knew the power of the media and he realized that he had to get his message out to the rest of Cuba and the world. He arranged for a reporter, Herbert Matthews of *The New York Times*, to come to the Sierra Maestra and interview him. Matthews's interview appeared on *The New York Times* on February 24, complete with pictures of the bearded Castro in army fatigues. This interview helped to create the legend and mystique of Castro as a hero, a modern-day Robin Hood fighting for justice and resisting oppression. It made him an international figure and all of Cuba finally knew that Castro was alive and well in the Sierra Maestra. Several other writers, journalists, broadcasters, and photographers followed Matthews into the mountains to find out about Castro and his guerrillas. By that time, Celia Sanchez, the daughter of a physician in Pilon, Haydee Santamaria, and Vilma Espin, the daughter of Bacardi executive Jose Espin, had joined the guerrillas in the mountains. Castro and his guerrillas also met with the leaders of the 26th of July Movement from across the island in late February. Pais promised Castro reinforcements and in March, he sent fifty-two new recruits from Oriente to join the *Fidelistas* in the mountains. Among these recruits was Hubert Matos, a local rice grower and teacher, who later would become a guerrilla commander.

In Havana, Echeverria and his Revolutionary Directorate staged a daring attack on Batista's palace. The goal was to assassinate Batista, capture the Havana radio station, and announce the end of the dictatorship. Echeverria and most of the student rebels were killed during the attack. Besides Castro, Echeverria was the most important opposition leader. With his death and the increasing repression and brutality, all of the opposition now looked to Castro for leadership. Interestingly enough, Cuba's elites, U.S. businessmen, and the U.S. government rallied to the support of Batista. World sugar prices were high, U.S. investment was increasing, and Batista continued an extensive public works program. The new Havana Hilton opened in April and the next month Batista was recognized as an honorary citizen of Texas.

Castro and his guerrillas captured a military outpost at El Uvero in May. This much-needed victory gave the rebels needed weapons, ammunition, and supplies, as well as a boost in morale. Castro's guerrillas had come of age, and they began to believe they could defeat Batista's army. Knowledge of the mountain terrain gave the guerrillas an advantage over the Cuban army. Repression by Batista's army and local police led peasants to join Castro and rural villages provided invaluable assistance to the guerrillas. On July 30, Pais was trapped in Santiago and shot. A general strike immediately started in the eastern provinces of Cuba.

Throughout 1957 Castro's force in the mountains continued to grow in size, and a headquarters was established at La Plata. At the same time, an underground in Havana and Santiago waged a brutal, terrorist war against Batista. Several groups including the 26th of July Civic Resistance and the Revolutionary Directorate engaged in bombings, kidnappings, assassinations, and propaganda distribution. Batista's indiscriminate and brutal retaliation against these groups turned much of the Cuban middle class against him. In September, segments of the navy in Cienfuegos mutinied and captured the naval installation at Cayo Loco. The rebel sailors worked with armed units of the *Autentico* underground and the 26th of July Movement. Batista was able to put down the rebellion only after extensive troop reinforcements arrived with tanks and aircraft. He then purged the officer corps of the navy. It was also found that some Cuban air force pilots had refused to bomb Cienfuegos during the naval uprising. With the Barquin conspiracy in the army and the navy and air force rebellion in Cienfuegos, it was clear to Batista that he could no longer count on the total support of the armed forces.

By the end of 1957, U.S. ambassador Earl Smith and the American business community wanted an end to the political crisis. The Catholic Church called for the creation of a government of national unity. The war widened when Raul Castro led rebels to the Sierra de Cristal on the northern coast of Oriente to set up a second front in March 1958. A few influential members of the U.S. State Department, including William Wieland, Roy Rubottom, and Robert Murphy, were not supportive of Batista and were upset that U.S. arms were being supplied to his repressive regime. On March 11, the United States suspended a shipment of arms to Cuba. In effect, the United States had put in place an arms embargo. Many Cubans viewed this as a change in U.S. policy and it clearly affected the morale of the Batista government and the armed forces.

A general strike in April failed largely due to the lack of support from the Popular Socialist Party. Batista then launched a major offensive against Castro's guerrillas in May. It consisted of 10,000 to 12,000 men moving into the Sierra Maestra. Naval units bombarded the mountains while planes strafed and bombed areas of suspected guerrilla activity. Batista's offensive had failed by August. Castro captured and turned over 443 prisoners to the International Red Cross. He also gained needed ammunition, guns, and tanks from Batista's soldiers. In October and November, Guevara and Cienfuegos set up additional guerrilla fronts in Las Villas. By this time, desertions and defections from the Cuban army were common. The *Fidelistas* treated the prisoners with respect, gave medical attention to the wounded, and returned soldiers unharmed. The end of the struggle was near as the Catholic Church, the business community, and others put pressure on Batista to find a peaceful solution. He held elections in November. With the victory of his self-appointed successor, Andres Rivero Aguero, through rigged elections, most Cubans came to the conclusion that only violence would bring an end to the Batista government.

Events moved quickly as the guerrillas chalked up one military victory after another over Batista's demoralized troops. Guevara and Cienfuegos set up a front with the guerrillas from the Revolutionary Directorate in the Sierra de Escambray, while Castro and Raul began to encircle Santiago. On November 30, Castro took Guisa near Bayamo. On December 28, Guevara captured an entire train of Batista's troops

Fulgencio Batista, left, with General Malin Craig, chief of staff of the U.S. Army, at a meeting in Washington, D.C., in 1958. Batista, who led the Sergeant's Revolt in 1934, dominated Cuban politics and maneuvered to secure U.S. support either as president or from behind the scenes until Fidel Castro's revolution in 1959. Coming to the presidency in a coup d'état prior to an election he was sure to lose in 1952, Batista ruled with increasing repression and corruption until he fled Cuba on January 1, 1959, just before Castro's rebels arrived in Havana. (Library of Congress)

while he was advancing on Santa Clara. Santa Clara fell on December 30. On New Year's Eve, Batista was told that Santiago was about to fall to Castro and his guerrillas. At 2:00 A.M. on January 1, 1959, Batista and his closest associates fled to the Dominican Republic. That evening Castro entered Santiago and called for a general strike. The next day Guevara and Cienfuegos entered Havana. The stage was set for Castro's triumphant parade across the island to Havana. On January 8, Castro, clad in fatigues, arrived and gave a speech at Camp Columbia. Three white doves, a symbol of peace, were released during his speech as he declared, "there is no longer an enemy." A new chapter in the history of Cuba was about to be written.

CUBA ON THE EVE OF THE REVOLUTION

Cuba had changed dramatically since independence, yet in many other ways it had not. The population had doubled to 6.3 million and most Cubans lived in urban areas. There were twenty-one cities with populations in excess of 25,000 and one-third of all Cubans lived in cities with a population greater than 50,000. Havana and Marianao, its suburb, had 1.4 million people.[4] Cuba had more television sets per capita than any other country in Latin America and was second only to Venezuela in the number of automobiles per capita. Its average per capita income was the third highest in all of Latin America and the number of telephones per capita was third highest. But these statistics masked the huge gap between the rich and the poor. Cuba was an island of stark contrasts. Havana was the industrial and commercial center; the eastern part of the island was primarily large landed estates dedicated to export-agriculture and cattle and the western part of the island was made up primarily of farmers working small plots of land.

One could see clear distinctions between the urban and the rural areas, Havana and the rest of the island and among social classes. Urban workers were well paid compared to their rural counterparts. The per capita income for urban workers had reached $374, yet for rural workers it was only $91.[5] Almost 87 percent of urban homes had electricity compared to only 9 percent in rural areas.[6] Most rural homes (*bohios*) were primarily made of palm and wood, lacked running water and bathroom facilities, and had earthen floors. Rural dwellers were four times more likely to be illiterate than urban dwellers.[7] Rural unemployment varied with the season—much of it based on the planting and harvesting of sugar. The urban areas, especially Havana, had become magnets that attracted those living in the rural areas to the promise of a better life.

Havana received nearly 75 percent of all investment on the island, excluding the sugar industry. Fifty-two percent of the non-sugar industrial sector was located in Havana. There was one doctor for every 1,000 people on the island, yet more than 50 percent of the doctors lived in Havana. Havana had 60 percent of the dentists, 65 percent of the nurses, and 66 percent of the chemists.[8] Cuba's elites and growing middle class lived there. The nightclubs, gambling casinos, and hotels of the city were playgrounds for wealthy Cubans and American tourists. On the surface, Havana was rich and prosperous with its world-famous ocean front promenade, the Malecon, its colonial forts, El Morro and La Cabana, its nightclubs, casinos, hotels, and its affluent neighborhoods in the western part of the city. Textiles, food processing, cosmetics, and the construction industries contributed to the city's economy. The busy port area with its shipyards was surrounded by oil refineries owned by Esso, Shell, Texaco, and gas and electric power companies.

At the same time, squatter settlements and shantytowns (*barrios insalubres*), such as Las Yaguas, Llega y Pon, and La Cueva del Humo, surrounded Havana and were fed by a constant stream of immigrants from the countryside. The city was not able to provide the necessary services to these shantytowns. The influx of people from the countryside created a surplus of labor pool that kept wages low. The vast majority of poor women worked as domestics (such as cooks and maids), for middle- and upper-class residents. This contributed to the lack of social mobility in Havana. The poor had to rely on charities for medical care.

Havana also had a dark, corrupt and sordid side to it. Organized crime from the United States owned or partly owned many of the gambling establishments. Such notable underground figures as Meyer Lansky and Santos Trafficante, who controlled the Sans Souci and the Casino International, were implicated to be part of the behind-the-scenes syndicate that controlled the Riviera, the Tropicana, the Sevilla Biltmore, the Capri Hotel, and the Havana Hilton. The casinos regularly paid off corrupt Cuban government officials. In fact, this was an accepted part of doing business. Prostitution was rampant and catered to all social classes as well as tourists and American sailors. Many people in Havana were forced to place a sign on their doors stating, "Don't Bother: Family House," because of the large number of prostitutes who worked out of their own homes.

By Latin American standards, Cuba had a large middle class. Its largest source of income was rental property in the urban areas. Sixty percent of all Cuban families and 75 percent of those in Havana paid rent on their residence.[9] The Cuban middle class of the 1950s was frustrated due to the lack of opportunities afforded it by a stagnant, sugar-based economy and this was especially true of those graduating from the universities. The University of Havana produced nearly 1,200 graduates per year, yet there were few real opportunities for them. Under-employment was the rule, as university graduates worked as clerks in the local Woolworth's Department Stores. In order to meet the rising costs of living, many middle-class women started to work outside the home. This occurred at precisely the same time that employment opportunities were shrinking. There was a surplus of lawyers. Many doctors worked as orderlies to help supplement their incomes. It was very difficult, if not impossible, for the middle class to maintain its standard of living in the 1950s.

Cuba's landed aristocracy had, for the most part, disappeared after the turn of the century and was replaced with large, productive estates with Cuban names but owned primarily by North American companies and absentee landlords. Twenty-eight percent of the largest sugar producers controlled one-fifth of the arable land. Yet, half the land on these estates was idle. Although a few landowning aristocratic families still existed (Calvos, Montalvos, Pedrosos, Agramontes, and Betancourt), most wealthy Cubans were in commerce and business and lived in Havana. They joined exclusive social clubs that had come to own much of the Havana waterfront. They sent their children to universities and schools in the United States or to the more prestigious private schools in the city such as Colegio de Belen (where Fidel Castro studied), Colegio de La Salle, Merici Academy, Sagrado Corazon, Ruston, and Phillips. The top-ten percent of wage earners accumulated 38.5 percent of all income in Cuba.[10]

The Cuban poor that lived either in the rural areas or in the shantytowns surrounding the urban areas lacked the means of social mobility. Twenty percent of all Cubans were illiterate and this figure was much higher in the rural areas. A small percentage of students attended schools in the 1950s than in the 1920s. Only 40 percent of school-age children attended school with only 44 percent of children ages six to fourteen and 17 percent of children ages fifteen to nineteen attending.[11] A large percentage of the Cuban poor were Africans and mulattos.

The Cuban economy depended on the export of agricultural products and sugar continued to dominate the economy of Cuba as it had since the late 1800s. The popular saying "without sugar, no country" indicated the importance of sugar to Cuba. More than 80 percent of its foreign exchange earnings were from the export of sugar. Relatively small changes in the price of sugar on the world market dramatically affected the Cuban economy, not to mention natural disasters such as hurricanes. Sugar production took up half of the arable land and a quarter of the labor force. Sugar workers suffered unemployment much of the year because of the seasonal nature of work on the sugar plantations and in the mills. By 1952, it was evident that Cuba was suffering from a stagnant economy. Per capita income fell by 18 percent between 1952 and 1954. The sugar industry was in need of modernization, as the last sugar mill was built in 1925. Cuba now produced 10 percent of the world's sugar, whereas it had produced 20 percent in the 1920s. In 1957 in Havana, the cost of potatoes increased by 37 percent, black beans by 88 percent, and rice by 30 percent. Cubans faced a declining standard of living across the island.[12]

Cuba had become economically dependent upon the United States by the turn of the century and by the 1950s that dependence was even greater. Through a quota system, Cuban sugar was guaranteed a market in the United States at above the world market price. In the 1950s, the United States purchased more than half of the sugar produced by Cuba. The United States had invested more than $1 billion in Cuba and owned half of the arable land. In fact, the United States controlled more than 40 percent of Cuba's sugar production, 90 percent of its utilities, and 50 percent of its railroads.[13] The United States also had interests in mining, oil refineries, rubber by-products, livestock, cement, tourism, and a quarter of all bank deposits. Eighty percent of Cuba's imports came from the United States. Foodstuffs amounted to 22 percent of all imports.[14] Although most foodstuffs could have been produced locally, U.S. producers pressured Cuba not to produce the foodstuffs locally so as to guarantee a market for its companies.

Not only was Cuba economically dependent on the United States, but also most Cubans had come to identify themselves with the American way of life. The pervasiveness of Americans, American companies and products, and American ideas since the turn of the century had left its impact on the island and its people. Baseball had replaced bullfighting as the Cuban national pastime. Cubans knew the best American players, and many Americans played in Cuba in the off-season. Many Cubans played with American professional teams. Baseball was so popular that when the World Series was first televised on the island in 1956, businesses literally closed. The Cuban sense of progress was measured in their ability to purchase American goods, such as televisions, radios, refrigerators, and automobiles. They had developed a sense of entitlement to the American standard of living. They admired the American democratic institutions and believed Americans to live up to those democratic ideals.

Yet, the economic stagnation of the 1950s forced many Cubans to realize that they would never achieve the American way of life. This, coupled with the realization that America would never view Cubans as equals, led to a growing disenchantment with and resentment toward the United States. This was especially true among the 150,000 Cubans, who were typically U.S.-educated, that worked for American companies on the island. By local standards, these Cubans were prosperous. Yet, they were able to see that the Americans on the island did not live up to their stated ideals and standards of fair play and equal treatment. They received firsthand the brunt of American discrimination and racism toward Cubans. Cubans were never in the top-level management, no matter how well they were qualified or educated. Cubans, who did the same job as Americans, received lower salaries. Louis Perez reports that one Cuban, who worked for the Cuban Electric Company as a bilingual clerk, stated his growing resentment, "North American clerks who know only English, and often with poor handwriting and performing inferior work, earned much more than Cubans." Another Cuban engineer who worked for Owens-Illinois Glass company stated, "The American engineers got higher salaries," although he and a friend "carried all the weight of the work on their shoulders . . . these were the rules of the game and you had to play in that way."[15]

Batista's *golpe* of 1952 and the U.S. recognition of, indifference to, and then support of Batista's repression served to increase the growing divide between Cuba and the United States. Cubans questioned America's commitment to democratic principles. They came to resent the depiction of Havana in *The Saturday Evening Post* and *Time* as a city of gangsters and sin, the brothel of the Caribbean. They came to recognize that Americans had played just as much, if not an even greater role as Cubans in creating the Havana of 1959. Cuba was searching for its own identity separate from the United States. Nationalism was growing and the United States was its target. The stage was set for Fidel Castro's revolution.

FIDEL CASTRO

Castro was born on August 13, 1926, on his father's sugar plantation near Biran on the northern coast of Oriente Province. The U.S. influence in this area of Cuba was pervasive with the United Fruit Company, the Dumois-Nipe Company, the Spanish American Iron Company, and the Cuba Railway Company dominating the economy. The U.S. government owned the Nicaro nickel deposits just a few miles south of the coast. The vast majority of Cubans lived in poverty while Americans enjoyed their own polo club, swimming pools, schools, stores, and hospitals. Angel, Castro's father, was originally from Galicia, Spain. He had fought the Spaniards and worked for the United Fruit Company before eventually accumulating a hacienda of 10,000 to 23,000 acres of land and as many as 500 workers. He was seen as someone who was both generous and severe with his workers and his children. Castro has never talked much about his father, but evidence indicates that they were neither close nor affectionate. He once referred to his father as "one of those who abuse the powers they wrench from the people with deceitful promises." In an interview with the noted biographer Lee Lockwood, Castro indicated that his father never paid taxes on his land or income and showed his contempt for him by saying that his father "played politics for money." Castro's father died in 1956. His mother, Lina, was a Cuban Creole whose family was also from Galicia. She protested when the 26th of July Movement burned sugar cane on the family plantation in 1957 and was outraged when the hacienda was nationalized under her son's agrarian reform policies. She and Castro's younger sister, Juanita, assisted anti-Castro groups in 1962 and 1963. These activities were overlooked by Castro. After his mother died in 1963, Castro arranged for Juanita to go to the United States. She never reconciled with her brother. Castro had seven brothers and sisters, as well as a half-brother and sister. The most important of these was Raul, who was four years younger, and has been with Fidel since the attack on the Moncada Barracks.

At an early age, Castro was sent off to school in Santiago where he stayed with godparents who mistreated him. His first memory of an event that "left a lasting impression" on him concerning the brutal nature of politics in Cuba occurred in Santiago. A group of sailors claimed that some students had said something about them. They followed the students into a nearby building, beat them with the butt of their guns, and hauled them to jail. Although not the best student, Castro loved the study of history. He was quite rebellious and at the age of thirteen, he tried to organize a strike of sugar workers against his father. In 1942, a tall, heavy, and powerfully built Castro attended the Colegio de Belen, the prestigious Jesuit preparatory school located in Havana where his best subjects were agriculture, Spanish, and history. One day he quarreled with an older and bigger student who beat him until he could not continue. The next day Castro came back for more and was beaten again until the two were separated. Castro came back for more on the third day and again he was beaten, but the other boy had had enough and conceded a moral victory to Fidel. Clearly, one of Castro's defining characteristics is that he will not accept defeat. He was a noted debater and voted the best athlete in the school in 1944. The school yearbook noted that he was a true athlete and had won the affection and admiration of all, and that he was of "good timber and the actor in him will not be lacking."[16]

He started studying law at the University of Havana in 1945. This period of Castro's life is very controversial and it is difficult to separate myth from reality. Cuban university students had been politicized since the presidency of Machado and the rivalry between the major groups on campus amounted to *gangsterismo*, with the use of guns, violence, and kidnappings being common. Castro became part of this environment and excelled at it by seeking a student leadership position. He took part in the failed invasion of the Dominican Republic organized by several student groups in 1947. The purpose was to overthrow the dictator Rafael Trujillo. The ships were to set sail from the Bay of Nipe and Castro was in charge of Dominican exiles. At the insistence of the United States, President Grau stopped the invasion and most of the participants ended up being arrested. Castro escaped by swimming across the shark-infested waters of the Bay of Nipe to his father's plantation.

Castro met Mirta Diaz-Balart in 1946 at the University of Havana and married her in 1948. Castro's son, Fidelito, was born in 1949. Mirta's father, Rafael, was a lawyer who worked for United Fruit Company and was a friend of Batista. After the Batista *golpe* in 1952, Rafael and her brother were given appointments in the new government. After Castro's ill-fated attack at Moncada, the Diaz-Balart family turned against Castro. While Castro was in jail, Mirta received a government stipend set up by her brother. When Castro discovered this, he was so angry that he turned against Mirta. The couple divorced in late 1954. The Diaz-Balart family, now in Florida, is a stalwart among the exiled, anti-Castro groups in the United States. Mirta's brother's son, Lincoln Diaz-Balart, served in Congress from 1993 through 2011 and was replaced by his younger brother, Mario.

In 1955 Castro had an affair with Natalia Revuelta. They had one child in 1956, Alina Fernandez, who now lives in Spain. He also had an affair with Maria Laborde who produced one child, Jorge Angel, in 1956. There is evidence that the same year he also fathered another son, Francisco Pupo. Unconfirmed liaisons produced another son, Alejandro or better known as Ciro, in the early 1960s, and another in 1970. During the literacy campaign of 1961, Castro met Dalia Soto del Valle, a school teacher. Since that time she has been his common law wife and is known by all as "la mujer de Fidel." They live a discreet, quiet, comfortable, but austere life in a small compound, known as Point Zero, in the western Havana suburb of Siboney. They have five sons.

These events early in his life shaped Castro's struggle with Batista from the attack on Moncada to prison on the Isle of Pines to the Sierra Maestra to his arrival in Havana in January 1959. They shaped his revolution once he was in power. The athletic and charismatic Castro is mischievous, rebellious, calculating, and opportunistic. He is ruthless yet kind. He never accepts defeat—it is only a temporary setback. He is both an idealist and a pragmatist. Castro has a flare for the dramatic and an intuitive sense of the importance of public relations and the use of the media to his advantage. He is somewhat of a loner and rarely confides completely in anyone. He typically learns by trial and error. Castro has a strong sense of the history of Cuba. Author Saul Landau who spent time with him in 1960 described him as "part Machiavelli, part Don Quixote, with a philosophy that was half Marxist and half Jesuit." Castro saw the need to "overturn the economic status of the nation from the top to the bottom—that is to say the state of the mass of the people, for it is here that one finds the root of the tragedy [in Cuba]." He saw the pervasive influence and domination of Cuba by the United States. His goal was to carve out a Cuban identity and nationalism separate from the United States—a true Cuban identity. Castro's opportunity arrived in January 1959.

NOTES

1. Fidel Castro, "December 12, 1953. To Luis Conte Aguero," in *The Prison Letters of Fidel Castro*, edited by Ann Louis Bardach and Luis Conte Aguero (New York: Nation Books, 2007), 11.

2. Thomas, *Cuba: The Pursuit of Freedom*, 826.

3. Perez, Jr., *Cuba: Between Reform and Revolution*, 221.

4. Ibid., 1094.

5. Roberto Segre, Mario Coyula, and Joseph Scarpaci, *Havana* (New York: Wiley, 1997), 88.

6. Ibid., 93.

7. Suchlicki, *Cuba: From Columbus to Castro*, 136.

8. Thomas, *Cuba: The Pursuit of Freedom*, 1105.

9. Ibid., 1096; Segre, Coyula, and Scarpaci, *Havana*, 92.

10. Segre, Coyula, and Scarpaci, *Havana*, 88.

11. Thomas, *Cuba: The Pursuit of Freedom*, 1131.

12. Perez, Jr., *On Becoming Cuban*, 453.

13. Segre, Coyula, and Scarpaci, *Havana*, 88.

14. Ibid., 89.

15. Perez, Jr., *On Becoming Cuban*, 465.

16. Marfeli Perez-Stable, "Fidel Castro," in the *Oxford Companion to Comparative Politics: 2-Volume Set*, edited by Joel Kriegel (New York: Oxford University Press, 2012).

6

Revolution, the New Socialist Man, and Cold War: 1959 to 1970

> In this period of the building of socialism, we can see the new man and woman being born. The image is not yet completely finished—it never will be, since the process goes hand in hand with the development of new economic forms.
>
> Che Guevara, *Man and Socialism in Cuba*[1]

When Fidel Castro and his bearded guerrillas triumphantly entered Havana on the evening of January 8, 1959, no one could have predicted the direction of the revolution or that this small island nation of 6.5 million people could become a flash point for the Cold War rivalry between the United States and the Soviet Union. Yet, by the middle of April 1961 the defining themes of the revolution were clearly in place. The charismatic Castro had come to dominate the political scene like no Cuban leader before him. He defied the United States and created the first communist government in the Western Hemisphere, although it clearly reflected his own revolutionary design and imprint. A socialist economy was developed with programs designed specifically to redistribute wealth and address the needs of the poor majority in Cuba. Fueled by the mutual suspicions of the Cold War, the relationship between the United States and Cuba rapidly deteriorated to the point of outright hostilities during the ill-fated attempt by the U.S. government-supported Cuban exiles to topple Castro in the Bay of Pig invasion in April 1961 and, later, the nuclear confrontation in October 1962. Mutually beneficial ties between Cuba and the Soviet Union were established and although the nature of these ties changed over the course of the Cold War, each country used the other to achieve its own national objectives.

THE CRUCIAL YEARS—1959 TO THE BAY OF PIGS

Castro was the man of the hour in January 1959. The major revolutionary groups, the 26th of July Movement, the rebel army and the Civic Resistance (the urban underground), looked to him for leadership. Middle-class reformers, the Popular Socialist Party, industrialists, and non-sugar agricultural interests turned to him. The Cuban people absolutely adored him. There were high expectations for dramatic change. Louis Perez points out that "while he [Castro] channeled popular forces for change, he did not create them."[2] This immense popular support gave Castro the power to radicalize the economy and challenge the powerful economic interests on the island, in particular, the sugar industry and major U.S. corporations. Although there would be a struggle within the new government to give the revolution its direction, it was clear to all that Castro would dominate the process.

Manuel Urrutia became the symbolic president of Cuba in January 1959. All of the former Batista supporters in the national, provincial, and urban governments were dismissed. Many of Batista's military and civilian leaders were given public show trials. Hundreds were executed and the government confiscated their properties. The Congress was dissolved. On February 7, the Fundamental Law of the Republic was passed, which basically gave all political power to the cabinet. Within a week Prime Minister Miro Cardona resigned and was replaced by Castro. The cabinet consisted of communists and noncommunists, reformers and revolutionaries. Its initial goals were to diversify the economy, weaken the pervasive U.S. presence and influence in Cuba, and reduce the tremendous economic inequality on the island.

Castro promised a revolution, a radical break with the past. Yet, the first reform program of the new government was not radical; in fact,

Fidel Castro, dressed in his classic revolutionary army fatigues, is shown here as he arrives in Washington, D.C., in 1959. Castro did not want to become another Cuban president who had little to no freedom to act under U.S. hegemonic power. He wanted Cuba to be able to pursue its own destiny. Cold War politics, the move toward a socialist economy, the elimination of any political opposition, and the U.S. embargo led to a dependent, if not mutually beneficial, relationship with the Soviet Union until the end of the Cold War. (Library of Congress)

much of it had been proposed in the 1940s: agrarian reform, industrialization, and employment expansion. Moderates and noncommunists in the cabinet, such as Columbia University–educated Felipe Pazos and University of Utah–educated Manuel Ray, played a major role in designing the reforms. Popular support for Castro and the rebel army soared with the passage of the initial reforms. Virtually every labor contract was renegotiated from January through April. In March, rents were slashed 30 to 50 percent, but landlords earning less than 150 pesos in rent income per month were excluded. In the urban areas, anyone who owned a vacant lot was forced to sell it either to the state (the National Savings and Housing Institute) or to anyone who wanted to build a house. That same month Castro began a major land redistribution project in Pinar del Rio in which he personally signed over land to peasants.[3] Tariffs were increased to protect local industries from foreign competition.

On May 17, 1959, the cabinet passed the First Agrarian Reform Law. The law was based primarily on Article 90 of the 1940 constitution and created the National Institute for Agrarian Reform (INRA). It placed a 1,000 acre limit on land holdings. All land beyond the limit was claimed by the government and controlled by the INRA. Expropriated land was either turned into cooperatives to be run by the INRA or distributed to individuals in sixty-seven acre plots. Sharecroppers and renters had first claim to the expropriated land. Owners were paid for their losses with twenty-year state bonds at 4.5 percent interest. This land limit did not apply to the cattle ranches and the sugar and rice plantations whose yields were greater than 50 percent of the national average. In these cases, the limit on land holdings was set at 3,333 acres. Thus, the law only applied to approximately 10 percent of all the farms, plantations, or ranches in Cuba but amounted to 40 percent of the land.[4] Foreign companies could own more land than the limit if the government deemed it was in the national interest. Sugar mill owners could no longer manage the sugar plantations unless all their shares were registered and owned by Cubans. Land could only be purchased by Cubans. The rebel army, which carried out many of the expropriations, the INRA, and the National Federation of Sugar Workers became the primary institutions that promoted and protected the interests of rural workers under the revolutionary government.

Tax policies were changed to favor Cuban over foreign and primarily U.S. investments, non-sugar over sugar sectors of the economy, small over large businesses, and the provinces over Havana. An ad valorem surcharge (a tax on the value of the item) of 30 to 100 percent was placed on all imported luxury items. The smaller sugar mills and rice growers were given larger quotas for export. As a backlash to the tremendous corruption of the Batista era, stealing from the government became a capital crime. The rampant sinecures system came to an end. Prostitution and gambling became illegal. Even the traditional Cuban practice of cockfighting was declared illegal.

Relations with the United States began to deteriorate rather quickly. The U.S. government opposed the summary trials and executions of Batista supporters largely due to the absence of established legal guarantees and due process. U.S. corporations and businesses opposed the wage increases and labor and land reforms. This resistance inflamed popular opinion against the United States. The seizure of the U.S.-owned Cuban Telephone Company in March 1959 became a symbol of defiance and stoked the passions of nationalism among the Cuban people. The May agrarian reforms contributed to U.S. suspicions of Castro and his revolution. It led to further U.S. opposition because many powerful U.S. interests lost land to the Cuban government and argued that they did not receive adequate compensation. This included the United Fruit Company, the Pingree Ranch, and the King Ranch of Texas that had influential ties to powerful people in the U.S. government.[5]

Castro visited the United States in April and even though Cuba needed aid, he did not ask for it. He did not want to be another Cuban leader who would discard his revolutionary principles, bow down, and become dependent upon the United States. After this visit, Vice President Richard Nixon, the State Department, and the Central Intelligence Agency (CIA) came to the conclusion that the United States could not have friendly relations with Cuba and efforts to overthrow the revolutionary government were supported and developed. For the next year, Castro and his rebel army fought counterrevolutionary groups and Miami-based Cuban exiles who used air bases in southern Florida to engage in assassination attempts, provide arms to counterrevolutionary groups, burn crops, bomb sugar mills, and attack ships bound for Cuba. The U.S. failure to disavow these groups and prevent their activities was enough evidence for Castro to assert U.S. complicity in these actions. In fact, the CIA developed at least eight different plans designed to assassinate Castro over the next five years.

Opposition to the agrarian reforms within Cuba began to appear among various groups. Sugar mill owners and cattle ranchers started a media campaign against the agrarian reform law. The media campaign used the imagery of a watermelon with the idea that the deeper you cut it (the Cuban government), the more red (communist) it becomes. Sugar mill owners, cane growers, rice plantation owners, and industrialists opposed the wage increases for workers. Refusing to meet with the union representatives, challenging the legality of the unions, cutting back on the number of employees, limiting worker access to credit, and engaging in lockouts were tactics used to fight the wage increases that workers demanded. The Labor Ministry mediated more than 5,000 labor management disputes in early 1959. These mediations were generally settled in favor of the demands of labor. Wage increases averaged 14.3 percent in 1959.[6]

Opposition began to appear within the ranks of the revolutionary leadership. This struggle pitted the noncommunists against the communists. The Popular Socialist Party did not play a major role in the revolution, and in fact, had condemned Castro's attack on the barracks at Moncada and had not become part of the Batista opposition until late 1958 when the final outcome of the struggle was evident. The initial agrarian reforms and nationalizations of foreign industries were made without consulting or informing the Popular Socialist Party and the initial reforms were more radical than the proposals of the Popular Socialist Party. Yet, Castro saw several advantages in using the Popular Socialist Party. It was well organized and could help control the labor movement in Cuba. Interestingly enough, Batista had used the party in the very same way. At the same time, Castro could purge the party of those whose primary loyalty was not to him. Finally, the Popular Socialist Party had ties to the Soviet Union and Castro knew that the Soviet Union could possibly deter a U.S. attack or action against Cuba similar to what had happened in Guatemala in 1954.

Vocal opposition to the perceived growing communist influence over the new government came from President Urrutia, who was forced to resign in July, and Pedro Diaz Linz, the head of the Cuban air force, who defected to the United States in June where the U.S. Senate promptly gave him a public forum to tell how the communists were taking over the island. Huber Matos, the commander of the rebel army in Camaguey Province, also expressed his concerns and opposition to the communists. Camaguey Province was the heart of the counterrevolutionary forces in Cuba. North American companies such as the King Ranch of Texas and the Manati Sugar Company had lost hundreds of thousands of acres of land and many of the more famous Cuban families, such as the Betancourts and the Agramontes, had their estates seized under the new agrarian reform law. Matos, who had fought with Castro in the Sierra Maestra, had publicly spoken against growing communist influence in the government in June. He resigned when Raul Castro was named minister of the armed forces in October. Raul and Che Guevara were already known for their revolutionary and pro-communist beliefs although neither of them were members of the Popular Socialist Party. Matos was tried for "uncertain, anti-patriotic, and anti-revolutionary" behavior and sentenced to twenty years in jail. Pazos, the president of the central bank, and Ray, the public works minister, resigned their positions and left as a result of the Matos affair.

Seeing increased divisions within the leadership of the revolution, fearing a repeat of the failed revolution of 1933, and expecting U.S. opposition and interference, Castro began to centralize the revolutionary power structure and emphasize loyalty, unity, and survival. Loyalty to Castro became the primary criterion for all future appointments. Revolutionary unity was defined as opposition to the United States and the Cuban elite, meaning the economic class with its historic ties to the United States. Unity also meant that members of the Popular Socialist Party were to be included in the revolution. The anticommunist resistance in Cuba had come to be more preoccupied and concerned with the role of the Popular Socialist Party in the government than with the revolutionary goals of ending U.S. dominance, reducing economic inequality, and meeting the needs of the poor majority on the island. Marifeli Perez-Stable, a noted scholar on Cuba, argues that the controversy over the communist influence in Cuba from 1959 to 1961 masked a "repudiation of radical change."[7] The anticommunists were moderates, not revolutionaries, and Castro swept them away. With the moderates gone and the revolutionary leadership unified, the U.S. hope of controlling the revolution faded. It is ironic that the U.S. opposition to the initial economic reforms helped to undermine the legitimacy of the moderates in the revolutionary government and paved the way for Castro to purge them and radicalize the economy—the very thing the United States did not want to happen.

During 1959 and 1960 Castro and his *fidelistas* began to move to control the existing mass organizations and to create new ones. The Popular Socialist Party came to control the Cuban Confederation of Workers. Other mass organizations included the University Students' Federation, the Federation of Cuban Women, Committees for the Defense of the Revolution, the Association of Young Rebels, the National Organization of Small Agriculturalists, and a civilian militia directed by the Cuban Revolutionary Armed Forces.

Castro began making more of the decisions. There were no more than two cabinet meetings held between October and March 1960. Several moderates in the cabinet—Manuel Ray, Faustino Perez, and Felipe Pazos—resigned. These people were well respected in the United States, in particular, Pazos, who also took with him many of his best technical advisers. These resignations left a shortage of skilled and technically competent administrators and planners in the new government. This clearly played a role in the turn to assistance from Eastern Europe and the Soviet Union. With the resignation of these moderates, the U.S. ambassador to Cuba, Phillip Bonsul, came to the conclusion that the United States could not reach an understanding with the new Cuban government. Survival for revo-lutionary Cuba during the Cold War meant developing closer ties to the Soviet Union.

In November and December, new laws were passed against foreign corporations. Foreign oil companies had to pay 60 percent of their earnings to the government. Lands from Bethlehem Steel and Inter-national Harvester were seized. More lands from the cattle ranches were also seized. It was the arrival of Soviet deputy premier Anastas Mikoyan in February 1960 that confirmed the suspicions of many in the United States that the Cuban revolution was clearly commu-nist. The Soviet Union and Cuba signed a five-year trade agreement in which Cuba would deliver 1 million tons of sugar annually in exchange for Soviet crude oil and the Soviets extended $100 million in credits to Cuba so it could purchase industrial equipment. On March 4, 1960, the ship *La Coubre*, loaded with weapons acquired in France, exploded in Havana harbor. Castro blamed the CIA and gave a defiant anti-American speech that day in which he ended with what would become the most important slogan of the revolution, *"patria o muerte"* (fatherland or death). Two weeks later, President Dwight Eisenhower approved the development of a covert operation designed to topple the Castro government.

By this time, the United States and Cuba were on a spiraling path of mutual fear and hostility toward an inevitable conflict and there was little possibility of accommodation. Events began to take on a life of their own. In May, Castro announced there would be no elections. He indicated that the Cuban people had already spoken. Given his tre-mendous popular support, there is no doubt that if elections had been held, he would have easily won. The U.S. House of Representatives approved a bill that would allow President Eisenhower to cut foreign sugar quotas at his discretion in June. Under instructions from the Eisenhower administration, Texaco, Shell, and Standard Oil refused to refine Soviet crude oil. On June 28, the Cuban government nation-alized the foreign oil companies. In July, President Eisenhower can-celled the remainder of the Cuban sugar quota for the year. It should be remembered that the United States purchased 40 to 60 percent of its sugar from Cuba under a quota system with fixed amounts and guaranteed prices above the world market price. Economic survival required Cuba to sell the remaining sugar that normally was sold to the United States. The Soviet Union agreed to purchase the sugar.

All the U.S. businesses such as Sears and Roebuck and Coca-Cola, as well as all the sugar mills, petroleum refineries, public utilities, tire plants, ranches, and banks were nationalized in August. This also included the U.S. government-owned nickel deposits at Moa Bay. The Eisenhower administration allotted $13 million to provide guerrilla warfare training to 400 to 500 Cuban exiles in Guatemala. The United States pressured the Organization of American States (OAS) to rebuke Cuba in September and, not surprisingly, Cuba strengthened its ties with the Soviet Union and Eastern Europe. Fearing a U.S.-led intervention, Castro organized the Committees for the Defense of the Revolution (CDRs). These local organizations served not only to mobilize the population in support of the government, but also to report any activities against the government. The next month the Cuban government nationalized all industry and commerce, and the United States announced an embargo of its exports to Cuba. In late October, a Guatemalan newspaper reported that the United States was training Cuban exiles in that country for an invasion of Cuba. By November there were more than 1,000 Cuban exiles being trained in Guatemala. In December, China agreed to purchase 1 million tons of Cuban sugar, and the Soviet Union agreed to purchase 2.7 million tons the following year. Nikita Khrushchev, the Soviet leader, expressed a willingness to defend Cuba from "unprovoked aggressions." By the end of 1960, the Cuban state controlled the primary means of economic production on the island. Cuban capitalism had come to an end and its ties with the communist world were expanding.

The Cuban economy performed quite well in 1959 and 1960. It grew at almost 10 percent a year and the sugar output of 6.2 million tons per year was greater than the average for the years 1950 through 1958. A trade surplus existed by the end of 1960. Wealth had been redistributed with 15 percent of the national income shifting from property owners to wage earners by the middle of 1960.[8] Housing and road in rural areas were improved. A great sense of optimism among the revolutionary leaders and the Cuban people led to an expectation that the economic goals of reducing Cuba's dependence on sugar and developing an industrial base for the island would prove to be successful.

The 1961 New Year's Day parade in Havana exhibited Soviet tanks and other weapons. Later that month, President Eisenhower severed diplomatic relations with Cuba when Castro demanded that the United States reduce the size of its embassy staff to eleven, the same size of the Cuban staff at its embassy in Washington, D.C. The incoming president, John Kennedy, and his advisers were anxious to prove to the world their anticommunist credentials and Cuba was their first target.

THE BAY OF PIGS—CONSOLIDATION
OF CASTRO'S POWER

The Bay of Pigs invasion in April 1961 represents the pivotal event in the early years of the Cuban revolution. It allowed Castro to consolidate his power and eliminate virtually all his opposition on the island. It gave Castro and the people of Cuba proof that the ultimate goal of the United States was to destroy the Cuban revolution. It convinced a reluctant Soviet Union that a relationship with Cuba could be very beneficial and entailed little risk. Finally, it led to the decision to place nuclear missiles on Cuban soil.

President Kennedy and his advisers inherited the plan for the invasion of Cuba by U.S.-trained exiles. On April 14, Cuban exiles who had been training in Guatemala boarded ships in Nicaragua and sailed for Cuba. Luis Somoza, the president of Nicaragua, encouraged and asked them to bring him back some of the hair from Castro's beard. On the morning of April 15, a group of B-26 bombers based in Nicaragua attacked key airfields in Cuba. The military damage was insignificant but it prompted Castro to move against his opponents on the island. All dissidents, both real and imagined, including all bishops, many journalists, the vast majority of the urban underground resistance, and most of the CIA's 2,500 agents and their 20,000 suspected sympathizers, were rounded up and thrown in jail. Castro used the air attacks to mobilize the Cuban public against the United States, concluding a speech in Havana with the phrase, *"Patria o muerte, venceremos!"* ("Fatherland or death, we will conquer!"). Castro received news of the landing of the invasion force at the Bay of Pigs at 3:15 A.M. on April 17. The towns near the Bay of Pigs had been the recipients of many of the initial benefits of the revolution—new roads and tourist centers had been built, a literacy campaign was in progress, and the standard of living had increased since 1959. It was unlikely place to start a counterrevolution against Castro. Cuban forces reacted quickly to the invasion. Two Cuban T-33 jet grainers and a B-26 bomber attacked the landing forces, sunk tow ships, and chased away the supply ships. Khrushchev threatened Kennedy, "The government of the United States can still prevent the flames of war from spreading into a conflagration which it will be impossible to cope . . . any so called 'small war' can produce a chain reaction in all parts of the world."[9] Kennedy hesitated to authorize air strikes from the USS *Essex* to support the invasion. Eventually, Castro captured 1,180 of the 1,297 who had landed.

It was the perfect victory for Castro. His often-predicted invasion by the United States had finally occurred. The Cubans had won a victory against the United States. The United States and its indecisive young president were humiliated by world public opinion. Castro's popularity among the Cuban people skyrocketed. He was able to enlist 100,000 people in a massive, nationwide literacy campaign. Thousands of urban residents volunteered to cut sugar cane. More than 300,000 local, civilian militias and 800,000 CDRs were developed to defend the island against future U.S. invasions. Housewives volunteered for the militias and the CDRs. Castro strengthened and consolidated his control over the political system and destroyed almost all of his opposition on the island. After the invasion, Castro declared the socialist nature of the revolution, an obvious attempt to encourage the Soviet Union to develop closer ties to Cuba. The United States with a slim majority suspended Cuba from the OAS in early 1962 and began pressuring its allies to end all trade and commerce with the island.

THE MISSILE CRISIS

The Soviet Union had initially been cautious in its relationship with Cuba. Its experience with revolutionary regimes that had come to power without its support indicated that these governments often pursued independent policies and were, at best, difficult to control. The Soviet Union was more concerned with promoting peaceful coexistence with the United States and gaining concessions in Berlin rather than with events in an area of the world that the United States had traditionally controlled and held an overwhelming strategic and military advantage. Yet, several factors led to the decision to place nuclear missiles in Cuba. The growing competition with China in winning the hearts and minds of revolutionaries in the developing world led the Soviet Union to tolerate and warm up to revolutionary leaders like Castro. It was the failed Bay of Pigs invasion by the United States that finally convinced the Soviet Union to take a chance in developing closer relations with Cuba. It appeared that the revolutionary government in Cuba now had a chance to succeed given that there was virtually no opposition left on the island. It convinced Khrushchev that the young U.S. president was weak and indecisive and lacked resolve. The Soviet Union believed that world condemnation of the failed invasion would make it difficult for the United States to use force against Castro, at least temporarily. It was seen as a window of opportunity to alter the nuclear balance of power that was in favor of the United States, to win concessions from the United States over issues in Berlin, and to deter a future U.S. invasion of Cuba. A closer relationship with Cuba would enable the Soviet Union to achieve these goals.

The Soviet Union increased its military aid to the island. This included aircraft that were capable of delivering nuclear bombs throughout the hemisphere. Even though the Cubans had not requested them, the Soviets began installing medium-range nuclear missiles in Cuba in October 1962. The Cubans had urged them to announce to the world that they were placing missiles in Cuba but the Soviets decided to install them in secrecy. Following the discovery of the missiles, the United States put in place a naval blockade (the United States called it a quarantine because a blockade is an act of war in international law) around the island. The Cubans fully expected a U.S. invasion and air attack. They expected to lose the initial battles and retreat to the mountains to wage a prolonged guerrilla war against the United States. They were ready to fight to the death and thought that the Soviet soldiers would fight and die with them. There was the expectation if the United States used nuclear weapons against Cuba or was about to overwhelm the island that the Soviets would use the nuclear weapons against the United States.

The agreement between Kennedy and Khrushchev to remove the missiles in Cuba in exchange for a pledge by the United States not to invade the island stunned and humiliated the Cubans. The reality is that Castro and the Cubans were pawns during the missile crisis. Neither the Soviet Union nor the United States consulted with them. Castro heard the news about the agreement to end the crisis on the radio. The Cubans were angry at the Soviets. In response, Castro set forth several demands that had to be met before he considered the crisis to be over. He called for an end to the U.S. economic embargo of the island, an end to all subversive activities of the United States, an end to U.S. support of Cuban exiles, respect for Cuban territory and airspace, and the return of Guantanamo Bay to Cuba. These demands were ignored by the United States and still are today. The Cubans felt betrayed by the Soviets but there was nothing they could do to stop the removal of the missiles. Relations between the Soviets and Cuba would be strained until August 1968 with the Soviet invasion of Czechoslovakia.

THE NEW SOCIALIST MAN AND THE RADICAL EXPERIMENT

Nearly 250,000 Cubans had fled the island between 1959 and October 1962. Almost all were members of the upper and middle classes, and this contributed to the "brain drain" and the lack of qualified personnel to help with the economic and political development of the country. This "brain drain" would hurt Cuba in the very near future. Still, there was much optimism about the economic future of Cuba in 1960 and the revolutionary leadership embarked on a strategy designed to reduce the island's dependence on sugar. This was to be achieved through rapid industrialization and the diversification of agriculture. The focus of rapid industrialization was to be in the areas of metallurgy, transportation equipment, chemical products, machinery, and sugar cane by-products. All of this required imported technology and materials. Sugar exports were to provide the necessary funds to purchase the needed imports.

By the spring of 1961, more than 33,000 peasants had become owners of land that they had previously worked as tenants, sharecroppers, or squatters. There were more than 266 state-run farms. More than 600 sugar cane cooperatives had been created.[10] Problems appeared when sugar output declined sharply in 1962 and 1963. The decline was largely due to mismanagement and the lack of skilled managers. Managers were often farmers with little or no experience in large-scale agriculture. Some were selected largely for political reasons. Cuban workers were simply not used to making decisions and taking the individual initiatives that were required for a cooperative to be successful. Other factors that contributed to the decline in sugar output included a reduction in the amount of land used to grow cane, a failure to replant much of the cane in 1960 and 1961, a rural labor shortage, and a prolonged drought in 1961. Just when Cuba needed sugar exports the most to finance its industrialization process, the sugar sector was not able to deliver. Diversification of agriculture did not meet the growing domestic demand for food (largely due to the downward distribution of income) and did not generate enough exports to make up for the sugar shortage.[11] Rationing of food began in 1962. The trade and balance of payments deficits ballooned. The lack of skilled personnel contributed to the chaotic and improvised nature of central planning in the Ministry of Industry. In 1963, Hurricane Flora devastated the island and the sugar crop. The attempt to achieve rapid industrialization failed.

There is no doubt that the U.S. embargo played a role in this failure as well. The existing industries in Cuba were almost totally dependent upon supplies and replacement parts from the United States. These were no longer available. The transportation industry (cars, trucks, buses, and trains) was perhaps hit the hardest but all suffered. The switch to supplies from Eastern Europe and the Soviet Union would take several years and most of the supplies and replacement parts did not fit the American-designed industries in Cuba. Changes to the Cuban port facilities which were designed to handle the smaller, freight ships from the United States as opposed to large ocean-going freighters from the Soviet Union, Eastern Europe, and China created many problems in the early years.

Recognizing that industrialization required foreign exchange or capital that only the sugar sector could provide, the revolutionary government adopted a new strategy of development in 1964. The strategy focused on sugar and agriculture. Increasing sugar production for export, the diversification of agriculture, and the focus on agriculture support industries became the model for national economic growth. The symbolic goal of this strategy was to be able to produce a massive 10 million ton sugar harvest in 1970. In order to accomplish this, the state would have to direct the majority of its resources, labor, and capital into the production of sugar.

This radical experiment had both internal and external components, as well as both practical and ideological motives. Within Cuba, Castro used his immense popularity and charisma to mobilize the passions and will of the people toward the creation of the "new socialist man." The new socialist man was to be committed to an egalitarian society and place the needs of the community before himself. Laborers were to work for the good of society rather than for personal gain. They were to work hard out of a moral commitment to the building of a socialist community. Labor unions under the Cuban Confederation of Labor became the primary vehicle to promote the new socialist man with its emphasis on moral incentives. Nonmaterial incentives, such as being recognized as a vanguard worker—those who had met the requirements of the so-called new socialist man according to the Cuban Confederation of Labor officials—were to compensate for overtime and volunteer work. Urban residents were encouraged to volunteer to work in seasonal agricultural activities such as cutting sugar cane. In support of this commitment to an egalitarian society, the government provided access to social services free of charge. Healthcare, educations, daycare, social security, and much housing were provided free to all Cubans.

By 1964, nearly 63 percent of the cultivated land was controlled by the state.[12] The remaining private farmers had to sell their goods to the state at low prices and volunteer to work on the state farms. Private farmers were encouraged to form their own credit and service cooperatives. In the spring of 1968, the remaining sector yet to be nationalized by the state—small retail businesses, such as food and service shops—came under state control. About 25 percent of the business owners in Havana who had their businesses nationalized went to work in agriculture.[13] Rationing of basic food guaranteed equality, although it did so in the middle of austere economic conditions. Thus, by controlling most of the cultivated land in the country, controlling the output on the remaining private farms, eliminating most private property, using *La Libreta* (the ration book), decreasing the wages for all except the poorest paid Cubans between 1966 and 1970, guaranteeing employment and providing free healthcare, education, and social security to all, the Cuban government created the most egalitarian distribution of income in all of Latin America. These policies also allowed the government to increase its revenues and resources to address the balance of payments deficit and to channel investment and more laborers into sugar production. In fact, gross investment by the government increased from 16 percent of the national product in 1962 to 25 percent in 1967.[14]

The radical experiment also consisted of a campaign against bureaucracy. The goal was to improve administrative efficiency in the government, trade unions, and other organizations by streamlining them. This, of course, would also increase the labor pool available to work in agriculture. The number of full-time administrators or bureaucrats in these organizations was reduced dramatically. Under the antibureaucracy campaign, the number of full-time union administrators in the Cuban Confederation of Labor was reduced by 53 percent.[15] By 1965, Castro had reorganized the Popular Socialist Party and had purged it of old-line Soviet communists, such as Anibel Escalante, who were less loyal to him. In effect, he had merged the 26th of July Movement, the Popular Socialist Party, and other revolutionary groups into the new Cuban Communist Party that could be used as an instrument of his personal power.

The new socialist man never materialized during the radical experiment. The victories and euphoria of the early years of the revolution were replaced with hard work and austerity. Due to the provision of free education, healthcare, social security, daycare, and housing, worker wages were almost meaningless. Yet, appeals to socialist ideals failed to motivate workers. Membership in unions declined to the point that less than 20 percent of the workers were members and these were primarily the vanguard workers.[16] Most of the workers were demoralized and resented the low pay, the long hours of work, and the lack of material incentives. They resented the back-breaking volunteer work in the sugar cane fields. Resistance took the form of foot-dragging and high absenteeism. This resistance, coupled with a lack of motivation, adversely affected the economic production of the state. Black market activity increased, with the private farmers often supplying the goods that were unavailable through the rationing system. Many private farmers became relatively wealthy. Even the growth in the number of Cuban Communist Party members was primarily from members of the military and government rather than average citizens. Perhaps the most successful organization during the radical experiment was the Federation of Cuban Women led by Raul Castro's wife, Vilma Espin, the unofficial first lady of Cuba. It was successful in increasing its membership to 1.3 million, managing day care centers across the island, educating rural women in healthcare and personal hygiene, and increasing the female percentage of the labor force to 18.3 percent in 1970.[17] The campaign against bureaucracy simply made economic planning more difficult and contributed to the chaos in the economy by the end of 1970.

Even though Cuba failed to meet the stated goal of 10 million tons of sugar in 1970, it did produce a record crop of 8.5 million tons. Yet, the Cuban economy was in shambles. Non-sugar agriculture and state industry suffered due to neglect and the vast amount of resources that had been redirected toward the production of sugar. In 1968, the world market price of sugar was below Cuban production costs and in 1970 it was less than half of what it had been in 1963. The Soviet Union would only purchase, at the most, 56 percent of the total Cuban sugar crop. Cuba was its own worst enemy. By increasing the world supply of sugar, its price remained depressed. During the radical experiment, sugar had not provided the necessary resources to diversify the economy. In fact, Cuba was as dependent as ever on one crop: sugar.

The external component of the radical experiment focused on the support of revolutionary groups throughout Latin America. The goal, in the words of Guevara, was to create "two, three, many Vietnams." This issue exacerbated the already strained relationship with the Soviet Union. The Soviet Union did not agree with Castro's efforts to promote violent revolution in Latin America. Castro believed that the Cuban revolution could be duplicated whereas the Soviets preferred the peaceful road to power via the traditional communist parties in the region. He denounced these parties for their lack of support for guerrilla movements in the region and chided the Soviet Union for its continued recognition of Latin American governments that were hostile to Cuba. Castro and the Cuban Communist Party refused to recognize the leadership of the Soviet Union and emphasized Cuba's right to develop its own foreign policy initiatives concerning revolutionary activities.

Venezuela with its vast oil reserves was a perfect target for an oil-hungry Cuba that was forced to rely on a less than dependable and faraway Soviet Union. Castro began to provide support to revolutionaries and urban terrorists in Venezuela in 1963. He hosted revolutionary leaders from across the world in Havana in 1966 and called for a continent-wide guerrilla struggle led by Cuba. Cuba provided training, arms, and funding for revolutionaries throughout the region. It is important to remember that this was taking place at the same time most of Latin America had come under control of repressive military governments and right-wing dictators who used the Cold War anticommunism to gain support and aid from the United States. The United States was more than willing to overlook the repressive nature of these governments and provide military training and support for them in their struggle against these revolutionary groups. In the end, Cuba's support for these revolutionaries failed to bring about victory. Revolutionary groups supported by Cuba could neither gain the support of the majority of the population, nor could they escape the military repression directed toward them. With the death of Guevara in the mountains of Bolivia in October 1967, it was clear that Cuba's revolution would not be duplicated in Latin America. The external component of the radical experiment had failed.

CHANGE IN DOMESTIC AND FOREIGN POLICIES

In August 1968, the Soviet Union invaded Czechoslovakia and crushed an attempt at liberalization. Castro spoke in support of the Soviet invasion in an attempt to create a closer, more cooperative relationship between the two countries. He began to show greater solidarity with the Soviet Union. He reversed the Cuban Communist Party's decision and allowed a Cuban representative to attend, as an observer, the World Conference of Communist Parties held in the Soviet Union in 1969. The purpose of the conference was to show solidarity against the Chinese Communists. The Soviet navy began to call on Cuban ports, while top-ranking Soviet officials visited Cuba. Castro and his brother, Raul, visited the Soviet Union and Eastern Europe for extended periods of time. Several factors led to this change in the relationship with the Soviet Union. The death of Guevara in Bolivia in 1967 ended Castro's dream of Cuban-led revolutions throughout Latin America. The Soviet Union had opposed Cuba's revolutionary policies in Latin America and this event removed a major area of disagreement between them. Poor sugar harvests in 1967 and 1968 had increased Cuba's need for Soviet economic aid. The Soviet Union announced a delay in petroleum shipments in January 1968. The island required petroleum and this announcement reminded the Cubans of their dependence on the Soviet Union. The presidential election of Nixon in 1968 also led Castro to a closer and more cooperative relationship with the Soviet Union. Castro saw Nixon as one of the chief architects of the Bay of Pigs invasion and believed that the new president would turn against Cuba. These factors, coupled with the failed economic strategy in 1970, set the stage for a change in both the domestic and foreign policies of Cuba.

ERNESTO "CHE" GUEVARA DE LA SERNA

Che Guevara, the oldest of five children, was born into an upper middle-class family in Rosario, Argentina, in 1928, where he developed asthma at an early age. As a youth he loved chess, developed a passion for poetry, and became an avid reader, especially books on philosophy. He moved to Buenos Aires to take care of his grandmother and after her death began studying medicine at the University of Buenos Aires. In 1951 he decided to take a break from his studies and took a motorcycle trip through Chile, Peru, Colombia, and Venezuela with his friend Alberto Granado. His notes from this trip later formed the basis for the book *The Motorcycle Diaries* and the hit movie by the same name. It was during this trip that Guevara witnessed the impossible living conditions, hardship and misery, extreme poverty, and injustices faced by workers and peasants. Many believe it was during this trip that Guevara came to believe that radical economic and political changes were the only solutions to meet the needs of the people. He returned to graduate from medical school in 1953 and then traveled through Chile, Bolivia, Peru, Ecuador, and Colombia and eventually ended up in Guatemala during the presidency of Jacobo Arbenz. The Arbenz government had engaged in massive land reform and legalized the communist party. While in Guatemala he met exiled Peruvian revolutionary Hilda Gadea, who introduced him to the study of Marxism. In 1954, the United States supported the Guatemalan military and other forces in the overthrow of the Arbenz government. This event further radicalized Che as he and Hilda fled to Mexico where he met Raul Castro, his brother Fidel, and Camilo Cienfuegos. Che, who quickly became close friends with Fidel and Cienfuegos, decided to join the 26th of July Movement.

Che was one of the eighty-two revolutionaries who boarded the yacht, Granma, and landed in Cuba in Oriente on December 2, 1956. Only a handful of men survived an ambush and made it into the mountains of the Sierra Maestra. Che, who was noted for his idealism, intellect, discipline, hard work, cleverness, toughness, and determination, led the guerrillas in the mountains in a defeat of Batista's military

Ernesto "Che" Guevara, medical doctor, intellectual, and revolutionary, is shown here on January 7, 1959, in Havana. Che
became the ideological lightning rod of the revolution until
his death at the relatively young age of thirty-nine while at-
tempting to stage a quixotic peasant's revolution in Bolivia
in 1967. Since that time his iconic image has inspired revolutionaries across the world. (Time Life Pictures/Getty Images)

offensive in the summer of 1958. Fidel, sensing that momentum was
in his favor, sent Che and his guerrilla force of 300 to take on Batista's
2,500 man army at Santa Clara. With the support of the people in Santa
Clara, Che defeated the Batista's military in three days. Che's victory
at Santa Clara, which gave the rebels control of one half of the island,
was the crucial event that led Batista to flee the island.

With Fidel in power, it was Che and Raul that led the executions of
former Batista supporters who were primarily in the military and the

police forces. Che played a major role in the early government of Fidel as the minister of industry and the head of the Cuban Central Bank. He played a primary role in developing Cuba's relationship with the Soviet Union. It was Che who inaugurated the so-called radical experiment in an attempt to create what he called the new socialist man. Che never liked his role as a government administrator and decided he was better equipped as a guerrilla commander who could help countries achieve anti-imperialist revolutions. He and a small group of Cubans went to the Congo where they failed miserably and barely escaped with their lives. In 1966, he took a small group of Cubans to Bolivia with the hope of gaining the support of the rural population and toppling the government. He ended up isolated with little support from the peasants. He was captured and executed by the Bolivian military on October 9, 1967, near La Higuera. U.S. Central Intelligence Agent Felix Rodriguez, who was with the Bolivian military, photographed the pages of Che's diary which later were published as *The Bolivian Diary*. His body was buried in a secret location but discovered in 1997 and returned to Cuba for burial in Santa Clara.

His death at such a young age and his image as a martyr to revolutionary change created a larger-than-life legacy. His iconic image can still be seen today on T-shirts worn by young Americans and revolutionary groups across the globe. His guerrilla strategies and revolutionary statements are well known by virtually all revolutionary groups. Yet, it is important to point out that he is still controversial as many see him simply as a failed revolutionary or failed communist who had no problems with executing those who disagreed with him. It was Che's death that signaled the end of any attempt by Cuba at leading revolutionary change throughout Latin America. It was the beginning of Cuba's turn to more orthodox communism and the Soviet Union. Some argue that the ideals of the Cuban revolution died with Che in Bolivia.

NOTES

1. Ernesto Che Guevara, "Socialism and Man in Cuba," in *The Che Guevara Reader*, edited by David Deutschman (Minneapolis: Ocean Press, 2005), https://www.marxists.org/archive/guevara/1965/03/man-socialism.htm.
2. Perez, Jr., *Cuba: Between Reform and Revolution*, 242.
3. Thomas, *Cuba: The Pursuit of Freedom*, 1201.
4. Ibid., 1215–1215.
5. Ibid., 1223.
6. Perez-Stable, *Cuban Revolution*, 68.
7. Ibid., 77.

8. Ibid., 85.

9. Suchlicki, *Cuba: From Columbus to Castro*, 165.

10. Thomas, *Cuba: The Pursuit of Freedom*, 1323–1324, 1326.

11. Perez-Stable, *Cuban Revolution*, 85.

12. Susan Eva Eckstein, *Back from the Future* (Princeton, NJ: Princeton University Press, 1994), 33.

13. Ibid., 34.

14. Ibid., 38.

15. Perez-Stable, *Cuban Revolution*, 114.

16. Eckstein, *Back from the Future*, 35.

17. Perez-Stable, *Cuban Revolution*, 116.

7

Economic Change, Institutionalization, Internationalism, and the Cold War: 1970 to the End of the Cold War

> The Cuban people hold a special place in the hearts of the people of Africa. The Cuban internationalists have made a contribution to African independence, freedom, and justice, unparalleled for its principled and selfless character.
>
> Nelson Mandela, July 26, 1991[1]

Revolutionary idealism, spirit, excitement, and fervor eventually gave way to the realities of everyday living. According to scholar Marifeli Perez-Stable, the 1960s' radical experiment was born of this revolutionary idealism as well as the concept of revolutionary social justice, the charisma of Fidel Castro, the challenge and hostility of the United States, and the growth of Cuban nationalism.[2] After the failure of the radical experiment and the move to closer relations with the Soviet Union, the realities of everyday living in a revolutionary socialist society became evident. Cuba was forced to turn to a more pragmatic strategy of development. From 1970 to the mid-1980s, the Cuban revolution moved to adopt a more institutionalized model of socialism, somewhat closer to the Soviet Union and Eastern Europe. Yet, it was clear that Cuba under Castro could never imitate this model. The attempt to institutionalize or formalize the role of the Communist Party of Cuba in society could never be complete as long as Castro ruled in such a personal manner and held such sway over party members and the people of the country. The Cuban economy was much more decentralized than the Soviet model, and Castro now emphasized that workers must have material incentives to improve production in addition to the moral, idealistic, and revolutionary incentives that had characterized the radical experiment. With sugar continuing to dominate its economy, Cuba became very dependent on Eastern Europe and the Soviet Union for necessary imports such as trucks, chemical fertilizers, pesticides, machinery, fuel (oil), and food. By the mid-1980s, strains in the relationship with the Soviet Union and Eastern Europe, coupled with debt problems, the lowest sugar prices since the Great Depression, corruption and growing economic inequality associated with growth of peasant markets, led Castro to adopt another strategy—rectification—that, according to Perez-Stable, "evoked the radical experiment of the 1960s."[3] Thus, Castro was still trying to find the right mixture and balance of revolutionary principles and market-oriented pragmatism as the Cold War came to an end.

Yet, at the brink of the end of the Cold War Cuba had established one of the highest standards of living in the developing world and led all other Latin American countries in the quality of life that it provided for children. Its infant mortality rate was among the lowest in the world, and it spent a higher percentage of its budget on education than any other country in Latin America. Rents were controlled and limited to 10 percent of income, rationed food prices were controlled, and 80 percent of Cubans owned their own homes.[4] The pillars of the revolution—free healthcare, education, and social security for all citizens—were rarely, if ever, found anywhere else in the developing world. At the same time, Castro, the revolutionary, was still firmly in control of the political decision making on the island.

ECONOMIC CHANGE IN THE 1970s

Castro announced the failure of the 10 million ton harvest on July 26, 1970, and took personal responsibility for it. It was clear that worker productivity had to be increased, government spending needed to be reduced, and government revenues (especially in foreign exchange or internationally accepted currencies) needed to be increased so that Cuba could pay for its imports and debts. The government implemented a series of changes in the country's economic strategy. Low worker productivity, absenteeism, and foot-dragging were to be corrected by providing more material incentives (wages and bonuses) based on increased production, the meeting of quotas, and overtime work. The government increased the availability of consumer goods (televisions and refrigerators) so as to encourage workers to be more productive. Market-related reforms were introduced into the state-run enterprises. They were given greater authority to hire and fire workers, purchase inputs from the private sector on the island, and hire workers on a piecemeal basis. Castro expanded the market-related reforms to include the agricultural and service sectors. The sugar industry became more mechanized with greater reliance placed on the use of combine harvesters to cut cane during the *zafra*. Castro became more tolerant of the private economic sector on the island. The growth of agricultural cooperatives was encouraged by providing them with greater access to new machinery while the growing of tobacco fell primarily to private farmers.[5] Farmers' markets were allowed so that cooperative and private farmers could sell their surpluses locally with prices based on supply and demand. The state also began to sell goods locally on a supply and demand basis. State-run stores with rationed goods at subsidized prices were still maintained to provide a social safety net for the poor. Self-employed individuals could provide certain services such as carpentry, plumbing, appliance and auto repair, and housing construction.

In order to meet growing housing demands, Castro created the minibrigade system in the early 1970s. Approximately thirty-five workers who were released from their work commitments made up each minibrigade. The workers not only built prefabricated houses for individuals in urban and rural areas, but also community projects such as day care facilities, schools, and medical clinics. The work centers or businesses that provided the workers for these minibrigades controlled 40 percent of the houses that were built and distributed them based on "social responsibility and merit." The level of family income determined the cost or rent to be paid for these units. Although the program had many problems, including the fact that these housing units were difficult to modify to meet the changing needs of families, and the national government controlled where these houses were built, it represented the first proactive state-financed approach to housing in all of Latin America.[6] By the end of the 1970s, more than 90 percent of the urban living units had running water and more than half had both running water and electricity.[7] These included projects in Ciudad Jose Marti in Santiago (housing for 50,000 residents) and Alamar East outside of Havana (more than 100,000 residents). Nonetheless, housing could not keep up with population growth, especially in the late 1970s and early 1980s when the 1960–1962 baby boom generation was ready to establish separate households.[8]

Castro expanded Cuba's trading ties by joining the Council for Mutual Economic Assistance (COMECON), an Eastern European and Soviet Union trading bloc, in 1972. He also began to trade more with countries in the West. In fact, by 1974 the Western bloc accounted by 41 percent of the island's trade.[9] That year the island was benefitting from record high sugar prices of 68 cents per pound.[10] Economic production increased dramatically. Between 1971 and 1975, the value of industrial output increased by 35 percent and the economy grew at an annual rate of 10 to 14 percent compared to 3.9 percent from 1966 to 1970.[11] Hard currency earnings from the sugar trade with the Western countries grew to almost $720 million in 1975.[12] Cuba began borrowing from Western banks during this period. It also benefitted from the preferential trading policies of the Soviet Union. The Soviet Union continued to purchase Cuban sugar at above world market prices and provided oil at a price lower than the price provided by the Organization of Petroleum Exporting Countries (OPEC). This helped protect Cuba from the oil shocks of the early 1970s that caused severe economic problems for the United States and West European countries. On the negative side, this relationship served as a disincentive for the diversification of the Cuban economy. Sugar remained the mainstay of the economy because of the lucrative price offered by the Soviet Union. In this manner, the Soviet Union, like the United States before it, structured trade as a disincentive to economic diversification on the island. The Soviet Union also provided Cuba with low interest, long-term loans and a postponement of the payment of its immediate debts.

The tremendous growth of the economy led to growing expectations of a better life among most Cubans, but by 1977 the world market price for sugar had fallen dramatically to 8 cents a pound and the growth of the Cuban economy slowed considerably. With Cuba earning less from its sugar and its debts to Western countries mounting, Castro had to institute austerity measures that included the reduction of imports from Western countries. The favorable trade relationship with COMECON countries provided some protection for Cuba from the downturn in the price of sugar. The fact that the Soviet Union and

COMECON countries only purchased few products from Cuba and continued to pay higher than world market prices forced the island to continue to depend on sugar as opposed to implementing policies designed to diversify its economy and to lessen its dependence on imports. With the slowdown in the economy, the number of houses built by the minibrigades, especially in the urban areas, had even more difficulty keeping up with demand. Dissatisfaction with the economy increased. At the same time, the government continued its commitment to the poor by providing its economic safety net of subsidized goods to all.

INSTITUTIONALIZATION

Castro attempted to institutionalize the revolution by drawing the jurisdiction lines of government more clearly. The Communist Party was to make political decisions, the state was to administer the policies, and mass organizations, such as the Confederation of Cuban Workers, were to provide popular participation. Cuba's first socialist constitution was adopted at the first Communist Party Congress in 1975 and approved through a referendum. It created the Popular Power system in which elected municipal assemblies elected members to the regional assemblies and the national assembly. Municipal assemblies were given the authority to oversee policy in a variety of local services such as garbage, schools, street maintenance, clinics, street maintenance, grocery stores, theatres, and small industries. According to William Leogrande, the municipal authorities have been quite successful in allowing for popular participation in these matters. The regional and national assemblies had limited power and for the most part ended up being a rubber stamp to major decisions already made within the Political Bureau of the Communist Party.

The Communist Party leadership organs (the Political Bureau, the Secretariat, and the Central Committee) that had not functioned in the 1960s began meeting regularly. The Central Committee, which was primarily made up of members from the military and the Ministry of the Interior in the 1960s, came to represent most sectors of Cuban society. The Communist Party experienced a dramatic increase in membership growing from 55,000 in 1969 to 211,642 in 1975, the year of Cuba's first Communist Party Congress. The Communist Youth became the primary avenue to party membership and by 1980 membership had reached 434,943.[13] The Confederation of Cuban Workers held periodic meetings. There was an increase in the number of local unions, and there was a massive turnover in local union leadership throughout the

1970s through elections that used the secret ballot. In order to encourage more workers to join unions, they were represented on economic management boards and helped to develop local production targets and deal with health and safety issues. Increasing worker production and the quality of the goods produced. Unions were represented at all levels within the decision-making processes of the Communist Party and the Popular Power system.

The Federation of Cuban Women held congresses in 1974 and 1980. In 1975, Castro initiated a policy of affirmative action designed to increase the number of women in the Communist Party, the Popular Power system, the Communist Youth, and the Confederation of Cuban Workers. Increased membership at all levels of these institutions was realized by the late 1970s. Women's share of the labor force increased and the Federation of Cuban Women was gradually successful in reducing the number of job categories that were reserved for men but still suffered from discrimination in achieving managerial positions.

CUBAN INTERNATIONALISM IN THE 1970s

Several factors contributed to the rise of Cuba as a force in international politics by the mid- to late 1970s. Throughout the first half of the decade, Cuba's Revolutionary Armed Forces (FAR) underwent major changes. Many active military personnel were poorly trained, had little education, and worked as agricultural laborers during the radical experiment of the 1960s. According to Richard Millett, a specialist on the Cuban military, in order to reduce these costs to the government the number of active military personnel of the FAR was reduced from 230,000 in 1970 to 117,000 in 1975. Training, equipment, and weaponry for the military were upgraded significantly, largely due to the influence of the Soviet Union. The threat of a U.S.-led invasion of the island disappeared with the winding down of the Vietnam War and arrival of détente between the Soviet Union and the United States and, as a result, the mission of the FAR became much more internationalist in orientation.

Cuba's isolation within Latin America also came to an end. Mexico never broke its relationship with Castro and eight other Latin American countries reestablished diplomatic ties between 1972 and 1975. The Organization of American States voted to end sanctions against Cuba in 1975. Castro was also busy establishing himself as a leader of the developing countries of the world. He traveled extensively throughout Africa in 1972 and 1973. His attendance at the Fourth Non-Aligned Summit in Algiers in 1973 marked Cuba's emergence as a leader among those countries. The Non-Aligned Movement (NAM) was made up of countries from Latin America, Africa, and Asia that focused on issues of anticolonialism and economic development. The charismatic Castro, Cuba's economic success, its defiance of the United States, and its anti-imperialist/anticolonial message played well among the NAM countries.

In late 1975, Cuban troops intervened into the Angolan civil war that had broken out when the Portuguese Empire in Africa began to crumble. Cuban troops were supported by the Popular Movement for the Liberation of Angola and were decisive in defeating the South African- and U.S.-backed groups. Cuban troops in support of Mengistu Haile Mariam's Ethiopian government also proved decisive in defeating a Somalian invasion of that country in 1977. Almost one out of every five Cuban soldiers served abroad in 1978 with most of them in Africa.[14] In July 1979, Castro's vision of a second in revolution in Latin America finally came to pass with the Sandinista victory over the U.S-supported Somoza dictatorship in Nicaragua. Cuban support of the Sandinistas during their struggle with Anastasio Somoza was very minimal when compared to efforts in Africa, and Castro advised the new Sandinista government to avoid conflict with the United States and diversify its trading partners. He urged it to make economic policy changes very slowly so as to avoid the massive emigration of skilled and professional people that Cuba suffered in the first few years of its revolution. In September of that year, the Sixth Non-Aligned Summit was held in Havana, with Cuba exercising the primary leadership role in developing the anti-American tone of the Final Declaration. Prime Minister Michael Manley of Jamaica and Maurice Bishop of the New Jewel Movement in Grenada openly courted Castro. Cuba was at the height of its power in terms of global political influence in the late 1970s and the FAR was a major military force in the developing world.

Cuban internationalism of this period had another component that received little notice in the Western countries. This component sent thousands of Cuban doctors, teachers, construction workers, agronomists, and other development project specialists (irrigation, mining, fishing, cattle raising, and sugar production) to Africa and other parts of the developing world. Most of this developmental aid was provided at either no cost to the host government or the host government simply covered the living expenses for the Cubans. By 1978, Cuba had more than 12,000 economic and technical aid specialists abroad and the number was greater than 14,000 in 1979.[15] These activities earned Cuba much prestige and respect among the developing countries of the world, especially those in Africa.

CUBA, THE UNITED STATES, AND THE
SOVIET UNION IN THE 1970s

In August 1970, a U.S. reconnaissance plane photographed the construction of a Soviet submarine base at the southern coastal city of Cienfuegos. President Richard Nixon argued that this violated the missile crisis agreement banning the introduction of offensive weapons in the Western Hemisphere. He successfully negotiated with the Soviet Union to stop the construction while the Cubans, once again, had little to say in the issue. Just as in the missile crisis, Cuba remained a junior player in superpowers politics. It was common in the United States to view the relationship between the Soviet Union and Cuba as one in which Cubans merely followed the orders of the Soviet Union. This is not only simplistic, but also historically incorrect. Cuba and the Soviet Union shared a more complex and interdependent relationship. Cuban foreign policy was clearly at odds with the Soviet Union during the 1960s, with the Soviet Union not supporting Castro's efforts to wage revolutionary wars in Latin America. The relationship that eventually developed was one of mutual benefit in which each country received support in the pursuit of its own national goals. This became quite evident throughout the decade of the 1970s. Cuba received economic development assistance, technology, preferential trading partners, and the means to upgrade its military. Cuban internationalism was a Cuban goal and the result of Cuban decisions. The intervention in Angola was a decision made by Castro. Development aid to Africa and other developing countries of the world was a Cuban decision. Because of its relationship with the Cuba, the Soviet Union received a presence in the Caribbean, an area that has historically been within the sphere of influence of the United States. Perhaps more importantly, the Soviet Union also gained entry into many of the developing countries of the world because of Cuba's leadership role in the NAM and the prestige and respect it had earned among those countries. Cuban foreign policy scholar H. Michael Erisman argues that Cuba established itself as a political broker between the Soviet Union and the developing countries of the world.

Castro, who did not trust Nixon and viewed him as the architect of the Bay of Pigs invasion, was quite pleased with his resignation in August 1974. This paved the way for a series of meetings between the United States and Cuba later that year and throughout much of 1975. These meetings reduced the tensions between the two countries temporarily. The Cubans preferred to focus primarily on specific issues that involved only the United States, such as payment for seized properties, immigration, the U.S. military base at Guantanamo Bay, the trade embargo, normalization of relations, and surveillance flights and radio interference. The tendency of the United States was to link changes in the bilateral relationship with other issues such as Cuban ties to the Soviet Union and Cuban policies in Africa. President Gerald Ford ended all discussions with the island when the Cubans decided to send troops to Angola in 1975.

President Jimmy Carter, who had a personal interest in Latin America, was elected in the wake of Watergate, Vietnam, and Ford's pardon of Nixon. In March 1977, Carter issued a presidential directive that indicated that the United States should move toward a normalization of relations with Cuba. Although not happy with the presence of Cuban troops in Angola, Carter began making overtures to Castro. The next month the United States and Cuba signed agreements concerning fishing rights and the marine boundary in the Straits of Florida. Carter created a U.S. Special Interests Section in Havana in September and removed some of the restrictions on travel to the island by U.S. citizens. He began negotiating with Castro for the release of political prisoners. But Carter's motives to normalize relations with the island soured with the introduction of 20,000 Cuban troops in Ethiopia in January 1978. In an effort to maintain the lines of communication with the United States, Castro announced in September his willingness to dialogue with groups from the Cuban exile community and to release political prisoners. He also allowed thousands of Cuban exiles to return to the island as tourists to visit their families and relatives. These moves were designed to appeal to the human rights agenda of Carter and the one group that had the most influence over U.S. policy toward Cuba. One of the consequences of these moves was a growing split within the Cuban American community in the United States. Some opposed the dialogue, while others supported it because they felt it would lead to the release of political prisoners. Many of those who participated in the dialogue with Castro received death threats from the militant Cuban American community, while others had to face boycotts of their businesses. Some even had their businesses bombed.[16]

By the end of 1979, it was impossible for Carter to make any more overtures to Cuba. The Sandinistas came to power in Nicaragua in July and some in the United States blamed Carter for the so-called communist victory in Central America. This, coupled with the growing rebel insurgence in El Salvador, made Carter appear to be weak in foreign affairs. This weakness was exploited by presidential candidate Ronald Reagan, who had staked out a hard line stance against not only communism, but also Carter's Panama Canal Treaties and the Soviet invasion of Afghanistan. Politically, Carter was forced to take a harder line in foreign policy to meet the electoral challenge of Reagan.

THE 1980s, RECTIFICATION, AND THE END OF THE COLD WAR

Castro knew that if Reagan were to be elected as president any meaningful accommodation with the United States would not be possible after January 1981. He allowed almost 125,000 Cubans to leave the country via the port city of Mariel in 1980. Among these émigrés were political prisoners, common criminals (less than 4 percent of the total), Cubans released from mental health facilities, and Cuba's poor. Most were from the Havana area. This group differed significantly from the largely elite professionals and middle- and working-class immigrants

Cuban refugees arrive in Key West on April 23, 1980. They are part of the third wave of almost 125,000 refugees known as the Mariel Boatlift that took place between April and October of that year. The initial wave of Cuban refugees from 1959 through 1962 largely represented those in positions of political power and economic elites, professionals, and managers. The second wave from 1965 through 1973 consisted of relatives of Cubans already in the United States and by 1970 were mostly blue-collar, service, or agricultural workers. Unlike the earlier emigres, the so-called Marielitos had lived most of their lives under Fidel Castro and represented younger, working-class, and poorer Cubans. (Bettmann/Corbis)

who arrived in Miami during the first (1959–1962) and second (1965–1973) waves. Whereas the early immigrants were received with open arms, the Mariel group added to the growing racial tensions in Florida between Cubans and non-Cubans. The overwhelming media attention focused on the criminal element among the Mariel émigrés and Florida officials indicated that they could not provide the services, schools, and jobs needed for them.

Several factors help to explain this large exodus. The decline of the economy in the late 1970s following a period of tremendous economic growth had deflated the rising economic expectations among many Cubans and increased their sense of frustration. The appearance of thousands of comparatively wealthy Cuban American tourists returning to visit the island added fire to the growing Cuban discontent. According to Susan Eva Eckstein, the demand for unmet housing also probably contributed to the mass emigration from the port of Mariel.[17] Castro's calculated decision to allow those who wanted to leave the freedom to do so was not only a last-minute appeal to the human rights agenda of the Carter administration and the international community, but also a clear opportunity to get rid of some of those who opposed him.

Ironically, the same year that tens of thousands of Cubans left the island from Mariel for economic reasons, the economy began to improve once again as the world price of sugar reached a yearly average of 28 cents per pound. Castro moved further to liberalize the Cuban economy by relaxing the regulations on foreign investment by allowing foreigners to have up to 49 percent in ownership in local businesses.[18] The production of steel, medicines, electronics, and chemicals increased. With the reduction in state-provided housing through the minibrigades, the private sector began meeting much of the demand. Housing construction in the early 1980s grew at a faster rate than any other sector and between 1981 and 1986 more than 60 percent of the housing units were privately constructed.[19] Production of agricultural goods increased largely due to the increase in price the state procurement agency paid to private farmers. In addition, both state and private workers realized increased profits from the farmers' markets.

The downside to the liberalization of the economy was that these lucrative markets encouraged farmers to sell their poorest crops to the state and their better-quality crops for even higher profits at the markets. This undermined the state's efforts to maintain the economic safety net for its poorest citizens. Public funds and resources used on state-run farms were often diverted illegally for private gain. Certain products were to be sold by the state and not supposed to be sold privately because they earned the government sorely needed foreign exchange or international currencies. These products, such as coffee, were routinely sold on the black market because of the profits to be earned. This practice cut into the state's ability to earn foreign exchange. Middlemen or vendors who bought from farmers and then sold goods at the markets appeared despite the fact they were illegal.

Cuban internationalism expanded in the early 1980s. Military equipment and training was provided to the Faribundo Marti National Liberation rebels in El Salvador, although the bulk of that was provided prior to the failed "final offensive" against the U.S.-supported government in 1981. Cuba provided military equipment, approximately 800 advisers, and technical expertise to the Sandinistas of Nicaragua in their struggle against the Contra forces supported by the United States. It provided construction workers to twenty countries in Africa, Latin America, the Caribbean, and Asia. Thousands of Cuban healthcare workers, doctors, and teachers provided assistance to countries in the developing world. In 1980, Castro announced a change in Cuba's military policy. He created a militia made up of nonmilitary personnel (much like the U.S. National Guard) that numbered 1.5 million people. Castro later justified this in terms of responding to the aggressive nature of the Reagan administration but scholars, such as Millett, argue that it was done largely to mobilize and reinvigorate popular support for the revolution.

President Reagan, who viewed the world strictly through the East-West Cold War perspective, brought a desire to "restore" U.S. power in the world and implement a hard line, anticommunist foreign policy. He viewed Cuban internationalism as simply part of the Soviet Union's "evil empire." U.S. defense expenditures escalated sharply and aid to countries under the threat of communist or communist-inspired insurgencies increased dramatically. Reagan moved to topple the Sandinistas in Nicaragua by organizing and funding the opposition group known as the Contras. The U.S. invasion of Grenada in October 1983 toppled the left-wing government of Bernard Coard who had just toppled the government of Maurice Bishop. One of the stated reasons for the invasion was the use of Cuban military and construction workers on an airport that, according to the United States, was to be used for military purposes. Reagan did not mention publicly that the Cubans had won the construction contract against British, Canadian, and French firms who all stated that the purpose of the airport was to increase tourism on the island. The United States increased military aid from $33.5 million in 1983 to $176.8 million the following year to prop up the government of El Salvador in it struggle against the

Faribundo Marti National Liberation Front.[20] Reagan moved quickly against Cuba by halting all air links with it and effectively banning travel to Cuba by prohibiting monetary expenditures by U.S. citizens.

By 1984, the world market price of sugar had fallen to 5 cents a pound and the Cuban economy was once again in recession. The country suffered from increasing international debts, an increased cost of hard-currency imports due to the devaluation of the U.S. dollar, and the need to increase foreign investments and government revenues. Even with the private construction of housing, there was still a shortage and the construction of clinics and day care facilities did not meet the nation's demand. Corruption had increased and was clearly associated with the growth of the peasant markets. Corruption took the form of stealing or diverting resources from state-run enterprises for private gain, the selling of the poorest crops to the state with the best crops being sold at the farmers' markets, the selling of illegal products on the black market, and the illegal use of state goods in the construction of houses by private individuals. Castro viewed this as a breakdown in revolutionary community conscience. He argued that this was caused by excessive reliance on market forces and the desire for individual gain at the expense of community and society. By the mid-1980s, the Confederation of Cuban Workers was also having accountability problems of workers of which nearly 50 percent either had been a child in 1959 or had been born after Castro came to power (the 1960–1962 baby boom generation).[21] In addition, growing economic inequality between those who could divert their products to the lucrative peasant markets and those who could not do so challenged the egalitarian principles of the revolution.

Mikhail Gorbachev's revolutionary changes in the Soviet Union, which included economic and political liberalization under the labels of perestroika and glasnost, appeared at a time when Castro was initiating his own campaign for rectification. Castro and the aging revolutionary leadership reacted with hostility to the reforms of the Soviet Union and in Eastern Europe. Although publicly this hostility was explained in ideological terms, Castro also knew that these changes were a major threat to the enormous economic subsidies and military support that Cuba received.

Castro initiated reforms in April prior to the Communist Party congress of December 1986 under the name of rectification—a return to the revolutionary idealism of the 1960s. He criticized the "profiteers" who were corrupt and had benefitted at the expense of others and the state. Revolutionary idealism with its emphasis on community rather than private gain was emphasized once again. Imports were cut and wages were reduced except in case of the poorest workers whose wages were actually increased. The peasant markets were eliminated although the state continued to sell some of its better products on a supply and demand basis in its *agromercados*. There was a return to the use of minibrigades to build houses, day care centers, and schools, rather than depending on private contractors. This time, the state reimbursed the economic enterprises that supplied the workers for the minibrigades. Between 1984 and 1988, nearly half a million Cubans who were leaseholders on government-owned housing had their rents converted to payments for outright home ownership and another 330,000 were simply granted titles to their houses at no cost.[22] Volunteerism was reemphasized as the Communist Party adopted the slogan, "forty hours of voluntary work on community projects." The state continued to provide its social safety net for all through its subsidized and rationed food stores. Ironically, at the same time Castro was criticizing Cubans for acting like individualists and capitalists, he was encouraging Western investors and the promotion of joint ventures in electronics, mechanical engineering, petrochemicals, pharmaceuticals, textiles, and tourism.[23] He also allowed private rentals and encouraged family-constructed housing units by making available low-interest building loans. Rectification was a mixture of revolutionary ideals and pragmatic market-oriented policies.

Corruption among high-level government officials and military personnel was publicly exposed during the period of rectification. With Cuba's constant need for foreign exchange and hard currency, those in crucial government positions who interacted with Western companies and financial institutions were prone to corruption. They used their preferential access to key resources for their own personal benefit, and many lived beyond their means of the typical Cuban citizen. Public trials combined with long-term prison sentences and some executions of top government officials were designed to deter future corruption. The most sensational and noteworthy trial was that of General Arnaldo Ochoa Sanchez, who was condemned to death for treason. The popular General Ochoa was a hero of Cuba's military triumphs in Angola and led missions to Ethiopia and Nicaragua. While in Angola, Ochoa had sold cane sugar, cement, and other goods on the Angolan black market as well as supplemented his budget with shipments of diamonds and ivory to Western Europe, although most of this was done to improve the living conditions of Cuban troops in the field. At the time, these activities were overlooked in the name of Cuban internationalism.[24] With rectification policies in place, Cuban internationalism had begun to contract. In particular, Cuba could no longer afford its large military presence in Africa. This policy caused resentment among many of the officers of the proud Cuban military. Returning military personnel faced a difficult economy when they returned home. General Ochoa was most vocal in his criticism of the cutbacks to the international mission of the FAR and the treatment of troops when they returned home from Africa to face economic auster-ity. Ochoa and other high-ranking military officials were also charged with drug trafficking. According to Millett, the evidence of drug traf-ficking against most of the defendants was strong, but that against Ochoa was extremely weak. Some scholars believe that the popular Ochoa had become a political threat either to Raul Castro, head of the FAR, or Fidel Castro himself. Regardless, his execution provided a clear signal that loyalty to Castro was still perhaps the most important aspect of the revolutionary Cuban political system.

CUBA ON THE BRINK OF THE END OF THE COLD WAR

Despite attempts to institutionalize the revolution through the Com-munist Party, the Popular Power Assemblies, and the Confederation of Cuban Workers, the personal and charismatic rule of Castro was still the most important factor in providing the legitimacy to the revo-lutionary government of Cuba. This was clearly evident in the fact that a special hand-picked Communist Party organ of his most loyal and trusted advisers, the Comandante en Jefe's Advisory Commission, existed. It was evident in the fact that rectification was Castro's idea. The Communist Party had little, if any, role in the decision. It merely approved Castro's policies. The fact that an extremely popular general could be executed also drove home the continuing importance of the personal significance of Castro to the revolution.

Although no one, including Castro, predicted the abrupt end of com-munism in Eastern Europe and the Soviet Union, it was clear that he knew that any change in the preferential relationship with these coun-tries could threaten his own revolution. With the collapse of the Ber-lin Wall and of communism in Eastern Europe and the Soviet Union, Castro found Cuba truly independent for the first time in its history. Yet, that very independence threatened his revolution like no other event since 1959. Castro faced another problem at home. He faced a once-proud military that had seen its international mission collapse under budget cuts and soldiers returning home to an island that was in recession. He was saddled with an aging revolutionary leadership while the majority of the Cuban population had been born after 1959.

In addition, in 1986 there was a massive turnover in the Central Committee of the Communist Party with almost 50 percent of the members being newly elected. The members were better educated than ever and almost 40 percent of the Communist Party had been in the party less than five years.[25] His challenge was to "retire" some of the aging leadership and appeal to the younger generation. Leaders within the younger generation had to be sought out and brought into the ruling circles. Castro, the aging, charismatic revolutionary, and the ultimate Machiavellian political survivor, was forced to rise to the challenge of a post–Cold War world.

NOTES

1. Nelson Mandela, "Speech by Nelson Mandela at the Rally in Cuba," in *How Far We Slaves Have Come*, edited by Nelson Mandela and Fidel Castro (New York: Pathfinder, 1991). Found at http://db.nelsonmandela.org/speeches/pub_view.asp?pg=item&ItemID=NMS1526.

2. Perez-Stable, *The Cuban Revolution*, 61–81.

3. Ibid., 153.

4. Benjamin Keen and Keith Haynes, *A History of Latin America*, 6th ed. (Houghton Mifflin, 2000), 448.

5. Eckstein, *Back from the Future*, 45.

6. Ibid., 158–160.

7. Ibid., 160.

8. Perez, Jr., *Cuba: Between Reform and Revolution*, 280.

9. Eckstein, *Back from the Future*, 47, 51.

10. Ibid., 50.

11. Keen and Haynes, *History of Latin America*, 446; and Eckstein, *Back from the Future*, 51.

12. Eckstein, *Back from the Future*, 52.

13. Perez-Stable, *The Cuban Revolution*, 146.

14. H. Michael Erisman, *Cuba's International Relations* (Boulder, CO: Westview, 1985), 73.

15. Ibid., 78–79.

16. Maria Cristina Garcia, *Havana USA* (Berkeley: University of California, 1996), 47–52.

17. Eckstein, *Back from the Future*, 160.

18. Ibid., 46.

19. Ibid., 161.

20. Peter H. Smith, *Talons of the Eagle* (New York: Oxford University Press, 2000), 215.

21. Perez-Stable, *Cuban Revolution*, 128.

22. Eckstein, *Back from the Future*, 160.

23. Ibid., 68.

24. Andres Oppenheimer, *Castro's Final Hour* (New York: Simon and Schuster, 1992), 141.

25. Perez-Stable, *Cuban Revolution*, 144.

8

Post–Cold War Cuba to Fidel's Farewell

> The imperialist powers cannot stand the fact that the Cuban Revolution did not collapse on the fourth day after the fall of the socialist camp and the USSR, and that, to the contrary, they see the years pass and without exaggeration we can say it is stronger.
> Fidel Castro, Havana, May 20, 1996[1]

Since the late 1860s Cuba had sought to become a truly independent country. In 1898, Spanish colonialism gave way to U.S. hegemony; and in the 1960s, U.S. hegemony gave way to dependence on the Soviet Union. With the collapse of the communist governments of Eastern Europe and the Soviet Union in the early 1990s, Cuba found itself truly independent for the first time in its history. But, there is an old adage that says that one should be careful for what one wishes. The end of Soviet subsidies and special trade relations affected Cuba as dramatically as the break with the United States in the early 1960s. Cuba could not stand by itself economically and new economic policies had to be implemented. The late 1980s policy of rectification, which was a return to the radicalization of the 1960s, gave way to austerity of the so-called special period and the implementation of a more pragmatic and market-oriented approach to Cuba's economic problems. It was during this period that one could begin to see the influence of Fidel's brother, Raul, who began to direct many of these economic changes modeled after economic reforms in China. Then, with Fidel near death with malignant diverticulitis, Raul was given provisional power over the country in July 2006. Raul then struggled to make policy changes under the shadow of his older brother until February 2008 when he became the official president of Cuba.

THE SPECIAL PERIOD AND ECONOMIC REFORMS

With the fall of communism in Eastern Europe and the subsequent fall of the Soviet Union during the period 1989 through 1991, Soviet petroleum exports to Cuba dropped by 25 percent in 1990 and by 1992 oil shipments had declined from a high of 13 million tons in 1989 to 1.8 million tons. Food shipments dropped by more than 50 percent in 1991 and the Cuban economy contracted by as much as 50 percent between 1989 and 1992.[2] In the short run it was impossible to secure alternative sources of assistance. Shortages of oil, gasoline, fertilizers, herbicides, animal feed, basic food, spare parts for manufacturing and industry, consumer goods, paper supplies, and many others appeared immediately. In the summer of 1990, Castro declared the "special period" in which Cuba was placed on a wartime economy. Austerity measures were put in place. Wages became stagnant and purchasing power plummeted. Fuel shortages, planned and unplanned electrical blackouts, factory shutdowns, and transportation problems were common. While food shortages were becoming a problem and rationing reappeared, it should be noted that rationing more than likely prevented the massive malnutrition and hunger that is common in many developing countries. Living standards that had improved tremendously the previous two decades were reversed. In 1992 and 1993, more than 7,000 balseros (the name given to those who braved the Straits of Florida in makeshift boats or rafts) made it to the United States from Cuba. According to interviews, the vast majority of the balseros were escaping the economic hardships of the special period.[3]

In order to survive, Cuba was forced to make major economic policy changes. It needed new sources for imports, new markets for its exports and access to technology, capital (funds for investment), and international currencies (foreign exchange). It needed to diversity its economy and increase food production for local consumption. At the same time, Castro and the Cuban people were convinced that these policy reforms had to be made without threatening the revolutionary social safety net of free education, healthcare, and social security benefits guaranteed to all.

One of the major problems for the island during the special period was that it lacked the foreign exchange to pay for its imports and debts. In perhaps the most significant reform, the U.S. dollar was legalized in August 1993. Before this, it was a crime for Cubans to hold U.S. dollars even though more than $400 million in U.S. currency per year was brought into the country via Cuban exiles living in the United States. These dollars (remittances) fed the local black market and served as an underground currency. Given that the government needed U.S. dollars to pay its debts and to purchase imports, the decision to legalize the dollar allowed the government to capture this foreign exchange. It could pay its debts and purchase products on the world market. In addition, one of the outcomes of this reform was that Cuba had two economies—one based on the U.S. dollar and the other on the Cuban peso with the dollar being the preferred unit of exchange. State shops were created for Cubans who had dollars to be able to purchase needed goods and services. Dollar bank accounts were authorized. The number of visas available to Cubans living in the United States was increased fourfold to encourage them to visit their relatives and bring dollars into Cuba.

Sugar was the largest source of foreign exchange for the government prior to the special period. Cuba was dependent on the discounted fuel (oil) and the higher-than-world market prices that it received from the Soviet Union and the Eastern European countries. With the arrival of the special period, this subsidy came to an end. Due to the bad weather and the lack of fuel, spare parts for machinery, and fertilizer, sugar production in 1993 was lower than any time since 1970. The dramatic decline in oil imports also hurt the nickel industry, which was also a major earner of foreign exchange. The decision was made to encourage the growth of tourism on the island. Foreign investment was needed to diversify the economy and promote the growth of the tourist industry.

In September 1995, the Cuban government dramatically changed the law concerning foreign investments on the island and the following year foreign banks were allowed to create branches on the island. Both joint ventures (a business owned in part by Cuba and in part by foreign investors) and complete foreign ownership of companies were legalized. Joint ventures were established in agriculture, hotels, telephones, natural gas, pharmaceuticals, construction, transportation, food processing, textiles, mining, and tourism. Most investment capital came from Spain, Venezuela, Canada, Italy, Mexico, Holland, and the United Kingdom, although fifty other countries invested on the island. Concessions, such as the repatriation of profits and tax exemptions, were offered to encourage this investment. Companies, such as Injelco SA (Chile), Sherritt (Canada), Joutel Resources (Canada), Miramar Mining (Canada), KWB Resources (Canada), ING Bank (Netherlands), Western Mining (Australia), Grupo Domos (Mexico), Unilever (UK/Netherlands), Labatt (Canada), and Pernod Ricard (France), made investments on the island. The French company Elf Aquitaine entered into a joint agreement with Cubapetroleo, Cuba's state-run energy firm, to pack liquid propane and butane gas mix in cylinders and distribute them to households in eastern Cuba.

In order to attract more investment from abroad, the government studied free trade zones in Latin America and the Caribbean. Three free trade zones were established in Havana and Mariel. Goods brought into these free trade zones from within Cuba or from abroad were exempt from taxes. Manufacturers were granted tax holidays. Reforms made it easier to invest in agriculture, including the production of citrus, tobacco, vegetables, and rice. By the middle of 1994, Spain had invested in the production of tobacco and Israel in the production of citrus.[4] The tourist industry attracted substantial foreign investment, including hotel chains from Canada (Delta, Commonwealth and Hospitality LTD), Spain (Iberostar SA, Sol Media, RUI Hotels SA, and Raytur), and Jamaica (Super-Club). Tourists began coming in substantial numbers from Canada and Europe. Funds from the tourist industry were used to renovate World Heritage Sites in Old Havana (*Havana Vieja*) and the city of Trinidad. The number of tourists grew from 350,000 in 1990 to 500,000 in 1992, to 740,000 in 1995.[5]

The traditional agricultural model, which had been in place since the early 1970s, emphasized large, mechanized, state-run farms and was almost totally dependent on imports of trucks, machinery, chemical fertilizers, pesticides, specialized feed, and fuel. The cutting of sugar cane was dependent upon combine harvesters. This traditional model played a role in the large number of Cubans who left agricultural work and moved to the urban areas in the 1970s and 1980s. During this same period, peasants, who traditionally supplied food for local consumption and were the primary beneficiaries of the revolutionary reforms, also began moving from the rural areas to the cities. As a result, production of food for local consumption declined and was replaced by imports. Cuba relied almost entirely on the Council of Mutual Economic Assistance countries (Eastern Europe and the Soviet Union) for these crucial imports. Its agricultural sector was thrown into a crisis when these imports were dramatically cut due to the end of the Cold War.

In response to the agricultural crisis, reforms during the special period included the setting aside of land on all state farms and cooperatives for the production of food for local consumption. State farms and cooperatives began developing livestock for consumption by their workers and members. By 1993, individual farmers were also beginning to grow food locally to provide for themselves and their workers. According to agriculture development specialist Laura Enriquez, the policy of providing food for workers on state farms, cooperatives, and individual farms helped to ensure the labor supply in the agriculture sector.[6] State farm managers were allowed to "loan" some of their lands to *parceleros*, who could use the land to grow crops for self-consumption. In 1993, the government started to move away from its traditional emphasis on large state-run farms. State farms have traditionally suffered from low productivity by workers, but with the problems created by the special period and the disastrous sugar crop of 1993, the decision was made to allow state farms to be transformed into member-operated cooperatives (Basic Units of Cooperative Production) in which the members have usufruct rights (they do not own the land, they only own the products produced from the land) and operate on a profit-sharing basis. By 1994, all of the state-run sugar farms had been transformed into member-operated cooperatives and state-run farms in other agricultural areas (tobacco, coffee, and cacao) were transformed.[7] These reforms, which decentralized agricultural production and moved to a more market-based operation, led to a 17.3 percent growth in agricultural production by 1996.[8]

Throughout the special period, the shortage of food crops created a very active black market. These goods were expensive and only Cubans who had access to dollars could purchase them. In October 1994, the government legalized, once again, the farmers' markets, where surplus crops could be sold for a profit. These *agropecuarios* sold everything, including cheese, milk, fruits, vegetables, and meat. As a result, black market sales declined, the availability of food at the markets increased, and food prices dropped. The government also overlooked the problem of health hazards and allowed the breeding of pigs in Havana Province. The purpose of this was to provide families with more pork (the favorite meat of Cubans and the source of lard) and to undermine its sale on the black market.

In December 1993, the government passed Law 141 which began to allow self-employment in different trades such as chauffeurs, hair stylists, shoemakers, photographers, carpenters, and auto and bicycle repair. By 1995 more than 200,000 individuals had obtained self-employment licenses in more than 160 government-approved activities.[9] Private home restaurants (*paladares*) were legalized the same year and have become quite common throughout the island as they cater to both tourists and locals. These private restaurants must be licensed by the state and they advertise primarily through word of mouth, especially among tourist groups. They are taxed by the state and if they conduct business in dollars they must pay the tax in dollars.

The government made major cuts in spending in state-run enterprises, government investments, and the military. State-run enterprises were also given autonomy and required to operate on their own accounts. In other words, state-run enterprises were now being asked to function on a for-profit basis. Many state-run enterprises were also given the ability to import necessary equipment and items without state permission. In order to improve its fiscal situation, the government levied a tax on some consumer goods. The government, to its credit, did not cut back spending on healthcare, education, and social security. This continues to set Cuba apart from the remainder of the developing world and even some wealthy countries.

By 1996, it was clear that the economy was growing once again and that Cuba had survived the worst of the special period and by 1998 the standard of living in Cuba was just about what it had been just before the end of the Cold War. Yet, the reforms were having some unanticipated outcomes. In particular, the dual existence of the dollar and the peso economies was beginning to bring about a visible gap between the rich or the privileged and the poor. The privileged Cubans either worked in the tourist and service industries that had access to dollars or were able to receive dollars from family members living in the United States. The poor were trapped in the peso economy of the ration card and state-run stores. Even though this provided a basic standard of living due to the guaranteed social safety net, the peso economy was not able to provide the "extras" that access to dollars can provide. In particular, this placed a difficult burden on white-collar professionals who worked for the state, such as doctors, nurses, teachers, engineers, government administrators, and others. Their monthly peso income provided only a basic standard of living but did not allow them to "get ahead." Many professionals began to take second jobs in the tourist sector, such as taxi drivers, where they could earn much more in U.S. dollars. In a discussion with one professional at that time, he indicated that he was having difficulty convincing his son that he should attend college and go to medical school. His son argued that he could make more money driving a taxi for tourists and questioned the value of further education.[10] This presents a major dilemma for a country that invests so much in education. What is most evident is that resentment among those in the peso economy was growing and the ideal of the revolution was being threatened by the dual dollar and peso economies.

THE SPECIAL PERIOD AND MILITARY AND POLITICAL REFORMS

The end of the Cold War and the special period dramatically affected the Cuban Revolutionary Armed Services (FAR). All military assistance, weapons, and supplies deliveries came to an end. Spare parts for military vehicles, ships, and aircraft became difficult to find. Fuel shortages forced reductions in vehicle and aircraft operations. Training exercises were reduced. The budget for the FAR was cut considerably. The FAR's highly successful internationalist mission came to an end in 1992 with the last personnel leaving Africa the previous year. Morale, which was already low due to the purges of the western army in the mid-1980s and the General Ochoa affair, plummeted even further. The last Russian troops left the island in 1993. Raul Castro, the head of the FAR, began to make major reforms.

One of the major reforms is that the mission of the FAR changed. In 1991, Castro announced that the FAR must help with the economy. This was not unprecedented in the revolutionary era, as it had exercised some administration of economic activities and provided labor for the sugar harvests of the 1960s. It was also already involved in the production of food by 1990 in order to meet its own consumptive needs during the special period. Soldiers returning from abroad were put to work on farms run by the state, while officers with technical expertise were put to work to find alternatives to the island's dependence on imported fertilizers. Raul sent many officers abroad to learn modern business practices. The FAR was given the authority to create economic enterprises to begin to meet some of its own budgetary needs. For example, Gaviota is a joint venture with foreign investment that plays a major role in the growing tourist industry. It also provides hard currency for the FAR and employment for retired service personnel. Since then, several subsidiaries have been created, such as Texnotec, which imports information technology and electronic equipment, and Tucrimex, which focuses on the movement of cargo. Another is the Army Labor Youth. The Army Labor Youth has two enterprises in Jaguey Grande and the Isle of Youth that was producing 58 percent of the island's citrus by 1998.[11] Another major reform was that the size of the military was reduced considerably. The Institute for Strategic Studies in London estimated that the Cuban military consisted of 105,000 troops in 1995. This represented a reduction of 100,000 troops since the mid-1980s. Mandatory military service for Cubans was reduced from three to two years. According to Richard Millett, the military was expressing concerns, if not doubts, of the ability of the Cuban air force and tanks to defend the island from invasion. The focus shifted to the practice of guerrilla warfare and the "retreat into Cuba's mountains and rural areas" to defeat an attack on the island.

According to Jaime Suchlicki, Castro dramatically streamlined the Communist Party during the special period.[12] The party had always been, to some extent, an instrument that Castro had molded simply to carry out his policies. He eliminated the secretariat position and the Central Committee rarely met. The Political Bureau was the only party organ making decisions. In 1991, the Political Bureau of the Communist Party was expanded in size but it excluded two important revolutionary figures: Vilma Espin, the president of the Federation of Cuban Women, and Armando Hart, the minister of culture. In 1992, Manuel Pineiro, a former guerrilla commander, lost his position as the head of the Central Committee's espionage service. Ramiro Valdes, a former guerrilla captain nicknamed Red Beard, was removed as the head of the powerful Ministry of the Interior in 1994. By 1995, ten of the fourteen provincial Communist Party secretaries were replaced with younger members. In the same year, seven younger individuals became heads of various economic ministries within the Council of State. In 1997, Carlos Rafael Rodriquez, a leader of the Popular Socialist Party in the 1950s, was removed from the Political Bureau of the Communist Party and in the same year Hart was relieved of his duties as minister of culture. It was clear that Castro was beginning to bring the next generation of loyal leaders into the ruling circles of Cuba. The civil government was reformed in 1993 by allowing the election of members to all levels of the Popular Power assemblies rather than just the municipal level.

The special period also brought about an increase in crime, corruption, and theft in the urban and rural areas. Dissident groups on the island increased and became more vocal in challenging authorities. The government responded with both repression and reform. In 1995, the Cuban Council, an umbrella organization for human rights groups, called for a national meeting of the more than 130 civic groups (with a focus on human rights, elections, and the environment) that it represented. The group was denied recognition by the government and in early 1996 more than 200 human rights leaders were harassed, arrested, and interrogated. One should note that the number of political prisoners had declined since 1991 and more than 300 were released after Pope John Paul II's historic visit in 1998. Amnesty International's 2002 Human Rights Report indicated a significant decrease in the number of political prisoners being held by Castro. At the same time, the report criticized Castro for his continued harassment of dissidents, the denial of civil rights to his people, and the fact that he was still holding political prisoners.

RELATIONS WITH THE UNITED STATES IN THE SPECIAL PERIOD

One may have expected the policy of the United States toward Cuba to change in the early 1990s with the collapse of communism in Eastern Europe, the establishment of a closer relationship between the United States and Mikhail Gorbachev–led Russia, and a continuation of the U.S. relationship with China despite the events of Tiananmen Square. In addition, three of the four stated conditions necessary for U.S. normalization of relations had been met by 1992. Castro was no longer supporting revolutionaries in Latin America, Cuban military ties to the Soviet Union were, in effect, eliminated, and all Cuban troops had been removed from Africa. The only condition left was an improvement in the protection of human rights on the island and a 1989 State Department report indicated improvement in this area. President George H. Bush even vetoed a bill in 1990 that would have made it difficult for subsidiaries of U.S. companies in other countries to trade with Cuba. In this case, the lobbying efforts of IBM, Exxon, ITT, and others that traded with Cuba via third countries were successful.[13] It looked like President Bush was moving to change U.S. policy toward the island.

The presidential election of 1992 and the power of the anti-Castro Cuban American National Foundation (CANF) brought an abrupt end to any thaw in U.S. policy. President Bush added the condition that Cuba must hold free and fair elections before the United States would consider normalizing relations. A similar version of the 1990 bill, the Cuban Democracy Act, also known as the Torricelli Act, was reintroduced in 1992. With Democratic candidate Bill Clinton catering to CANF, President Bush decided to support the passage of the bill and signed it in Miami just before the election. The Torricelli Act prevents subsidiaries of U.S. companies in other countries from trading with Cuba even if those countries allow trade with the island. It also prevents ships that dock in Cuba from coming to the United States for six months and allows the president to stop U.S. foreign aid to any country that conducts business with Cuba. Finally, it allows the president to give assistance to Cuban dissidents. Even though Canada and U.S. allies in Europe opposed the Torricelli Act and resented what they considered to be U.S. intervention into their own trade policies, President Bush and the incoming president Clinton continued to take a hard line against Cuba. Perhaps more importantly, policy toward Cuba and any change in that policy now required an act of Congress, not just a presidential decision.

Due to the crisis created with the arrival of the *balseros* during the special period, President Clinton worked with Cuban officials to promote safe, legal, and orderly immigration to the United States. For more than thirty years the U.S. policy was a grant of automatic asylum to Cubans who could make it across the Florida Straits. One could argue this immigration policy served as a magnet that attracted Cubans to the United States. Clinton agreed to allow a minimum of 20,000 legal Cuban immigrants per year. He then moved to promote more people-to-people contacts between the United States and Cuba by allowing private organizations to develop relationships with Cuban organizations. The Cuban Liberty and Democratic Solidarity Act, also known as the Helms-Burton Act, made its way through Congress in 1996. Fearing an adverse reaction from U.S. allies in Europe and Canada, Clinton threatened a veto, but on February 24 of that year Cuban planes shot down two U.S. civilian aircraft belonging to the anti-Castro, Miami-based group Brothers to the Rescue in international waters. In reaction to this event, the U.S. Congress passed and President Clinton signed the Helms-Burton Act in March. This act allows American citizens to sue foreign corporations whose trade or investments profit from any properties expropriated by the Castro government after 1959. It allows the U.S. government to penalize foreign companies that conduct business in Cuba. Finally, the act added another condition for the normalization of relations with Cuba: that no government with Castro or his brother Raul would be acceptable to the United States. The assumption is that it would be unacceptable to the United States if either Castro were elected president through free and fair elections. This act, similar to the Torricelli Act, further placed U.S. policy toward Cuba in the hands of the Congress which is much more susceptible to lobbying by anti-Castro groups than the executive branch.

Yet, some dissenting voices concerning U.S policy toward Cuba were raised. The same year the Torricelli Act was passed, the United Nations General Assembly voted overwhelmingly to condemn the

U.S. embargo and each year since then it has done the same. At a summit meeting in 1993, Latin American, Spanish, and Portuguese leaders unanimously called for an end to the embargo. The Organization of American States condemned the Helms Burton Act and the Inter-American Juridical Committee ruled that it violated international law on at least eight counts. Most international law specialists argued that it violates several international treaties, and Canada and the European countries argued that the United States has no right to extend its laws to their countries (extraterritoriality). They threatened to take the dispute before the World Trade Organization, but the Clinton administration worked out an agreement with them that he would not enforce the part of the Helms-Burton Act that allows U.S. citizens to sue foreign corporations that have benefitted from expropriated properties in Cuba if they would support the demand for political reform on the island.

By the mid-1990s, it was clear to many agriculture and tourist businesses in the United States that they were missing out on the economic opening of Cuba under its reform investment and trade policies. The United States-Cuba Trade Economic Council testified to Congress in support of ending the U.S. embargo. Other large multinational corporations such as Archer Daniels Midland, Time Warner, Carghill, and Caterpillar are on record in support of an end to the embargo. In 1998, Pope John Paul II urged the United States to end its embargo. In reaction to the Pope's visit to the island, the Clinton administration allowed an increase in direct flights to the island, gave authority for direct food and medicine sales to Cuba, and established direct mail service.

CHANGES IN CUBA AFTER THE SPECIAL PERIOD

By the mid- to late 1990s the Cuban economy had recovered from the special period. More than twenty-two contracts had been awarded to develop domestic oil production. Almost 400 joint business ventures between Cuba and foreign firms had been established. Most foreign investment was in the tourist sector with investments largely coming from Canada, Mexico, and Spain. Rice production increased as did tobacco, nickel, and cobalt exports and economic growth reached 7 percent of gross domestic product. Electricity output increased. Foreign investments on the island began to pay off. The Clinton administration then raised the amount of remittances from U.S. families to relatives in Cuba to $1,200 per year. This had a dramatic effect on the daily lives of those families in Cuba fortunate enough to receive the cash. Remittances increased from $500 million in 1995 to more than $1 billion in 2004.

By the year 2000 Cuba had established a special relationship with the Hugo Chavez–led and oil-rich Venezuela. Chavez, an ideological soul-mate to Castro, viewed him as a father-like figure. During the attempted *golpe* against Chavez in 2002, Castro was in constant contact with Chavez and encouraged him to never give in to the demands of those trying to oust him. Castro and Chavez became close, remained in contact with each other, and visited each other on a regular basis. Their close relationship led to mutual economic benefits for their countries. Cuba began to provide training to the Venezuelan military and sent large numbers of teachers, doctors, and nurses to assist in Chavez in his efforts to transform his country. Venezuelans gained access to Cuban medical facilities and care. In return, Venezuela sold discounted oil to Cuba. Joint business ventures in nickel, electrical power, and rice were established. A joint venture for the development of oil refining capabilities in Cienfuegos and to explore for oil of the

This billboard near the Plaza of the Revolution in Havana welcomes President Hugo Chavez to Cuba for the revolutionary celebrations of May Day, 2005. Chavez and Fidel Castro were ideological and geopolitical soul-mates, although Chavez viewed Fidel as a father-figure. Venezuela continues to provide discounted oil to Cuba in return for medical personnel and doctors. (Courtesy of Ted Henken)

northern coast of Cuba was established. Venezuela began to provide foodstuffs, farm equipment, and transportation equipment to Cuba.

While Cuban sugar production increased in 1995, it continued to face problems and production declined from 1996 through 2003. This was largely due to inefficiency, the lack of fertilizers and insecticides, the need to update equipment, and declining world prices from 1996 through 2003 due to increased global production and the increased use of corn syrup and artificial sweeteners. In fact, by 2002 the world price of sugar was 6 cents per pound and the average sugar production costs in Cuba were 20 cents per pound.[14] In April 2002, the government closed 71 of the 156 sugar mills in the country representing more than 60 percent of the land used for sugar production and representing 100,000 workers. This land was used to diversify agricultural production both for export and for local consumption. Cuba began investing in the remaining mills to update the technology and make them globally competitive. It was the end of King Sugar; scholar Louis Perez states that

> A way of life was coming to an end in countless tens of thousands of households. Hundreds of communities across the island had historically formed and functioned around the rhythms of sugar production, including many of the oldest zones on the island, with antecedents deep in the nineteenth century, suddenly found life as they had known it for generations profoundly and permanently changed.[15]

Ironically, with tourism earning more foreign exchange than sugar, some of the old sugar plantations became tourist attractions. Hurricanes in 1998, 1999, 2002, and 2004 did not help as they caused substantial crop loss and property damage to the ailing sugar industry.

During the last part of the Clinton administration, U.S. relations with Cuba improved. By 1997, more than 400 U.S. companies had organized USA Engage, which was designed to lobby the Congress to end the embargo. In 2000, Congress passed the Trade Sanctions Reform and Export Enhancement Act which allowed U.S. companies to sell foodstuffs to Cuba on a cash basis only. By 2003, the United States provided 25 percent of Cuba's total food imports consisting primarily of corn, rice, wheat, soybeans, eggs, cattle, pork, and poultry. The number of U.S. citizens traveling to Cuba increased and reached 210,000 by 2003. There was a dramatic expansion of sister-city programs. Academic cooperation increased in the form of U.S. college-study abroad programs, faculty exchange programs, and the establishment of library and archival ties. Cuban musicians, such as the internationally known Buena Vista Social Club, artists, and dance groups, such as the National Ballet, came to the United States. U.S. musicians, such as Jimmy Buffet, began performing in Cuba. U.S. news organizations, such as CNN, the Associated Press, and *The Chicago Tribune*, created bureaus in Havana. Governing agencies and individuals began to support a move to engage Cuba in an even more positive relationship. These included a review in 1998 by the Richard Clarke, the national coordinator for counterterrorism; assessments made by retired General Barry McCaffrey who had met extensively with the Castro brothers in March 2002; assessments by General Charles Wilhelm, the former commander in chief of the U.S. Southern Command; assessments by General Jack Sheehan, the former commander in chief of the U.S. Atlantic Command; and assessments by the Central Intelligence Agency, the Defense Intelligence Agency, the National Security Agency, the State Department's Intelligence and Research Unit, and all military intelligence.

Despite the growing cooperation and improvements in the relationship between Cuba and the United States and U.S. government assessments and recommendations favoring an even more cooperative policy toward Cuba, the Bush family history and presidential election politics of 2000 all but guaranteed a change in U.S. policy to one of hostility toward Cuba. The Bush family had been a major stockholder in the West Indies Sugar Corporation in the 1940s and 1950s. The company's vast sugar holding was next to the Castro family farm or *finca*. A member of the Bush family, "Uncle Herbie," managed the family's sugar interests until the Cuban revolution and it was Fidel Castro who nationalized the West Indies Corporation early in the revolution.[16] This family history was not lost during the presidency of George H. W. Bush and was clearly not going to be lost with George W. Bush.

It could be argued that the election of George W. Bush in 2000 was largely due to the Cuban American vote in Florida. The Cuban American community, Congressmen Mario and Lincoln Diaz-Balart and Congresswoman Ileana Ros-Lehtinen, and, of course, Governor Jeb Bush had closed ties to the Bush administration. Bush publicly placed Cuba within the so-called axis of evil. In mid-2002 President Bush expelled four Cuban diplomats. He provided aid to families of political prisoners and dissidents and the U.S. Interest Section in Havana openly began to support dissidents and opposition groups in Cuba. By the 2004 election year, Bush had virtually halted the people-to-people contacts with Cuba, despite the release of a report by the private and Republican-led Cuba Study Group that a majority of Cuban exiles favored diplomacy with Castro. American scholars, journalists, artists, and college students found it almost impossible to obtain a Treasury Department license to travel to Cuba. Cuban American families were restricted in their travel back to Cuba to visit relatives to one time in a three-year period. The amount of dollars that could be sent to Cubans from Americans (remittances) was reduced. Hard-line, anti-Castro groups in Miami lined up to eagerly receive government money to "foster democracy in Cuba." In 2008, more than $45 million was granted to groups such as the Cuban American National Foundation, the Cuban Liberty Council, the Center for a Free Cuba, and the International Republican Institute.

Not all Cuban Americans supported the Bush policies toward Cuba. The *Cambio Cubano, Puentes Cubano*, and Brothers to the Rescue condemned those policies that limited travel by Cuban Americans to visit relatives and the limits placed on remittances. The once monolithic exile community in Cuba was beginning to show divisions. Opposition to the hard line anti-Castro groups began to appear in younger generations of Cuban Americans and those exiles who arrived after the 1980 Mariel boat lift.[17] Leading dissidents in Cuba, such as Oswaldo Paya, Miriam Leiva, and Yoani Sanchez, opposed the Bush administration's hostile policies toward the island.

THE GROWING AND DIVERSE DISSIDENT MOVEMENT

Dissident groups began to play a more visible role in Cuba despite the harassment, intimidation, and the possibility of being arrested. Many of these groups are supported by groups outside Cuba. Some of these include the Lawton Foundation, the Rosa Parks Feminist Movement for Civil Rights, the Cuban Democratic Directorate, and the Manuel Marquez Sterling Society of Journalists led by Oscar Espinosa Chepe and his wife, Miriam Leiva. One of the first open dissident groups was the Cuban Committee for Human Rights which developed in the 1980s in the prisons of Cuba. Independent journalists Raul Rivero and Yndamiro Restano created the first independent Cuban press agency. The Cuban Council in the mid-1990s sought to organize the growing number of independent professional organizations. Although many of its leading activists were intimidated and arrested, the Cuban Council was able to get its message of a unified opposition in support of a peaceful transition to democracy to foreign heads of state who were in Havana in 1999 for the Ibero-American Summit. Despite harassment, imprisonment, and exile of its leaders, an independent library movement with access to uncensored literature and information was started in Las Tunas and there are now at least 135 independent libraries across the island today. Many of these are in private homes.

The Christian Liberation Movement, started by Oswaldo Paya in Cero Parrish in Havana in 1988, is a human rights and Catholic Church–based organization. It focuses on issues of freedom of religion and lobbies to obtain the release of Cubans held in prison for their political activities. Paya also started the Varela Project in 1998. The goal of the project was to use Article 88 G of the Cuban Constitution which allows for amendments to be made via a referendum. The necessary requirement to call for a referendum was to get 10,000 signatures on a petition. Paya suggested amendments that included guarantees of free speech, assembly, and press; amnesty for political prisoners, and new election laws. In 2002 he submitted the petition to the national assembly with 11,000 signatures on it. Many of the project's supporters were harassed and put in jail, and Castro declared the petition to be illegal.

In the spring of 2003, now known as Black Spring, several nonviolent protest marches were staged by human rights activists and journalists. In March, seventy-five human rights activists were arrested for "complicity with the enemy." Prison sentences for individuals in the group ranged from six to twenty-eight years. It was the wives of those who were arrested who created the Ladies in White. Initially led by Laura Pollan, Miriam Leiva, Angel Moya Acosta, and Berta Soler, they dress in white, meet as a group, and walk down Quinta Avenue (5th Avenue) in Miramar to the Church of Santa Rita where they pray for the release of their husbands and other political prisoners. While all of the original seventy-five husbands have either been released or exiled, the Ladies in White still walk today. They are reminiscent of the Mothers of the Plaza de Mayo in Argentina. In 2005 the Assembly to Promote Civil Society was created as a coalition of 365 independent society groups. It held a congress in May of that year. A rural women's group, known as FLAMUR, gathered 10,000 signatures on a petition to call for an end to the two-currency system in Cuba.

Younger dissidents in Cuba have taken advantage of the Internet. Despite government attempts to limit or deny access to the Internet, scores of dissident bloggers, such as internationally famous Yoani Sanchez and her Generation Y blog, are now in the front of the opposition movement to the communist government. Their blogs reach a global audience and are often translated into several languages. Although not considered to be dissident groups, the Citizens Committee for Racial Integration works within the Cuban political system to fight racial discrimination. The Federation of Cuban Women, although a mass organization controlled by the Communist Party, has worked within the system to promote women's rights and to prevent discrimination against women. The research wing of the organization regularly provides data on the obstacles to women in official leadership positions in the government and economic enterprises.

Bloggers reported that dissidents had been warned by state security officials that they would be jailed "immediately" for any activities at the July 26, 2006, celebration of the anniversary of the Cuban revolution. After several speeches that day, it was clear to observers at his speech in Holguin that something was wrong with Fidel Castro. Only a few people knew he was in crippling pain. The next day he was flown back to Havana and underwent extensive, intestinal surgery for malignant diverticulitis at the Center for Medical-Surgical Studies Hospital. During and after the surgery, abscessed material had leaked into the peritoneal cavity and blood poisoning set in.[18] It was not known if Fidel would survive. Nearly a week of silence on his status set the stage for the historic announcement on July 31, 2006.

THE "LONG DYING" OF FIDEL CASTRO AND RAUL'S RISE TO POWER[19]

At 9:15 P.M. that evening, a young Carlos Valenciaga, Castro's personal aid, announced that Castro, *El Comandante*, was ill and had undergone intestinal surgery. He then announced a temporary transfer of power to Raul Castro. The shockwaves of the announcement radiated across the island to Miami and the rest of the world. Raul put into effect "Operation Caguairan" in which more than 200,000 troops were mobilized to take to the streets and prevent any disturbances during the situation. There were few, if any, disturbances. Many among the Cuban elite and most Cubans believed Castro to be dead or soon to be dead. Similar rumors among Cuban exiles in Miami were rampant. Some analysts in the U.S. Central Intelligence Agency concluded that Fidel would be dead by 2007 and regime collapse was near. Only a few people were allowed in Castro's hospital room. These included long-time friend and revolutionary Dr. Jose Miyar Barruecos, Fidel's wife, Dalia Soto del Valle, and, interestingly, his first wife Myrta Diaz-Balart who had flown in from Miami.[20]

By August, the Council of State declared a peaceful and successful succession, while at the same time Castro began showing signs of improvement from the bungled surgery. In order to silence the rising tide of those who believed Castro was dead, a video of a very frail Castro was shown on October 28. Many Cubans and U.S. intelligence analysts argued the video confirmed that Castro was near death. In December, Jose Luis Garcia, a Spanish surgeon who specialized in colon cancer, flew to Havana and treated him. Garcia confirmed that Castro was not suffering from colon cancer, as had been widely reported and speculated. On January 30, 2007, Cuban television broadcast a short video of Castro and Hugo Chavez, the president of Venezuela, embracing. By early spring pictures of a frail Castro walking in the hospital gardens began to temporarily silence the rumors of his impending death. Yet, Castro's failure to attend the May Day celebration and the funeral of Vilma Espin, Raul's wife and former guerrilla in the Sierra Maestra, fueled even more death rumors only to be silenced when dignitaries from other countries would come to the island and pictures and videos would appear on television and in *Granma*. In August 2007, Castro, dressed in a tracksuit, appeared on Cuban television. When asked about his "impending death," he responded, "Well, here I am!"[21]

In March 2007, *Granma*, the official paper of the Communist Party, began publishing "Reflections" of Fidel Castro. For the next two and one-half years, Fidel's essays touched upon a variety of subjects and issues such as U.S. imperialism, George Bush, the Central Intelligence Agency, Ronald Reagan, Hugo Chavez, and Cuban policies. Raul sometimes found his provisional authority undermined by Fidel's essays in "Reflections." Raul had approached the United States concerning a change in the relationship. Fidel, in one of his "Reflections," squashed the idea of a rapprochement with the United States. It was clear that Fidel still had the final word on significant matters. It was during this time that Raul, who believed that the future of economic reform in Cuba needed to follow the Chinese model of economic reform, wanted to implement more meaningful economic reforms.

Raul had visited Beijing in 1997 and met with Zhu Rongji who was responsible for the dramatic economic reforms in China. Other Chinese officials followed to assess the Cuban economy and to provide advice. As head of the Cuban armed forces, Raul had sent hundreds of military officials abroad to study modern business management in the 1990s and he began to insist upon economic enterprises being run by modern business principles. In 2003, Raul invited then Chinese premier Zhu Rongji for a series of lectures across the island. That same year a visit by Xu Sicheng of the Chinese Academy of Social Scientists led to the advice that Cuba must "establish mechanisms of the socialist market economy . . . and smash egalitarianism." Visits by then Chinese president Hu Jintao in 2004 reinforced Raul's belief that Cuba must adopt the Chinese model of economic reform. In

2007, Cuba-Chinese trade represented $2.6 billion. Because Raul was the provisional president and Fidel was still alive, Raul did not have the full power of the presidency and it was difficult to promote the major reforms that he sought. Yet, Raul began making some changes. Cubans were granted the right to rent cars, buy electronic goods and cell phones, stay in tourist hotels, operate private taxis, and develop private farms of up to 100 acres on unused state-owned land. Factions began to appear between hardliners such as Ramiro Valdes and the leadership of the Communist Party and the so-called reformers in the Council of State such as Vice President Carlos Lage. Castro's essays in "Reflections" clearly supported the *duros* or hardliners who did not want to dismantle socialism in favor of the Chinese "socialist market economy."

Fidel would never fully regain his health, and the on-again and off-again rumors of his impending death interspersed with pictures of the numerous dignitaries coming to visit him dominated much of the Cuban and Miami media. Much of the discussion over his future was also fueled by the fact that Fidel had not appeared in public since July 26, 2006. On February 19, 2008, still with health problems, he announced that he would not stand for reelection to the presidency and on February 24 Raul Castro was officially elected President of Cuba. Raul moved quickly to build his support within the Communist Party and the government. He replaced twelve of Fidel's loyalists in February 2009 with *Raulistas,* many of whom were from the FAR.

The global recession which began in 2008 affected the Cuban economy as the number of tourists to the island declined and the global price of nickel and sugar dropped. Raul began to make dramatic changes to implement the Chinese model in Cuba. President Hu Jintao of China visited in the fall of 2008 for economic discussions. Cuba and China signed agreements in the sale of sugar and nickel and port reconstruction. Massive hurricanes in 2009 and 2010 destroyed more than a half a million homes and devastated the already ailing sugar industry. In October 2010 Raul stated that "without an increase in efficiency and productivity, it is impossible to raise salaries, increase exports, substitute for imports, and sustain the enormous social expenditures of our socialist system." He then stated the following which clearly distanced himself from his brother, "In the economic policy that is proposed, socialism is equality of rights and opportunities for the citizen, not egalitarianism." With this statement there was no doubt to anyone that the transition from Fidel to Raul was complete. It was officially sealed when Raul was also selected as the first secretary of the Communist Party on April 19, 2011.

NOTES

1. Fidel Castro, "Workers in Cuba Stand Firm," *The Militant* no. 20 (May 20, 1996) found at http://www.themilitant.com/1996/6020/6020_4.html.

2. Laura Enriquez, "Cuba's New Agricultural Revolution: The Transformation of Food Crop Production in Contemporary Cuba," *Food First, Development Report* no. 14 (May 2000), 4.

3. *Christian Science Monitor*, February 6, 1991; *Boston Globe*, January 2, 1994, 9.

4. Maria Antonia Fernandez Mayo and James E. Ross, "Cuba: Foreign Agribusiness Financing and Investment, "International Working Paper IW98–7, EDIS, University of Florida, 1998, 13.

5. Perez, Jr., *Cuba: Between Reform and Revolution*, 309.

6. Enriquez, *Cuba's New Agricultural Revolution*, 4.

7. Ibid., 4.

8. Keen and Haynes, *A History of Latin America*, 453.

9. Perez, Jr., *Cuba: Between Reform and Revolution*, 306.

10. Interview by the author, Havana, May 2001.

11. Mayo and Ross, *Cuba*, 13.

12. Suchlicki, *Cuba: From Columbus to Castro*, 248.

13. Economic Intelligence Unit, Cuba Country Report, no. 3 (1990): 16.

14. Perez, Jr., *Cuba: Between Reform and Revolution*, 320, 321.

15. Ibid., 322.

16. Ann Louise Bardach, *Without Fidel* (New York: Scribner, 2009), 58.

17. Perez, Jr., *Cuba: Between Reform and Revolution*, 328.

18. Bardach, *Without Fidel*, 4.

19. Ibid., 1.

20. Ibid., 5, 12.

21. Ibid., 56.

9

Cuba in Transition

Beans are more important than cannons.

Raul Castro, 1994[1]

Cuba is in a period of economic transition toward the so-called Chinese socialist market model. This includes the development of a more diverse and mixed economy (both private and state-run enterprises), the adoption of modern business and market-based practices, a continued role for the military in the economy, encouragement of foreign investment on the island, and the development of a diverse number of trading partners. It includes the maintenance of political control by the Communist Party. What makes the Cuban version unique is that it also seeks to do all this and maintain the three pillars of the revolution: free education for all, cradle to grave free healthcare benefits to all, and social security for all. One of the primary problems in applying the Chinese model in Cuba is that the island, unlike China, does not have a large internal market and must, as it has historically been forced to do, find external markets for its products. Raul Castro, the loyal brother of Fidel, is managing the transition. The questions that remain are how well will he manage the transition and what will happen in

2018 when the first post-revolution generation under the chosen successor, Miguel Diaz-Canel, assumes power in the country.

RAUL CASTRO

Throughout all the years that Fidel Castro led Cuba, his brother Raul was seen as an enigma by many observers. Some portrayed him as an ideologue and hardliner, others saw him as pragmatic and open to change. Both characterizations are correct. Raul Castro was the youngest son of Angel Castro and Lina Ruz. Born on June 3, 1931, he was his mother's favorite and is four years younger than Fidel. Fidel and Raul have always been close with Fidel serving as a mentor to Raul at an early age. He enrolled in a military prep school and then, like his brother, attended the Jesuit-run Dolores School in Santiago and the prestigious Colegio de Belen in Havana. Raul attended the University of Havana but was not a strong student. He dropped out in 1952 and returned home to work with his father and his brother, Ramon. Raul, who had been involved in the Communist Party while at the university, attended a Communist Party conference in Vienna, Austria. He was briefly detained by the Batista government when he returned home. Since that time Raul has always been at the side of Fidel, but always in his shadow.

Raul joined Fidel in the failed attack on the Moncada Barracks on July 26, 1953, and spent twenty-two months in prison on the Isle of Pines. He and his brother were released in May 1955. He then went to Mexico with his brother to plan their revolution. Raul, who was a marksman and gifted military strategist, introduced Che Guevara to Fidel in Mexico City in July. According to author and journalist Ann Louise Bardach, it was during this period that their collaborative role-playing of hero and villain began.[2] Throughout the early years of the revolution Fidel was the hero and Raul was the villain. Raul was willing to be the fall guy for unpopular decisions and policies. He served as the ultimate communist hardliner and Fidel's henchman.

Juanita Castro, the sister of Fidel and Raul, suggests that in everyday family life the roles are just the opposite. Raul is the hero and Fidel is the villain. Raul married Vilma Espin in 1959 and they had four children. Espin, the daughter of Jose Espin who was a lawyer and executive for the Bacardi Rum Company in Santiago, was considered the unofficial first lady of the revolution. A chemical engineer by training, who spent a year in postgraduate school at Massachusetts Institute of Technology, she joined Frank Pais and the 26th of July Movement in 1956 and later joined Fidel and Raul in the Sierra Maestra. It is Raul, not Fidel, who is the patriarch of the extended and often-divided Castro family. He was the toastmaster at weddings and the negotiator at divorces and the one who calmed all in family crises. He attended all the family functions from graduations to birthday parties. He sent comforting letters and notes during difficult times. The Castro family in Cuba and Miami is loyal and protective of Raul because of his instinctive empathy.[3]

Raul, who is very uncomfortable in public speaking, worked tirelessly behind the scenes for his brother and served as the commander in chief of the Cuban Revolutionary Armed Forces (FAR). According to scholar Brian Latell, the pragmatic and cautious Raul managed the FAR in a "self-effacing, consultative, and collegial fashion."[4] He developed a deep and loyal following in the FAR. He modernized the FAR by making sure it received the best weapons from the Soviet Union. Troops were thoroughly trained. He was largely responsible for the professionalism and distinguished international record of the FAR in the 1970s and 1980s, in particular, its roles in Angola and Ethiopia.

The dramatic changes coming to the Soviet Union in the 1980s with Mikhail Gorbachev's decision to implement perestroika and glasnost directly affected the political debate in the other communist countries in the world. Perestroika referred to a fundamental restructuring and decentralization of the economy. Glasnost referred to a greater opening and transparency in the political processes. Fidel rejected perestroika and glasnost. Norberto Fuentes, Cuban author and journalist, stated, "In the 1980s, Fidel and Raul would argue about perestroika and the country's economic problems. Raul was, and remains in favor of perestroika, and to an extent, he believes in glasnost."[5] According to Jesus Renzoli, his long-time secretary and Russian translator to the Castro brothers, the Solidarity Movement in Poland had a tremendous impact on Raul's belief in the need for reform. The harsh realities of the special period on the Cuban people and Raul's trip to China in 1997 led him to believe that for Cuban socialism to survive it must adopt the Chinese socialist market model. Raul had become a socialist reformer but major reforms would have to wait until he was no longer in the shadow of his brother.

RAUL AS LEADER OF CUBA

Raul has made it very clear to the people of Cuba that he is not his brother and that they should adjust their expectations to his style of leadership. He lacks the charisma of his brother and, unlike Fidel, shuns the spotlight. In a speech to students, Raul stated, "Sometimes people fear the word disagree, but I say the more debate and more disagreement you have, the better decisions will be."[6] This statement is indicative that he is not his brother. Raul has several factors working in his favor in terms of his legitimacy and ability to lead Cuba through this transition. His loyal following in the FAR coupled with its major role in the Cuban economy virtually negates the possibility of a *golpe*. Scholar Jaime Suchlicki argues that Raul, different from his brother, has "nurtured" the development of the Communist Party in recent years.[7] Raul believes that the institutionalization of the party is necessary if he is to be successful in this transition. This began in 2006 with the re-establishment of the secretariat organ within the party. He has brought strong provincial leaders to the secretariat to implement the decentralization of the economy. Miguel Diaz-Canel, his chosen successor, is an example. Diaz-Canel was a communist youth leader

Raul Castro, the younger and loyal brother to Fidel, served most of his career as head of the Cuban Revolutionary Armed Forces. It was the realities of the so-called special period that caused him to to see the need to reform Cuban socialism. As president, he is managing the economic transition on the island with Chinese economic reforms serving as a model. (AP Photo)

and has held several positions in the party, including provincial party leader who implemented the economic reforms in Villa Clara and Holquin. Yet, other scholars point out that Raul has made sure that the leadership is full of those loyal to him and question the extent of the institutionalization of the Communist Party. On April 19, 2011, Raul became the first secretary and has since replaced virtually all of the former *Fidelistas* in the Communist Party leadership positions with *Raulistas*. He has effectively controlled the Ministry of the Interior, which includes the intelligence gathering agencies, the police, and security organizations since the early 1990s.[8] Raul controls all the levers of power and no longer has to look over his shoulder for his big brother. Most observers believe that he will be able to maintain his power base and carry out his reforms until 2018 when, and if, he steps down as he has promised. He brings a management style developed while he was the head of the FAR. He depends on family, old friends, and trusted colleagues. He is not afraid of delegating authority and responsibilities with both military and civilian leaders who reciprocate his confidence. Raul is publicly more honest than Fidel in his assessment of the island's challenges and opportunities, stating that Cuba is rife with problems that must be overcome and opportunities of which it must take advantage if economic reform is to be successful.

ECONOMIC REFORM

Raul Castro has indicated that the Chinese socialist market model of development is the only way for Cuba to survive in the twenty-first century. In essence, this means that Cuba is moving to liberalize its economy with both a state sector and private sector that operate on market principles. As he explained in a somewhat joking but very serious manner to the national assembly, "We cannot hope that two plus two are five. Two plus two are four. . . . Sometimes, actually, in socialism, two plus two comes out to three."[9] The Chinese model also means continued political control by the Communist Party and a major role in the economy by the military. In the summer of 2007 Raul issued a decree that the more than 3,000 state-run enterprises would begin to operate under market-style management. Salaries and payments would be based upon merit, achievement, and profit. Caps on state salaries were removed. Some consumer goods, such as television sets and air conditioners, were made available to all Cubans. The state made major investments in infrastructure, and China provided new buses for public transportation. Private taxis were allowed. The growth rate in GDP reached 12.1 percent in 2007.

The global recession, which began in 2008 coupled with four hurricanes that hit the island that summer, had a dramatic effect on Cuba. Much of the sugar, citrus, and tobacco crops was destroyed. More than one-half a million people were without shelter and one third of the population had no electricity. Aid from Venezuela, Brazil, China, and Russia was crucial to overcome the effects of the storm. Gross domestic product growth fell to 7.3 percent in 2008 and reached a low of 1.4 percent in 2010. The economy has since gradually improved with the GDP growth rate at 3 percent in 2013. At the April 2011 Communist Party Conference, Raul announced the primary goals of his economic reforms. He indicated that the state or government had to be downsized by as many as 1.2 million workers. He announced that these displaced public workers should be able to find employment in the growing self-employment private sector as more and more entrepreneurial opportunities were opened up through further economic liberalization. There are hundreds of these opportunities that range from restaurateur to beautician, to seamstress, to renting rooms to tourists, to automobile mechanic, and to real estate and telecommunications agents. Estimates are that close to a half a million new private sector businesses or *cuentapropistas* have been created, although many observers believe that the private sector of the Cuban economy is not growing at a sufficient rate to absorb these former state employees who are looking for work. Individuals in the new business opportunities need access to credit and supplies if they are to be successful. Raul recognized this need and is moving to develop and expand banking facilities and access to credit across the island. That same year Cuban real estate laws were changed. Cubans could own, buy, and sell their homes. In 2012 it was announced that state companies could keep 50 percent of the profits for recapitalization and had the freedom to make decisions about wages.

One area that is in desperate need of reform is the two-currency system in Cuba. There are two currencies in Cuba, the convertible peso (CUC) and the regular Cuban peso (CUP). The value of the CUC is pegged to or equal to the U.S. dollar and is used extensively in the tourist sector and foreign trade. The CUP is used only in the local economy. The two-tiered system was originally designed to protect the local economy. It has done nothing but has angered those Cubans who are paid in the much lower-valued CUP and denied access to many consumer goods that are only available for those who have CUCs. Those Cubans who work in the tourist sector or in the foreign trade sector have access to CUCs or dollars and are able to raise their standard of living considerably. Those who are unable to work in these sectors have access only to the CUPs and find it almost impossible to raise their standard of living. The system runs counter to the egalitarian principle of the revolution. Raul recently announced the goal of currency reunification in 2015. He also identified several crucial areas concerning the economy that Cuba must address. These are the issues of foreign debt, foreign investment, the potential of oil and nickel, biotechnology, local food production, and tourism.

FOREIGN DEBT

Cuba's economy has always depended upon the ability of its exports to earn foreign exchange (international currency such as dollars or Euros) to be able to pay for its imports and other debts. Foreign debt has plagued Cuba since the end of the Cold War, and beginning in 2002 the island began to renegotiate much of its debt with Mexico, Panama, Spain, and Italy. In 2008, Cuba defaulted on its trade credit debt to Japan and this was renegotiated. Debt was estimated to be about $72 billion in 2010, which represented about 125 percent of the island's GDP (U.S. debt in the same year stood at 109 percent of GDP). Almost 39 percent of that debt was to Russia and another 20 percent to Venezuela.[10] There has been some improvement in the last two years largely due to debt forgiveness. In 2012 Japan forgave about 80 percent of Cuba's debt, approximate $1.4 billion. In November 2013 Mexico forgave 70 percent of Cuba's debt, close to $487 million. In July 2014 Russia forgave 90 percent of Cuba's Cold War debt of almost $32 billion. The death of Hugo Chavez in May 2013 makes the Cuban-Venezuelan relationship somewhat problematic and dependent upon future events in Venezuela. Chavez never worried much about Cuban debt, but with Chavez gone the relationship could change very quickly. Venezuela is Cuba's second-largest creditor. Cuba's ability or inability to pay its debts plays a major role in the island's ability to attract foreign investment, in particular in the export sectors of the economy such as oil, nickel, agriculture, and tourism.

FOREIGN INVESTMENT

Cuba has recently made dramatic policy changes to encourage foreign investment. From 1995 through 2002 foreign investment grew with the number of joint ventures reaching 403. This number declined to 218 by 2009. Former economic minister Jose Luis Rodriguez indicated that this was largely due to the expiration of contracts, breach of terms, and negative economic results from the ventures. Other scholars point to the excessive "red tape" associated with these agreements. Jose Azel of the Institute for Cuban and Cuban-American Studies states that the Cuban economy faces an uphill battle to gain the investments that are needed. Most of the investments in Cuba are in the more lucrative, export-oriented sectors of oil, nickel, tourism, and agriculture. For example, Great Britain and Brazil recently invested in upgrading the technology used in the sugar industry. Investments that will help the majority of the Cuban people are those that provide wide-ranging employment and provide goods to the local market. Yet, investment in Cuba to take advantage of low labor costs is problematic because there are an abundance of low-labor cost countries in the world with which Cuba must compete. Investment to supply or sell to the local market al.o has its problems because Cubans have little discretionary or disposable income and the Cuban market is relatively small.

Recognizing the great need for investment and that he has no other alternative, Raul has moved to provide more incentives. Symbolic of this is the opening, in November 2013, of the "Chinese-style" economic development, free trade zone, and container terminal in Mariel Bay. It will be the largest industrial port facility in the Caribbean. In the heart of the special economic zone is the container terminal which was funded largely by Brazil. It has state-of-the-art technology which can handle cargo from the largest ocean-going container ships and supertankers that currently cannot traverse the Panama Canal but will be able to do so in December 2015 upon completion of the work on the canal's expansion. This will dramatically open up Cuba to trade with Asia and Latin America. The port is directly tied into an extensive and modern railroad, highway, and communications infrastructure system on the island. The first of eight zones in the special economic zone will consist of a modern technology park for biotechnology and pharmaceuticals. Two other zones will focus on alternative energies and agriculture and food. Proposals from Europe, Asia, and the Americas are already being evaluated for the special economic zone. More incentives were announced. Foreign investors were given an eight-year tax holiday. After the tax holiday, the taxes on profits are to be 50 percent of the standard rate. The tax on Cuban labor was eliminated as well. It remains to be seen if these incentives will attract the necessary foreign investment. In March 2014, Raul told the nation that it must attract at least $2 billion in foreign investment each year to spur adequate economic growth.

THE CHALLENGE OF DEVELOPING THE
OIL INDUSTRY AND THE SUCCESS OF NICKEL

Cuba currently provides for about 50 percent of its oil needs and relies largely upon Venezuela for the remainder. With the continuation of heavily subsidized Venezuelan oil dependent upon the unknowns of post-Chavez politics, the development of oil fields in the very deep northern waters of Cuba could be a major factor in the success of Raul Castro's reforms and the future of the island in the long run. The U.S. Geological Survey estimates that the North Cuban Basin has between 4.6 billion and 9.3 billion barrels of oil, as well as 1 trillion cubic feet of natural gas. It was discovered initially by Repsol YPF, a Spanish oil company in 2004. Several oil companies have signed agreements with Cuba's state-run oil company, CUPET. These include Respol (Spain), Petrobras (Brazil), PDVSA (Venezuela), ONGC Videsh (India), Nordsk Hydro (Norway), Petrovietnam (Vietnam), Petronas (Malaysia), Canada's Sherritt International Corporation, Sonangol (Angola), as well as Zarubezhneft (Russia) and CNPC (China). The problem is that the search for oil in deep water (5,000 to 12,000 feet) requires a tremendous amount of investment capital and technology that is, for the most part, dominated and controlled by the United States. According to Cuban oil specialist, Jonathon Benjamin-Alvarado, the U.S. embargo is affecting the search for oil because virtually all oil platforms contain U.S. parts and technology and by U.S. law they cannot be used in Cuban waters.[11] In 2012, the drilling platform Scarabeo 9 (built specifically with less than 10 percent parts and technology from the United States and at a tremendous cost) was hauled from China to the deep waters off the north coast of Cuba. Three companies—Respol, Petronas, and PDVSA—leased the platform at a cost of $500,000 a day and found no oil. Zarubezhneft used the drilling platform Songa Mercur and failed to find oil in 2013. The current unrealized potential of oil in the North Cuban Basin continues to keep Cuba dependent upon external sources such as Venezuela.

Nickel is a crucial ingredient in the production of stainless steel, and nickel deposits in Cuba are among the largest in the world. Mining for nickel requires significant time and investment and extraction is difficult due to the presence of other metals in the nickel ore. In 1994, Sherritt International (Canada), in defiance of the U.S. embargo, engaged in the Moa joint venture with Cuba. It successfully linked Cuba's nickel resources with one of its nickel refineries in Fort Saskatchewan, Alberta. Interestingly enough, Cuba is now a joint owner of the Canadian refinery. Sherritt has become so successful that it is playing a major role in upgrading the old Soviet era mining, oil, and gas technology of Cuba. Its former CEO, Ian Delaney, was often called Fidel Castro's favorite capitalist. Sherritt is also the largest private-sector energy producer on the island. Nickel earns more foreign exchange than sugar for Cuba. Joint ventures with China's Minmetal Group should increase Cuba's exports. Currently, China receives more than 50 percent of Cuba's nickel exports.

BIOTECHNOLOGY

One of the major success stories in the Cuban economy is the biotechnology industry. It was developed to diversify the economy and end Cuba's almost complete dependence on commodities such as sugar and nickel. The industry emerged in the early 1980s to meet the growing demand for chronic disease drugs with the creation of the West Havana Scientific Cluster of more than forty organizations, 12,000 employees, and 7,000 scientists and engineers. The primary focus of its research and development is in the fields of oncology, cardiovascular technology, and HIV/AIDS. Cuba has invested more than $1 billion in the past twelve years in its biotechnology industry. More than forty therapeutic biological compounds and immunodiagnostic systems are manufactured in the program. It controls more than 900 patents and markets pharmaceutical compounds and vaccines in more than forty countries generating more than $300 million per year. Despite its critics in the United States, the European Union is developing an oncology research program with Cuba. The program is not without problems. In the 1990s, the global pharmaceutical industry went through a period of consolidations and mergers. Many European firms which worked with Cuba were bought by U.S. firms and under U.S. law were then no longer allowed to work with the island.

LOCAL FOOD PRODUCTION

For most of its history, agricultural production, in particular sugar, was primarily for export. It was based upon large private plantations that were tied directly into the international market. This model of development historically led to the importation of food for local consumption. From the beginning of the revolutionary era in 1959 to the end of the Cold War, agricultural production, in particular sugar, was based primarily on large state-run farms that were dependent upon imported tractors, parts, fertilizers, pesticides, and oil. This model of development also historically led to the importation of food for local

consumption. With the collapse of the Soviet Union, export agriculture based upon state-run farms has virtually collapsed due to the
unavailability of tractors, parts, fertilizers, and oil. Food imports for
local consumption collapsed. Cuba not only had to redevelop its
export agriculture but it had to learn to feed itself. The development
of urban agriculture to increase the supply of vegetables to cities like
Havana and Santa Clara is beginning to make a difference. Cuban
agriculture has become much more ecologically oriented as it has had
to learn to grow crops with fewer imported chemical fertilizers. Production on small farms and by peasants has increased. Reforms such
as allowing individual farmers to cultivate up to ninety-nine acres of
government land and keep their profits and increasing the number of
farmer's markets have been implemented. Yet, Cuba still must import
60 to 70 percent of its food while millions of acres of arable land are
unused. While Raul has referred to Cuba's inability to feed its people
as "a national security issue," this is an issue that must be resolved.
Interestingly enough, the United States is the largest single supplier of
food products for the island through the Trade Sanctions Reform and
Export Enhancement Act. Under this law Cuba must pay for this food
in dollars and it must be paid in advance.

TOURISM

Joint ventures between the Cuban government and foreign hotels
have developed since the mid-1990s. The industry, which is still predominantly controlled by the government and, in particular, the military through GAESA and GAVIOTA, earns nearly $3 billion a year
in revenues. Nearly 3 million tourists visited Cuba each year in 2011,
2012, and 2013. In the first half of 2014 more than 1.6 million tourists visited the island earning it more than $1.6 billion in revenue.
Havana, Varadero, Santiago, Holquin, Manzanillo, Santa Lucia, Cayo
Santa Maria, Cayo Coco, and Cayo Largo are some of the favorite
destinations. Most of the tourists are Canadian and European with
Mexican and South American tourism increasing. The Cuban government has started a process of privatization, but most believe it will
never be completely privatized because the industry has direct access
to hard currency, such as dollars and the Euro. Nonetheless, in 2013
the state-run tourist industry began to contract lodgings, excursions,
and other activities to private businesses. This was viewed as a way
to boost the growing private sector. Tourism is responsible for more
than 10 percent of the employment in Cuba. Most analysts believe that
the future of Cuban tourism is tied to the United States. Despite the

restrictions by the U.S. government, record numbers of Americans are traveling to Cuba under the people-to-people programs, which must have an educational or cultural focus. The tourism industry is one of the major lobby groups pushing the U.S. Congress to end the embargo. Should the United States end its travel restrictions, some analysts predict that a million Americans per year will travel to Cuba.

THE CHALLENGE OF RACE

Tourism is tied into the challenges of race on the island. While the revolution may have ended official or legal discrimination, unofficial discrimination is still a major problem. Raul asked for an assessment of race problems in Cuba and received a report in 2008 which clearly contradicted the mantra of the revolution that racism no longer exists. The report was quite blunt in its assessment of the status of the 62 percent of Cubans who are "black" (this includes those who identify as mixed or mestizo). It found that black impoverishment had increased over the past twenty-five years and Cuban leadership was largely white with 80 percent of the faculty at the University of Havana white and 72 percent of the nation's scientists and technicians white. Ninety-eight percent of the private land in Cuba was held by whites. Only 5 percent of the state cooperatives were controlled by blacks. The prison population was 85 percent black. It noted that 85 percent of all Cubans who had fled the island to the United States were white. Thus, remittances benefitted white Cubans rather than blacks. These remittances have aided in the establishment of "white" businesses in Cuba and have contributed to the economic gap between whites and blacks.

Heriberto Feraudy, the former Cuban ambassador to Zambia, Botswana, Nigeria, and Mozambique, and Esteban Morales, an economist who writes on race, fear that Raul's move toward a Chinese model with state payrolls being slashed and an increase in private entrepreneurship on the island will hurt Afro-Cubans. They argue that blacks are not well positioned to take advantage of these changes.[12] The tourist sector, because of the access to hard currency such as dollars, allows many Cubans to get ahead economically. The problem is that this sector has not been open to hiring Afro-Cubans. Documented cases of hiring discrimination are quite common. Among Afro-Cubans there is also a real fear of the return of the exiled "white" and wealthy Cubans from Miami. Like many of the youth in Cuba, young Afro-Cubans have withdrawn from the political processes and others show their resistance in other "underground" ways. Among the younger blacks the popularity of Afro-Cuban religions, such as the rebellious Rastafarianism, are increasing dramatically. Afro-Cuban artists, musicians, and writers are in the forefront of exposing and challenging the unofficial racial discrimination on the island. This issue festers just under the surface of Cuban society and must be addressed as economic change comes to the island.

A FRUSTRATED YOUNGER GENERATION

Brian Latell argues that one of the major groups that Raul must somehow "win over" is the so-called lost generation, the young people of Cuba who were born primarily in the post-1975/1980 era, the eighteen to forty year olds.[13] This is a generation that could be the most explosive social group that the government faces during this period of transition. They have no historical memory of the revolution; they have grown up in an era of economic hardship and, to some extent, global isolation; and according to scholar Damian Fernandez they are frustrated adults.[14] This frustration is a result of the mismatch between their expectations and reality. Their high expectations are driven by their high levels of education and the inability of the government to deliver on its promises. Many have become disenchanted, disappointed, and alienated from the system. It is evident in their music, fashions, slang, tattoos, graffiti, and their informal resistance to and withdrawal from the Cuban political system.[15] Their individualism is at odds with the collectivist ideal of the revolution. They often evade agriculture volunteer work, do not attend neighborhood organizational meetings, do not vote, evade the draft, drop out of school, and engage in criminal activities and drug usage. Political participation is viewed as meaningless. As one young man who had recently left the University of Havana confided,

> My grandfather is still a true believer . . . My parents followed the rules and worked hard but have never gotten ahead . . . For me, it is obvious that Raul does not care or he would be moving faster to make change. Everything is for the future, but the future never gets here. For me, I don't even have any dreams of the future. There is no future here.[16]

Yet, the continued failure of the government to provide change and a meaningful future for these young people could turn this frustration from political apathy to active political opposition. There is an underground rock movement, led by the punk band Porno Para Ricardo, which is highly critical of the government. Its music and albums are best sellers across the island in the underground (illegal) market. Since 2006 students who attend the unauthorized concerts by the dissident Carlos Varela wear white bracelets with the word *cambio* (change) written on it. The very popular Varela is known for his antigovernment protest songs and he is regularly denied a government permit to put on a public concert. In fact, a few university students are beginning to show some overt opposition to government policies. In late 2007 disgruntled students at the University of Oriente staged a sit-in and detained the dean of the school after complaining of crime on campus and the rape of three women. The government sent representatives to Santiago, met with the students, and met their demands for greater security on campus and the dismissal of the dean. Shortly after this incident, students in Cienfuegos organized a protest demanding greater civil liberties. Student leaders of this protest were "quietly" dismissed from the university. In January 2008 then national assembly Chief Ricardo Alarcon was confronted by angry students at an elite computer school. Students complained about one-party elections, the lack of work opportunities, the lack of access to the Internet, and the inability to travel outside Cuba.[17] In October 2009 students at the Superior Institute of Art protested censorship, the lack of freedom, and the living conditions at the school. In December 2010 students chanted antigovernment slogans when they were denied the ability to watch a soccer match in a theater in Santa Clara. Student-led uprisings and protests in Egypt (2011), Ukraine (2013), and Venezuela (2014) have affected university students in Cuba. One student stated, "Seeing the marches or strikes on television is something that I envy. That freedom of protesting in front of the governmental institutions, as in Ukraine or Venezuela, we need it in Cuba."[18] Given that many in the revolutionary generation were students when they became active against Batista, the government is very sensitive to student demands and protests. Young Cubans have increasingly turned to the Internet to express their dissatisfaction with the government.

THE YOUNGER GENERATION, THE INTERNET, AND DISSIDENT BLOGGERS

The Internet in Cuba is controlled by the Telecommunications Company of Cuba (ETESCA). While Cubans have access to the Internet via the government-run Internet cafes, they are expensive, slow, and the content is controlled. Freedom House estimates that only about 5 percent of Cubans have access to the open Internet and these include government officials, doctors, engineers, and regime-approved journalists.

Internationally known dissident and blogger Yoani Sanchez indicates that it is common for those who have access to the open Internet to copy newspaper articles and news accounts to pen drives and share them widely with those who lack this access. While the overall dissident movement has grown and become more diverse (see Chapter 8) since the mid-1990s, it is led by the post-1980 generation's blogger underground. Despite the intimidation, beatings, and jail sentences and the Cuban government's attempts to restrict their access to the Internet, these bloggers continue to get their articles and reports out to the international community often via illegal satellite dishes and proxy servers that are located outside Cuba. In May 2014 Sanchez and her husband, Reinaldo Escobar, unveiled *14ymedio*, the first dissident-run, independent online newspaper that is produced in Cuba. At this point in time the vast majority of Cubans on the island still do not have access to the new *14ymedio* or any of the dissident blogs. The "cat and mouse" game played by the Cuban government and the dissident bloggers will continue as technology improves and as Cuba continues its transition under Raul Castro. Cuba has turned to China in an effort to upgrade its Internet infrastructure which is still in the dial-up access era.

CHINA AND CUBA

It is China that is now having the most impact on the economy of the island. Raul believes that the application of the Chinese model will allow Cuba to prosper in the twenty-first century. He has sought advice from the Chinese for more than ten years. China is Cuba's second-largest trading partner and its largest source of credit today. China financed the new fiber-optic Internet cable that now runs from Venezuela to Cuba. It has invested in energy, agriculture, nickel, and biotechnology on the island. The visit of current president Xi Jinping in July 2014 was symbolic of the deepening economic ties between the countries. During the visit he inaugurated a factory that makes biosensors to monitor the blood sugar of diabetics. More than fifty entrepreneurs from China accompanied Xi Jinping to investigate investment opportunities. While there is clearly an ideological affinity between China and Cuba, most observers see China's policy toward Cuba driven by pragmatism and strategic economic interests. They point out that Chinese investments in Latin America and the rest of the world are in both left and right leaning governments. While China may have the most impact on the immediate economic future of Cuba, most observers recognize that this could change overnight with a change in U.S. policy toward Cuba.

UNITED STATES AND CUBA

In the election of 2008 Barack Obama campaigned on a policy of willingness to engage in diplomacy with friends and enemies without preconditions. He received 38 percent of the Cuban American vote in Florida and about half of the Cuban American vote under the age of forty-four. Initial reforms in 2009, such as ending the travel restrictions by Cuban Americans to see their families and the restrictions on sending remittances to their families coupled with 2011 reforms which made it easier for Americans (journalists, academics, students, business groups, church groups, and others) to travel to Cuba, led many to believe that a dramatic change of U.S. policy toward Cuba had begun. Yet, beyond this, little has changed in U.S. policy. In the 2012 election, Obama received 49 percent of the Cuban American vote, while Mitt Romney received 47 percent. Hopes were raised once again in December 2013 when President Obama shook hands with Raul Castro at the funeral of Nelson Mandela. Recent cooperation in areas of drug interdiction, oil spill mitigation, and immigration has created a network for greater interaction at the official level.

Yet, the Obama administration has not seen Cuba policy as a priority and it has not been willing to take on the hardline Cuba lobby in the U.S. Congress. In fact, it has continued many of the Bush administration policies such as using the United States Agency for International Development (AID) programs to stir up political dissent. Alan Gross, who worked for Development Alternatives Incorporated which had received a $6 million grant from AID to "promote democracy," deployed sensitive government-controlled technology to a secret communications system. His job, as he explained it to CNN, was to set it up and "test to see if it works." Gross was arrested in December 2009 and sentenced to fifteen years in prison for acts against the territorial integrity of Cuba. AID created a "Cuban Twitter" program to foment dissent among the young in Cuba. It also used Venezuelan, Costa Rican, and Peruvian youth to pose as aid workers in various health and civic improvement programs. The real intention of these "workers" was to meet with dissidents and foment political opposition to the regime. Exposure of these programs to the international media has not only been an embarrassment to the Obama administration but it has undermined the legitimacy of many of the authentic health and civic programs sponsored by the United States and other international agencies. Hardline anti-Castro members in Congress are in key positions to block the Obama administration's limited attempts to change the policy. The leaders of this opposition group include Democratic senator Robert Menendez from New Jersey,

Republican senator Marco Rubio from Florida, and Republican representatives Ileana Ros-Lehtinen and Mario Diaz-Balart from Florida. They have either routinely blocked Obama's few initiatives that were designed to relax U.S. policy or blocked any Obama executive branch appointees that support a liberalization of U.S. policy.

Most scholars see the U.S. embargo and other economic sanctions against Cuba as a failure no matter how one measures the term failure. The embargo has allowed Cuban officials to place the blame for the economic failures on the United States rather than themselves. It has not prevented a majority of the countries in the world from trading with Cuba. It limits U.S. business opportunities in terms of trade with or investment in Cuba. It serves only to restrict American travel to the island. Perhaps the only so-called benefit is that U.S. sanctions have made it difficult for Cuba to fully develop its oil and biotechnology industries and have not allowed Cuba to reach the full potential of its growing tourist industry.

The U.S. embargo is routinely condemned by virtually every country and major international organization in the world. There is rapidly growing support within the United States for the normalization of relations with Cuba. A majority of Americans, Floridians, Cuban Americans, and Cuban Americans in Miami support an end to the U.S. embargo of the island. The tourist and agribusiness industries routinely lobby Congress to change the trade laws with Cuba. Many notable Cuban American business leaders, such as Andres Fanjul, who, with his three brothers, is the head of the Fanjul Corporation, the largest sugar company in the world, have publically urged the Obama administration to expand trade ties with the island. Noted Cuban specialist, Julia Sweig, and many others indicate that with the dramatic economic changes currently taking place, the United States has chosen to remain on the sidelines while other countries have entered the game and are taking advantage of the economic opportunities and the possibility of shaping the future of Cuban development. The U.S. International Trade Commission estimates that the United States is losing at least $1.2 billion in revenues from trade with Cuba. This is to say nothing of the millions of government dollars wasted in enforcing the more than fifty-year-old, failed embargo.

CUBA ON THE BRINK OF THE POST-CASTRO ERA

Raul Castro, with the support of the major power brokers on the island and the increasing economic support of China and, currently, Venezuela, will be able to implement his economic changes through the end of his own self-imposed term as president. The dominance of the Communist Party in Cuban politics and the continued role of the military in the economy will no doubt be maintained. The pace of economic changes will depend largely upon Raul and his own political instincts. The question with which he will struggle is how much he can decentralize and open up the economy to the private sector and foreign investment, yet assure the continued political dominance of the Communist Party and the role of the military in the economy after he leaves office in 2018. At the same time he must continue to maintain the promise of the three pillars of the revolution: free education, cradle-to-grave healthcare benefits, and guaranteed social security.

At this point there is no reason to doubt Raul's promise to step down and turn Cuba over to his self-appointed successor Miguel Diaz-Canel, who will be the first leader in the revolutionary era born after 1959. Diaz-Canel, an engineering professor and former minister of education, is a reformist within the mold of Raul and has a reputation for being able to negotiate with provincial party leaders. Having been a successful provincial leader in Holguin and Villa Clara, Diaz-Canel understands that these leaders are very protective of their own power bases, who, according to scholar Arturo Lopez-Levy, are "kings in their own provinces." The evidence indicates that he also has strong ties to the military. Raul has a reputation for picking the best man for the job and it appears that he has set the stage for an orderly change within the Communist Party elites in Cuba. Yet, it is important to note that there is a history of those who are being groomed for the top leadership positions finding themselves removed from favor with little notice. Fidel protégés Carlos Lage (former secretary of the Council of Ministers) and Felipe Perez Roque (former foreign minister) are cases in point. The next leader of Cuba will face the daunting and risk-filled task of trying to lead and implement his own vision for Cuba within the shadows of Fidel and Raul Castro as long as they are alive. Overcoming the legacy of more than a half a century of Castro brothers' dominance and rule, the next leader will more than likely have to look over his shoulder periodically and how he handles the first situation in which his policies are opposed by the Castro brothers will speak volumes as to the nature of the political transition.

There are two primary institutions that will play a primary role in success or failure of political and economic continuity in the post-Castro era: the Communist Party and the military. Scholars differ in assessing the degree of institutionalization of the Communist Party with some seeing it dependent upon the Castro brothers and subject to collapse should they no longer control the key positions or should they die and others seeing the recent efforts of Raul Castro as successfully making the party independent of individual leaders. The key challenge in the post-Castro era is standardizing the leadership selection process of the Communist Party. Another problem is that the Communist Party has little legitimacy among the Cuban people with less than 3 percent of the population serving as members. This, coupled with a failure to standardize the party leadership selection process, could present political problems. The FAR, on the other hand, has legitimacy among Cubans as it has never been deployed to crackdown on political opposition or demonstrations. As long as it retains a key position in the economy, the FAR should work to continue the current system. That key position is maintained by the presence of trained technocratic military managers in key state-run organizations and so-called entrepreneurial soldiers who are charged with making a profit in the large joint ventures. With access to international currencies (the dollar and the Euro), widespread corruption and a growing economic gap between these military entrepreneurs and other members of the military could serve to delegitimize the FAR. There is also the possibility of a split between the politically favored generals who now lead economic enterprises and a young, officer corps that sees this as a threat to the professionalization of the military. These "young Turks" may play a role in demanding changes in the military and its role in the economy just as they did in the post-communist transition in Eastern Europe. A question that is often asked is how the FAR would respond to widespread political unrest of the nature that the secret police and domestic intelligence could not contain. While the FAR clearly would act to protect its own interests, Cuban specialist Brian Latell and most observers argue that the FAR will not use violence against the local population. There will be no Tiananmen Square in Cuba.

Whether it is Diaz-Canel or someone else, the new leader will face a different Cuba. He will face a changing civil society (organized groups in society) consisting of the traditional communist-controlled mass organizations and an increasing number of autonomous groups. Mass organizations were designed as instruments of control and include the Cuban Federation of Women, the Committees for the Defense of the Revolution, the National Association of Small Farmers, the Federation of University Students, the Confederation of Cuban Workers, and others. The mass organizations are losing legitimacy among young people who skip meetings and see the leadership as unresponsive to their needs. Members of the official labor unions express their dissatisfaction through tardiness, stealing or destroying government property, and moonlighting to earn hard currency. Despite intimidation and harassment, there has been a growth in the number of independent groups such as the United Council of Cuban Workers (education, healthcare, and transportation workers in fifteen provinces) and the Independent Workers Confederation (agriculture, healthcare, education, and social service workers from sixty-five unions in twelve different provinces) that function in the open. There is also political space available for new groups to organize independently of the government such as those that have engaged in cooperative farming (referred to as the Basic Units of Cooperative Production) and the new private sector consisting of restaurants (*paladares*) and hundreds of other small businesses. There is a growing and diverse dissident movement (see Chapter 8) that operates in the open, even though it is still intimidated and harassed by the government. Many of these groups have developed strong ties to support groups off the island.

Within Cuban civil society is a younger generation that is frustrated and alienated from a political system in which they no longer believe in the official ideology nor support its institutions. It is the younger generation that could become politically active under the right circumstances. Students, who have played a role in Cuban politics since the Generation of 1930, could possibly form the basis of a broad social movement should some acute political crisis or economic event occur that could serve as a catalyst to give rise to key, well-known student leaders. It is this generation of students that longs for a new Cuba in which there are greater choices and opportunities to live a productive and meaningful life on the island. It is this generation that the new, post-Castro Cuban leader will have to begin to respond despite the island's authoritarian history. Yoani Sanchez stated it best in her Generation Y blog of September 2, 2014,

Born during the Special Period, they have grown up trapped in the dual currency system, and when they get their degrees Raul Castro will no longer be in power. They are the more than one hundred thousand young people just starting college throughout the country. Their brief biographies include educational experiments, battles of ideas, and the emergence of new technologies. They know more about X-Men than about Elipidio Valdes [the Mambi colonel cartoon character on state-run television in the 1970s who fought for the liberation of Cuba from Spain] and only remember Fidel Castro from old photos and archived documentaries. They are the Wi-Fi kids with their pirate networks, raised with the "packets" of copied shows and illegal satellite dishes. Some nights they would connect through routers and play strategy video games that made them feel powerful and free. Whoever wants to know them should know that they've had "emerging teachers" [a failed Cuban program designed to upgrade the quality of education in the schools] since elementary school and were taught grammar, math and ideology via television screens. However, they ended up being the least ideological of the Cubans who today inhabit this Island, the most cosmopolitan and with the greatest vision of the future.

The constants in Cuban history will continue to influence the post-Castro era. The country is an island nation with a small local market that must depend on its ability to export products to the global market to be successful. It must seek to diversify its economy to allow it to weather global economic crises. It must continue to seek foreign investment. Adequate foreign investment can only come from economically powerful countries. Despite the fact that Cuba currently is developing strong ties to China and is moving toward the so-called Chinese model, it is the United States that still holds the wildcard to the future of the island. If, or perhaps when the United States plays its wildcard and ends the embargo, the future of the island will change radically. An economic opening with the United States will have almost an immediate impact on three of the most important industries on the island: oil, biotechnology, and tourism. In addition, it will begin to address the local food issue. The tremendous potential of future U.S. investments on the island will add pressure for greater economic and political transparency in Cuba. In a post-Castro Cuba, playing the U.S. wildcard will, without a doubt, alter the political and economic decisions of the military and the Communist Party. One of the constants in Cuban history has been the struggle for all Cuban voices to be heard in its political system. A change in U.S. policy will affect the growing and diverse dissident movement on the island. Most agree that a change in U.S. policy will enhance that struggle at this point in time. From 1898 through 1959 U.S. relations with Cuba were hegemonic in nature and were one of the reasons for Castro's revolution. Should the United States re-engage with Cuba, the question that remains is will that relationship be one based upon a return to hegemony or will revolutionary Cuba insist upon a relationship based upon mutual political respect and economic interests.

POSTSCRIPT

President Obama made an historic announcement at noon on December 17, 2014, that the United States will reestablish full diplomatic relations with Cuba. In his announcement he stated that "these

50 years have shown that isolation has not worked . . . it's time for a new approach." The negotiations that led to this announcement were encouraged by Pope Francis and were facilitated by the Canadian government. The decision by Obama will ensure that the United States will have a greater role in the Cuban transition under Raul Castro and his successor.

NOTES

1. Manuel Roig-Franzia, "Raul Castro, Leader with a Freer Hand," *Washington Post*, February 19, 2008, found at http://www.washingtonpost.com/wp-dyn/content/article/2008/02/19/AR2008021902962.html.

2. Bardach, *Without Fidel*, 191.

3. Ibid., 193

4. Brian Latell, "Raul Castro: Confronting Fidel's Legacy in Cuba," *Washington Quarterly* 30:3(Summer 2007) found at http://ctp.iccas.miami.edu/website_documents/washington%20qtrly%20may%2007.pdf.

5. Bardach, *Without Fidel*, 216.

6. Anthony Boadle, "Raul Castro Calls for More Policy Debate in Cuba," *Washington Post*, December 20, 2006, found at http://www.washingtonpost.com/wp-dyn/content/article/2006/12/20/AR2006122001825.html.

7. Jaime Suchlicki, "The Party Is On," *Cuba Transition Project*, 135 (December 9, 2010) found at http://ctp.iccas.miami.edu/FOCUS_Web/Issue135.htm.

8. Bardach, *Without Fidel*, 186.

9. Ibid., 260.

10. Hans de Salas del Valle, "Cuban Debt Crisis," *Cuban Transition Project of the Institute for Cuban and Cuban-American Studies, University of Miami* 147 (August 9, 2011) http://ctp.iccas.miami.edu/FOCUS_Web/Issue147.htm.

11. David Lagesse, "Cuba's Oil Quest to Continue Despite Deep Water Disappointment," *National Geographic News* (November 19, 2012) found at http://news.nationalgeographic.com/news/energy/2012/11/121119-cuba-oil-quest/.

12. Juan O. Tamayo, "Racism Remains an Issue in Cuba, Officials Say," *Cuban Human Rights* (June 3, 2011) found at http://cubarights.blogspot.com/2011/06/racism-remains-issue-in-cuba-officials.html.

13. Latell, "Raul Castro Confronts Fidel's Legacy in Cuba," 53–65 found at http://ctp.iccas.miami.edu/website_documents/washington%20qtrly%20may%2007.pdf.

14. Damian Fernandez, "The Good, the Bad, and the Ugly," in *Looking Forward: Comparative Perspectives on Cuba's Transition*, edited by Marifeli Perez-Stable (Notre Dame: University of Notre Dame Press, 2007), 109–113.

15. Ibid.

16. Interview by the author, Havana, June 4, 2012.

17. Bardach, *Without Fidel*, 258.

18. Ivan Garcia, "Opposition Protests in Venezuela Worry Not a Few Ordinary Cubans," from the blog *Diario de Cuba*, Febuary 23, 2014. Translating Cuba: English Translations of Cuban Bloggers. http://translatingcuba.com/opposition-protests-in-venezuela-worry-not-a-few-ordinary-cubans-ivan-garcia/.

Notable People in the History of Cuba

All of the individuals listed are discussed in the text where you will find additional information. Those marked with an asterisk have a formal biography in the text. Spanish names often include the primary name of the mother. For example, in Fidel Castro Ruz, Ruz refers to the primary last name of his mother and Castro refers to the primary last name of his father. These names are arranged by alphabetical order based upon the father's primary last name which is normally used as the last name in everyday conversation.

Reinaldo Arenas (1943–1990). Arenas was a poet, novelist, and writer of international reputation who was convicted in 1973 for ideological deviation and publishing abroad without official consent. He came to the United States in 1980 during the Mariel exodus and died of AIDS. He is perhaps best known for his book *Before Night Falls*, but others include *The Doorman, Singing from the Well, The Assault, Old Rosa*, and *Mona and Other Tales*.

Francisco de Arrongo y Parreno (1765–1839). Arrongo was a Creole planter and Cuban nationalist who promoted the development of the sugar industry (in particular applying the steam engine for use at the mills) and infrastructure to support it in the late 1700s and early 1800s. He successfully lobbied Charles III of Spain to allow free and unlimited importation of slaves to Cuba.

Fulgencio Batista y Zaldivar (1901–1973).* Batista was a mulatto army sergeant who came to dominate Cuban politics from 1933 to 1959. He led the sergeants' revolt that toppled Gerardo Machado in 1933 and then a *golpe* in 1952 to seize the presidency. His corrupt and repressive government was toppled by Fidel Castro in 1959. He died in exile in Spain.

Fidel Castro Ruz (1926–).* Fidel Castro was the charismatic, bearded leader of the revolution that toppled the Batista dictatorship. He led the country until 2006 when an illness led him to allow his brother Raul Castro to become president. His father owned a sugar plantation in Oriente Province. He studied law at the University of Havana and led the attack on Moncada Barracks in Santiago in 1953.

Raul Castro Ruz (1930–).* Raul Castro is the brother of Fidel Castro who was the leader of the Cuban Armed Forces until becoming president in 2006 upon the illness of his brother. Raul believes that Cuba should pursue the Chinese model of socialist development.

Carlos Manuel de Cespedes (1819–1874). Cespedes was a Creole lawyer and planter from Bayamo who declared Cuban independence and started the Ten Years' War in 1868. He supported an end to slavery on the island and some consider him to be the father of modern Cuba.

Eduardo Chibas (1907–1951). Chibas was a charismatic student leader and leader of the Ortodoxo Party. He greatly influenced Fidel Castro and was a candidate for the presidency in 1952. He accidentally killed himself in 1951 during a radio broadcast.

Camilo Cienfuegos (1932–1959). Cienfuegos was a very popular commander of the 26th of July Movement who was killed in a plane crash in 1959.

Jose Antonio Echeverria (1932–1957). Echeverria was a charismatic student leader who was president of the Federation of University Students and organized the Revolutionary Directorate that waged an urban terrorist war against Fulgencio Batista. He was killed in 1957 leading an attack on Batista. He was perhaps the only person capable of challenging Fidel Castro as the leader of the revolutionary groups.

Bishop Jose Diaz de Espada y Fernandez (1756–1832). Espada was one of the founders of the Economic Society in the early 1800s. He was responsible for liberalizing the curriculum at the Real Colegio Seminario de San Carlos in Havana that became a breeding ground for Cuban nationalists in the 1800s.

Vilma Espin (1930–2007). Espin was the daughter of a lawyer for the Bacardi Rum Company and an original member of the 26th of July Movement. She was an assistant to Raul Castro in the Sierra Maestra and later married him. She became the unofficial first lady of revolutionary Cuba. She served as president of the Cuban Federation of Women.

Evaristo Estenoz (?–1912). Estenoz was a former slave and veteran of the Cuban wars of independence. He became the leader of the Independent Party of Color that led an African uprising in 1912 that was crushed by Cuban and U.S. troops.

Tomas Estrada Palma (1835–1908). Estrada was the first president of the Republic of Cuba from 1902 until 1906, when the second occupation of the island by the United States began.

Jose Miguel Gomez (1858–1921). Gomez was the leader of the Liberal Party and second president of the Republic of Cuba from 1909 to 1913.

Maximo Gomez (1836–1905). Gomez was a Dominican who led the rebel military forces during the Cuban wars of independence against Spain.

Ramon Grau San Martin (1887–1969). Grau was the dean of the medical school at the University of Havana, leader of the Autentico Party, and president of the Republic of Cuba from 1933 to 1934 and 1945 to 1949. When Grau was president in 1933, he came to represent the goals and dreams of the Generation of 1930. His second term in office was characterized by much corruption.

Ernesto "Che" Guevara (1928–1967).* Che Guevara was an Argentinian medical doctor who was a commander of the 26th of July

Movement and a confidant of Fidel Castro. He was an intellectual who wrote extensively on guerrilla warfare. He died in an ill-fated attempt to stage a revolution in Bolivia in 1967. He died young and has become the iconic face of revolutionaries across the world.

Antonio Maceo (1845–1896). Maceo is known as the "Bronze Titan"; he was perhaps the most effective rebel general during the Cuban wars of independence. He was an expert in guerrilla warfare. Today he is considered one of the most revered and beloved figures in Cuban history.

Gerardo Machado (1871–1939). Machado was the president of the Republic of Cuba from 1925 to 1933. His corrupt and repressive regime set the groundwork for the sergeants' revolt of 1933 led by Fulgencio Batista.

Jose Marti (1853–1895).* Marti was an intellectual, poet, statesman, and revolutionary. He is considered to be the father of Cuban independence.

Jose Antonio Mella (1905–1929). Mello was a charismatic student leader, secretary of the Federation of University Students, and the first student leader of the Generation of 1930 to become a national figure. He was exiled in 1927 and murdered in Mexico two years later on orders from Cuban president Gerardo Machado.

Mario Garcia Menocal (1886–1941). Menocal fought in the Cuban wars of independence and was president of the Republic of Cuba from 1913 to 1921.

Arnaldo Ochoa Sanchez (1930–1989). Ochoa joined the 26th of July Movement and fought with Camilo Cienfuegos during the revolution. His distinguished military career included command of Cuban troops in Angola. He was accused of drug trafficking and treason in 1989 and executed. Some argue that he had become so popular that he was a political threat to either Fidel or Raul Castro.

Frank Pais (1934–1957). Pais was a school teacher and the leader of an underground group in Santiago which later merged with the 26th of July Movement. He then became the leader of the 16th of July Movement in Oriente. He was killed in Santiago in 1957.

Carlos Prio Socarras (1903–1977). Prio represented the Autentico Party and was the president of the Republic of Cuba from 1949 to 1952.

Jose Antonio Saco (1797–1879). Saco was a leading intellectual and nationalist in the 1800s. He supported Cuban self-rule and an end to slavery.

Celia Sanchez (1920–1980). Sanchez served with Fidel Castro in the Sierra Maestra. She was Castro's personal secretary and confidant until her death from cancer in 1980.

Yoani Sanchez (1975–). Sanchez is an internationally known for her Generation Y blog which is a critical portrayal of everyday life in Cuba. The University of Havana graduate was named by *Time* magazine in 2008 to its list of 100 Most Influential People in the World.

Haydee Santamaria (1923–1980). She and her brother, Abel, were with Fidel Castro in the attack on the Moncada Barracks in 1953. She ran the 26th of July Movement's fund-raising activities in Miami, served as a member of the Central Committee of the Communist Party, and headed the revolutionary government's cultural center. She committed suicide in 1980.

Tomas Terry y Adan (1808–1886). Terry was an immigrant from Venezuela and the first Cuban planter to use electricity in his sugar mill outside Cienfuegos in the mid- to late 1800s. He amassed a fortune from sugar.

Father Felix Varela Morales (1788–1853). Varela was a leading intellectual and nationalist. He supported self-rule and an end to slavery.

Diego Velazquez de Cuellar (1465–1524). Velazquez was the first Spanish governor of Cuba until his death in 1524.

Alfredo Zayas y Alfonso (1861–1934). Zayas was a member of the Liberal Party and president of the Republic of Cuba from 1921 to 1925.

Bibliographic Essay

The literature on the history of Cuba is unbelievably extensive and diverse. For those who want access to archives in the United States concerning Cuban history, Louis A. Perez, Jr.'s *A Guide to Cuban Collections in the United States* (Westport: Greenwood, 1991) is perhaps the best. For scholars or those who want an overview of the past research on Cuba, I would initially suggest looking at Louis A. Perez, Jr.'s *Essays on Cuban History: Historiography and Research* (Gainesville: University Press of Florida, 1995) and Damian Fernandez's (ed.) *Cuban Studies since the Revolution* (Gainesville: University Press of Florida, 1992). Although somewhat dated, these volumes are an excellent place to start. For a general and scholarly historical overview, Hugh Thomas's *Cuba: The Pursuit of Freedom* (New York: Harper and Row, 1971) is meticulously researched, detailed, and well written, although the general reader may find it rather lengthy at more than 1,500 pages. More accessible general histories include Louis A. Perez, Jr.'s *Cuba: Between Reform and Revolution*, 3rd ed. (New York: Oxford University Press, 2006) and Jaime Suchlicki's *Cuba: From Columbus to Castro*, 5th ed. (Dulles, VA: Potomac Books, 2002). For a cultural history of Cuba focusing on its relationship with the United States, Louis A. Perez, Jr's *On Becoming Cuban* (Chapel Hill: University of North Carolina Press,

1999) is a masterful work that is already considered by many to be a classic.

For a study of the early history of Cuba, one should see Irene Wright's *The Early History of Cuba, 1492–1586* (New York: Macmillan, 1916). The edited book *Slaves, Sugar, and Colonial Society: Travel Accounts of Cuba, 1801–1899* (Wilmington, DE: Scholarly Resources, 1992) by Louis A. Perez, Jr., gives the reader insightful firsthand travel accounts of Cuban society in the 1800s. On the topic of slavery, an excellent scholarly study is Arthur Corwin's *Spain and the Abolition of Slavery in Cuba, 1817–1886* (Austin: University of Texas Press, 1967). I would also suggest David Murray's *Odious Commerce: Britain, Spain and the Abolition of the Cuban Slave Trade* (London: Cambridge University Press, 1980), Rebecca Scott's *Slave Emancipation in Cuba* (Princeton, NJ: Princeton University Press, 1985), and Miguel Barnet's and Esteban Montejo's *The Autobiography of a Runaway Slave*, Revised Edition (Willimantic, CT: Curbstone Press, 1994).

The best study of the role of race during the struggle for Cuba's independence is Ada Ferrer's *Insurgent Cuba: Race, Nation, and Revolution, 1868–1898* (Chapel Hill: University of North Carolina Press, 1999). Other studies of Cuba's struggle for independence include Louis A. Perez, Jr.'s *Cuba Between Empires, 1878–1902* (Pittsburgh: University of Pittsburgh Press, 1983), Philip Foner's *The Spanish-Cuban-American War and the Birth of American Imperialism*, 2 Volumes (New York: Monthly Review Press, 1972), and Louis A. Perez, Jr.'s *The War of 1898: The United States and Cuba in History and Historiography* (Chapel Hill: University of North Carolina Press, 1998).

For an overview that focuses on Cuba in the first part of the twentieth century, once should see Charles Chapman's *A History of the Cuban Republic* (New York: Macmillan, 1927), Louis A. Perez, Jr.'s *Cuba under the Platt Amendment* (Pittsburgh: University of Pittsburgh Press, 1986), and his *Intervention, Revolution, and Politics in Cuba, 1913–1921* (Pittsburgh: University of Pittsburgh Press, 1978). For an excellent study of the sugar industry during this era, one should see Alan Dye's *Cuban Sugar in the Age of Mass Production: Technology and the Economy of the Sugar Central, 1899–1929* (Palo Alto, CA: Stanford University Press, 1998). For another overview of the sugar industry before the revolution John Paul Rathbone's *The Sugar King of Havana* (New York: Penguin Press, 2010) is a fascinating read. For a similar overview of the rum industry before the revolution, I would suggest Tom Gjelten's *Bacardi and the Long Fight for Cuba* (New York: Penguin Books, 2008).

One should see Louis A. Perez, Jr.'s *Army Politics in Cuba, 1989–1958* (Pittsburgh: University of Pittsburgh Press, 1976) for the best scholarly study of the role of the military as it developed in twentieth-century Cuba and its role in the revolutionary upheavals of 1933 and 1959. For the best studies of the role of students in Cuba from the Generation of 1930 to the revolution see Jaime Suchlicki's *University Students and Revolution in Cuba* (Coral Gables, FL: University of Miami Press, 1969) and Justo Carillo's *Cuba 1933: Students, Yankees, and Soldiers* (Coral Gables, FL: University of Miami North-South Center, 1994).

For an overview of the Batista years leading up to the revolution one should see Samuel Farber's *Revolution and Reaction in Cuba, 1933–1960* (Middletown, CT: Wesleyan University Press, 1976) and Robert Tabor's *M-26, the Biography of a Revolution* (New York: Lyle Stuart, 1961). Tabor was a journalist who lived with the guerrillas in the 26th of July Movement. Julia Sweig's *Inside the Cuban Revolution* (Cambridge: Harvard University Press, 2002) supports the argument that the Cuban urban underground played just as much a role in the revolution as Castro's guerrilla warfare in the countryside. In an earlier work that discusses the same theme, one should see Carlos Franqui's *Diary of the Cuban Revolution* (New York: Viking Press, 1980). Two other important books are Ernesto "Che" Guevara's *Episodes of the Cuban Revolutionary War, 1956–1958*, edited by Mary-Alice Waters (New York: Pathfinder, 1996) and *Revolutionary Struggle, 1947–1958*, volume one of *The Selected Works of Fidel Castro*, edited by Rolando Bonachea and Nelson Valdes (Cambridge: MIT Press, 1972). Other books that discuss the historical events of the 1950s include Neil McCauley's *A Rebel in Cuba: An American Memoir* (Chicago: Quadrangle, 1970), Rufo Lopez-Fresquet's *My Fourteen Months with Castro* (New York: World Publishing, 1966), Gladys Mariel Garcia-Perez's *Insurrection and Revolution: Armed Struggle in Cuba, 1952–1959* (Boulder, CO: Rienner, 1998), and Anthony DePalma's *The Man who Invented Fidel* (New York: Public Affairs, 2006).

For studies that focus on Cuba during the 1960s, one should see K.S. Karol's *Guerrillas in Power: The Course of the Cuban Revolution* (New York: Hill and Wang, 1970), Efran Cordova's *Castro and the Cuban Labor Movement: Statecraft and Strategy in a Revolutionary Period, 1959–1961* (Lanham, MD: University Press of America, 1987), Theodore Draper's *Castroism: Theory and Practice* (New York: Praeger, 1965) and his *Castro's Revolution: Myths and Realities* (New York: Praeger, 1962), Andre Suarez's *Cuba: Castroism and Communism* (Cambridge: MIT Press, 1967), Rene Dumont's *Socialism and Development* (New York: Grove, 1970), Richard Fagen's *The Transformation of Political Culture in Cuba* (Stanford, CA: Stanford University Press, 1969), Edward Gonzalez's *Cuba under Castro: The Limits of Charisma* (Boston: Houghton Mifflin, 1974),

Carmelo Mesa-Lago's (ed.) *Revolutionary Change in Cuba* (Pittsburgh: University of Pittsburgh Press, 1971), Maurice Zeitlin's *Revolutionary Politics and the Cuban Working Class* (Princeton, NJ: Princeton University Press, 1967), and Mario Llerena's *The Unsuspected Revolution: The Birth and Rise of Castroism* (Ithaca, NY: Cornell University Press, 1978).

For other very insightful overviews that emphasize the Castro years during the Cold War, one should see Juan M. Del Aguila's *Cuba: Dilemmas of a Revolution* (Boulder, CO: Westview, 1984) and Jorge I. Dominguez's *Cuba: Order and Revolution* (Cambridge: Harvard University Press, 1978). For the two best scholarly analyses of the political economy of Cuba under Castro, one should see Susan Eva Eckstein's *Back from the Future* (Princeton, NJ: Princeton University Press, 1994) and Marifeli Perez-Stable's *The Cuban Revolution: Origins, Course and Legacy* (New York: Oxford University Press, 1999). For a study of the relationship between the Catholic Church and Cuba under Castro, one should see John M. Kirk's *Between God and the Party* (Tampa: University of South Florida Press, 1989).

There are many biographies of Fidel Castro. Some tend to be overly sympathetic toward Castro and others highly antagonistic. Some of the better biographies include Robert Quirk's *Fidel Castro* (New York: Norton, 1993), Tad Szulc's *Fidel: A Critical Portrait* (New York: William Morrow, 1986), Lee Lockwood's *Castro's Cuba, Cuba's Fidel* (New York: Vintage, 1969), Enrique Meneses's *Fidel Castro* (New York: Taplinger, 1966), and Herbert Matthews's *Fidel Castro* (New York: Touchstone, 1969). More recently the works of journalist Ann Louise Bardach such as *Cuba Confidential: Love and Vengeance in Miami and Havana* (New York: Vintage, 2003) and *Without Fidel: A Death Foretold in Miami, Havana, and Washington* (New York: Scribner, 2009) focus on the Castro family and the family relations that touch both Miami and Havana.

For an excellent biography of Guevara, see Jorge Castaneda's *Companero: The Life and Death of Che Guevara* (New York: Knopf, 1997). Guevara wrote extensively and his most important include a compilation of his major works on guerrilla warfare entitled *Guerrilla Warfare*, with an introduction by Marc Becker (Lincoln: University of Nebraska Press, 1998) and *Che Guevara on Revolution*, edited by Jay Mallin (Coral Gables, FL: University of Miami Press, 1969). *The Complete Bolivian Diaries of Che Guevara*, edited by Daniel James (New York: Cooper Square, 2000) is also recommended.

For a substantive and balanced study of the exile and immigrant Cuban community, one should see Maria Cristina Garcia's *Havana USA* (Berkeley: University of California Press, 1996) and for a look at the Cuban American community and its relationship to the mass media, one should see Gonzalo R. Soruco's *Cubans and the Mass Media in South Florida* (Gainesville: University Press of Florida, 1996.

Cuba's relationship with the United States and the Soviet Union during the Cold War can be studied in many books, including Daniel F. Soloman's *Breaking Up with Cuba* (Jefferson, NC: McFarland and Company, 2011), James G. Blight, Bruce J. Allyn, and David Welch's *Cuba on the Brink: Castro, the Missile Crisis and the Soviet Collapse* (New York: Pantheon, 1993), H. Michael Erisman's Cuba's *International Relations: The Anatomy of a Nationalistic Foreign Policy* (Boulder: Westview, 1985), Laurence Chang and Peter Kornbluh's (eds.) *the Cuban Missile Crisis, 1962: A National Security Archive Documents Reader* (New York: New Press, 1992), Peter Wyden's *Bay of Pigs: The Untold Story* (New York: Simon and Schuster, 1979), Wayne Smith and Esteban Morales Dominguez's *Subject to Solution: Problems in Cuban-U.S. Relations* (Boulder: Rienner, 1988), Donna Rich Koplowitz's *Anatomy of a Failed Embargo: U.S. Sanctions against Cuba* (Boulder: Rienner, 1998), and Sergio Diaz-Briquets's (ed.) *Cuban Internationalism in Sub-Saharan Africa* (Pittsburgh: Duquesne University Press, 1989).

For an excellent study of the historical development of Havana, one should see Roberto Segre, Mario Coyula, and Joseph Scarpaci's *Havana: Two Faces of the Antillean Metropolis* (New York: Wiley, 1997). James A Michener and John King's *Six Days in Havana* (Austin: University of Texas Press, 1989) is also recommended. One should see M. Acosta and J. E. Hardoy's *Urban Reform in Revolutionary Cuba*, translated by M. Bochner (New Haven, CT: Yale University Press, 1973). John Gilderbloom of the University of Louisville has contributed many articles in newspapers and journals concerning Cuban architecture.

There are many websites that focus on Cuba. One of the most useful is the Latin American Network Information Center (LANIC) at the University of Texas (http://lanic.utexas.edu/la/ca/cuba). Another excellent and informative site is the U.S.-Cuba Trade and Economic Council, which was established in 1994 and is one of the best sites on how to do business with and in Cuba (http://www.cubatrade.org). Another excellent site is *Havana Times* (http://www.havanatimes.org) which is edited in Nicaragua but the majority of its writers and photographers live in Cuba. For a look into the future of Cuba, Marifeli Perez-Stable's (ed.) *Looking Forward: Comparative Perspectives on Cuba's Transition* (Notre Dame: University of Notre Dame Press, 2007) is excellent. The website of the Cuba Transition Project at the University of Miami (http://ctp.iccas.miami.edu) has the most up to date and scholarly analyses of the economic and political changes taking place on the island. I also would suggest the Cuba Study Group (http://www.cubastudygroup.org).

In recent years dissident bloggers have become an important source of information on everyday life in Cuba. A place to start is Yoani Sanchez's *Havana Real* (Brooklyn: Melville House, 2011) which is a collection of some of her entries in her internationally famous blog Generation Y (for the English version see http://generacionyen.word press.com/). There are other important bloggers who have had their blogs shut down several times such as Claudia Cadelo, Lia Villares, Reinaldo Escobar, and Miriam Celaya.

Index

United States-Cuba Trade
  Economic Council, 145
University Student Directorate,
  67, 68, 76
University Student Federation,
  62, 66, 75
Urrutia, Manuel, 98, 102
U.S. trade relations with Cuba:
  increasing trade between
  the two Cuban wars for
  independence, 40–42; U.S.
  trade policies and effects on
  diversification of the Cuban
  economy, 10, 65. *See also*
  Batista, Fulgencio; Cuban
  Democracy Act (Torricelli
  Act); Cuban Liberty and
  Democratic Solidarity Act
  (Helms Burton Act); Embargo;
  Machado, Gerardo; Platt
  Amendment; Slavery; Sugar;
  Union of Soviet Socialist
  Republics; United States

Valdes, Ramiro, 142, 153
Valenciago, Carlos, 1

Varela, Carlos, 13, 151
Varela, Felix, 12, 31
Varela Project, 150
Velazquez, Diego, 18
Venezuela, 12
Veradero, 8
Vietnam, 7

Welles, Sumner, and the
  crisis with the Machado
  government, 67, 68, 69, 70
Weyler, Valeriano, 42, 43, 44
Wieland, William, 87
Women. *See* Federation of
  Cuban Women
Wood, General Leonard, 46, 47,
  48, 49

Year of the Lash, 29
Yellow journalism, 42
Young, Samuel, 46
Younger generation and future
  of Cuba, 167–69

Zafra (sugar harvest), 29
Zayas, Alfredo, 59, 60, 61, 62, 66

About the Author

CLIFFORD L. STATEN, PhD, is professor of political science and international studies at Indiana University Southeast in New Albany. His published works include ABC-CLIO/Greenwood's *The History of Cuba* (first edition) and *The History of Nicaragua* as well as numerous scholarly articles. He is the recipient of the Distinguished Teaching Award, the Distinguished Research Award, and the Chancellor's Diversity Award from Indiana University Southeast. He is also a member of the Indiana University Faculty Colloquium on Excellence in Teaching. Professor Staten received his PhD from the University of North Texas.

Titles in the Greenwood Histories of the Modern Nations
Frank W. Thackeray and John E. Findling, Series Editors

The History of Afghanistan
Meredith L. Runion

The History of Argentina
Daniel K. Lewis

The History of Australia
Frank G. Clarke

The History of the Baltic States
Kevin O'Connor

The History of Brazil
Robert M. Levine

The History of Bulgaria
Frederick B. Chary

The History of Cambodia
Justin Corfield

The History of Canada
Scott W. See

The History of Central America
Thomas Pearcy

The History of the Central Asian
Republics
Peter L. Roudik

The History of Chile
John L. Rector

The History of China, Second
Edition
David C. Wright

The History of Congo
Didier Gondola

The History of Costa Rica
Monica A. Rankin

The History of Cuba, Second
Edition
Clifford L. Staten

The History of the Czech Republic
and Slovakia
William M. Mahoney

The History of Ecuador
George Lauderbaugh

The History of Egypt
Glenn E. Perry

The History of El Salvador
Christopher M. White

The History of Ethiopia
Saheed Adejumobi

The History of Finland
Jason Lavery

The History of France
W. Scott Haine

The History of Germany
Eleanor L. Turk

The History of Ghana
Roger S. Gocking

The History of Great Britain
Anne Baltz Rodrick

The History of Greece
Elaine Thomopoulos

The History of Haiti
Steeve Coupeau

The History of Holland
Mark T. Hooker

The History of Honduras
Thomas M. Leonard

The History of Iceland
Guðni Thorlacius Jóhannesson

The History of India, Second
Edition
John McLeod

The History of Indonesia
Steven Drakeley

The History of Iran, Second Edition
Elton L. Daniel